THORNY
ENCOUNTERS

THORNY
ENCOUNTERS

A HISTORY OF
ENGLAND
V THE
ALL BLACKS

MATT ELLIOTT

First published by Pitch Publishing, 2018

Pitch Publishing
A2 Yeoman Gate
Yeoman Way
Worthing
Sussex
BN13 3QZ
www.pitchpublishing.co.uk
info@pitchpublishing.co.uk

© 2018, Matt Elliott

A CIP catalogue record is available for this book
from the British Library.

ISBN 978-1-78531-446-9

Typesetting and origination by Pitch Publishing

Printed and bound in India by Replika Press Pvt. Ltd.

Contents

The Professional Era

*This book is dedicated to my big
little brother, Peter*

and to the memories of

*Prince Alexander Sergeevich
Obolensky (1916–1940)
and
Jonah Tali Lomu (1975–2015)*

'Nowhere else have I come across the one-eyed bias you find in the southern hemisphere. In New Zealand's case, they just didn't respect our rugby and couldn't really get their heads around the fact we can actually play the game in the northern hemisphere.'

– *Lawrence Dallaglio (ENG 1995–2007)*

'For me there's something special about playing England. Maybe it's because they're always talking themselves up. Maybe because it's the "mother country" – the home of the game. Whatever, playing England really spins my wheels.'

– *Jonah Lomu (NZ 1994–2002)*

'Rugby is a democratic game. One has the right to play it in any way one chooses.'

– *Andrew Mulligan (IRE 1956–61, 1959 Lions in New Zealand)*

Acknowledgements

My sincere thanks are due to the following for the various ways in which they have helped with this project:

I am indebted to Mike Slemen, Phil de Glanville, Nigel Redman and Izzy Noel-Smith for generously sharing their thoughts and reminiscences.

Toby Goodman's enthusiasm and introductions are greatly appreciated.

Dinah-Lee Tui, Henry Liu and Phil O'Malley (Glenfield Library); Keith Giles (Principal Photographs Librarian, Auckland Libraries).

M.J. Ford (Cambridge); Howard Ahmun (Cardiff).

Paul and Jane Camillin, Pitch Publishing; Duncan Olner; Graham Hales; Becca Wells; Dean Rockett.

As always, my wife, Melissa, son Peter – 'How's your rugby book going, Dad?' – and Murray for his ongoing interest.

Introduction

EXCLUDING a Rugby World Cup (RWC) final, is there any bigger occasion for the Rugby Football Union (RFU) than hosting the All Blacks at Twickenham?

After the anthems, the All Blacks take their places for the haka, an important piece of cultural and sporting theatre and a tradition that connects the All Black teams of the 21st century with those who first stepped out onto the muddy Crystal Palace field in 1905. As the men in black begin their challenge of 'Ka mate' or 'Kapa o pango', in response a large proportion of the crowd begin singing the low notes of the appropriated negro spiritual, 'Swing Low, Sweet Chariot'. The crowd is announcing their own challenge to the visitors. They will be heard.

This is where fevered sporting rivalry combines with another English tradition, that of theatrical pantomime. There will be booing and hissing of the 'villains' and rousing cheers for the heroes.

The crowd will get in the ear of the referee, too. Even the best officiators can't resist looking at a big screen when repeated boos ring out across the ground. ('He's behind you!')

There is no venue the All Blacks have a greater dislike of losing at, though many also name Twickenham as their favourite venue outside New Zealand. There is no greater scalp for England to claim on their hallowed ground than that of the All Blacks.

The rivalry between the two teams, their respective administrators and supporters, is not based on geo-political histories. It is mostly about differing philosophies of how the game 'should' be played or governed. It is a rivalry of opposites. White v black. The traditional home of the game against the colonial upstarts who have claimed it as their own. Players representing the largest, wealthiest union with the biggest home ground from a country of 50 million people in which rugby is not the number one sport, against players from a country with a tenth of the population, a smaller player base and a number of small (by comparison) regional stadia that host their national team, allowing fans of the country's main game to see their heroes. England's players are contracted to their clubs, New Zealand Rugby (NZR, previously the New Zealand Rugby Football Union and New Zealand Rugby Union) centrally contracts players.

In the amateur era, rugby fans attended Twickenham, the ground variously known as Rugby Football Ground or 'Headquarters', with much hope but little glory when it came to defeating the men in black. Match programmes were in praise of the rugby gods who had arrived from the bottom of the world. (The use of the word 'gods' is no exaggeration by the author.) Tries by the visitors brought great cheers from the attending English public.

The visitors held an advantage. They had been travelling together for a number of weeks and had been able to field 'shadow' Test teams against the more highly regarded district combinations they faced.

On the contrary, the England team had to abide by the rules of the International Rugby Board (IRB) which prevented Test teams assembling more than a couple of days before a match. Thus, the well-drilled side that had been able to try tactics and planned moves in the match environment ran out against 15 players who had enjoyed little time together. Most of the English Test XV would have faced the All Blacks in tour matches but in some instances that only added to the awe in which they viewed their opponents.

In the professional era, with ten-month seasons, the challenges of end-of-year tours to the northern hemisphere have never been greater for the All Blacks.

England didn't send a team to New Zealand until 1963. The subsequent once-a-decade visits, with challenging itineraries of time and opponents, were a curiosity for local fans and warmly welcomed.

Then along came a tournament called the Rugby World Cup. At last a team could justifiably call themselves the world champions. For four years. Being the traditional team of excellence, or the best in your hemisphere, no longer counted. There was a trophy and with it came bragging rights. For national unions and their coaches, it became THE measure of achievement.

The rivalry between the All Blacks and England changed, much of it fuelled by ever more strident, parochial media. The 1993 win by England at Twickenham was a key game in that change. England went into the game wanting revenge for defeat in the 1991 RWC pool game. Then, at the 1995 RWC, the All Blacks sought revenge for the 1993 loss.

Surprisingly, perhaps, England's record of wins against the All Blacks is worse in the professional era than in the amateur days. It is small consolation that it remains superior to the combined results of neighbours Wales, Ireland and Scotland. Should it be better than it is?

A reading of the opportunities missed and player reactions to losses within this book suggests that it should. But then, it isn't by accident the All Blacks have fashioned the best winning record across the history of the game. As former Scottish international, coach and four-time coach of the British and Irish Lions, Sir Ian McGeechan, has said, 'All Blacks are created by the system and the environment, not just by pulling on the jersey ... every player in the country understands the game so well, and that is why they are difficult to beat. Sometimes you might have a better team, but the All Blacks might have a better understanding, and that can be crucial.'

In recent years, a succession of England coaches have provided plenty of work for carpenters and interior designers at Twickenham. The England dressing room and surrounds have frequently been remodelled, with reminders of the nation's rugby history in a variety of forms put up and taken down. Even the dressing room door has been moved twice. At the end of the day, though, the position of the door doesn't make a team win. It's who goes through it and what physical and mental skills they possess.

Notes to the text

Positional names are those used by the respective teams i.e. England use the terms scrum-half, fly-half and inside-centre. New Zealand use halfback, first-five and second-five.

+ denotes a player's international debut.

* denotes a player or coach whose international career was still going at the time of writing.

Numbers after players' names in the team lists are; time spent off the field due to yellow (Y) or red (R) cards; or, when they came onto the field as a replacement.

Touch judges are listed from when they became international appointments.

In the early years of tours, the word 'coach' was a blasphemy, an Americanism, a nod to feared professionalism. On All Black tours, the assistant manager undertook the role of coach. Thus, I have referred to assistant managers by the unofficial term of coach, where it is clear that was their role and increasingly the media were referring to them as such.

As a historian, I firmly believe that the voices of participants in events are key stitches in historical tapestries. Writing this book, having piled my writing studio high with the acknowledged sources and working from my own notes and memories of matches, has been a big task. Any errors are entirely my own.

On Facing the All Blacks

WHAT is it like to play the All Blacks, and win? How can England be more successful against the team that is the best in the history of the game? Three former England internationals share their reminiscences and advice.

Mike Slemen (MS) played on the wing a (then) record 32 times for England from 1976–84 and for the British and Irish Lions in South Africa in 1980. Playing out of the Liverpool club, Slemen was tall, lean and very quick. A superb defender, he was great with ball in hand, though he only scored eight tries for his country in an era when 'there were a few forwards who liked to hang on to the ball'. A great exponent of the art of following up kicks, he was well respected by the All Blacks who he faced a number of times, including for the Northern Division side that beat them 21-9 at Otley in 1979.

Nigel Redman (NR) accumulated 20 England caps across 14 seasons, from 1984–97. A lock, he made appearances in the 1987 and 1991 Rugby World Cups and was called up to the British and Irish Lions during their 1997 tour of South Africa. A dominating lineout figure in the 1993 Twickenham victory over the All Blacks, Redman's erudite views on rugby have been heard in match commentaries and an assortment of television programmes. He has coached England age-group rugby teams and in 2014 took up the position of Elite Coach Development Manager for British Swimming.

Phil de Glanville (PdG) partnered Jeremy Guscott in Bath's midfield for a number of seasons but his appearances in the England jersey from 1992–99 were somewhat restricted by the Guscott-Will Carling combination. Renowned for his speed, handling and coolness under pressure, de Glanville captained England in 1997 following the retirement of Carling. His 38 caps included a win and a draw against the All Blacks. He famously started and finished a great counter-attacking try against the All Blacks in the 1999 Rugby World Cup.

MS: 'I played three times against the All Blacks in 1978, which was hard work. I played in the Barbarians game and scored two tries. It's the only time I've ever been cheered at Cardiff! New Zealand won it with a drop-kick, the last kick of the game. When you play people that many times, you get to know them and respect them. We had some brilliant times.'

Facing the haka:

MS: 'We used to say that the haka was a bit like Morris dancing, and I don't think they practised it very much back then.'

PdG: 'I always loved it, as did most of the team. That day in 1997 when Richard Cockerill did get carried away, he was so pumped up before the game.

'It always spurred me on and I looked forward to facing it. Even now when I watch matches on TV, I never miss the haka. What I never really knew until going to New Zealand was how it was used to welcome people to communities, and I saw it in a whole different light. My sister is married to a Kiwi, too, so we have a good understanding of the Kiwi culture now. We even performed it for their wedding!'

Beating the All Blacks:

MS: 'The North had beaten New Zealand before but not many England county sides did. The day we did in 1979, conditions weren't great. Otley, not the best ground in the world, but the crowd got very much involved in the game. It was really windy. We played very well. It was fantastic. It's one of those things, when I look back and think of some of the internationals I played in, this was a better game than a lot of them. We had a good set of forwards and a good backline. A good side. We scored four tries which was outstanding, as you can imagine.

'On that particular day, I was up against Stu Wilson. He scored their only try. I got on very well with Stu. We had the wind in the second half and wanted to keep them down in their half. At one point some of our players said, "What are we going to do here?" I said, "Come blind with me, kick into the corner and I'll chase it down. Hopefully they'll just kick it into touch." We did that and as I ran past Stu, he grabbed hold of me. I took a semi-swing at him and didn't hit him, obviously. He took a swing at me and missed completely. The referee was Alan Hosie, the Scottish referee. He ran past as we had hold of each other and said, "Will you two f****** stop messing about and get on with the game." Stu and I just burst out laughing.

'Steve Smith scored our first try. He belted the ball down and I chased it. Stu went back and he and Richard Wilson passed the ball between them and it went down. I kicked it through and picked it up and passed to Steve Smith, who was never the fastest man in the world, and he scored under the posts.

'Stu Wilson and I were nice small people. The first time I played an international side, against the touring Australians for the North, I was only 11st 2lb. I never got above 12½st.'

PdG: 'Having only done it once [1993] out of four matches, with one draw, it is a very special feeling as the All Blacks have consistently been the best side in the world. They keep their standards so high and move the game on before the rest of the world has worked out what they are doing as real innovators. They are still the benchmark team to beat. For me personally it was special in 1993 because of what had happened before in the South-West Division match [*De Glanville suffered a serious cut to his face from a controversial stray All Black boot*]. Also, it was my first starting cap for my country, which is a proud moment regardless of who you are playing.'

The 15-9 win at Twickenham, 1983:

MS: 'Scotland drew with the All Blacks the week before. The Scots weren't a bad side at the time. I hadn't played for England at the end of the previous season. I felt I was getting a bit past it. But we had a new coach, Dick Greenwood, who was a northern lad and he brought me back in. I'd played quite a lot at fly-half before I moved to the wing. As I could kick the ball quite well the lads used me behind the lineouts near to the line to get the ball away. That particular day, our forwards played as well as I'd ever seen England forwards play. Maurice Colclough had a particularly good game. He's passed away now but on that day he was very much alive!'

NR: 'I grew up in South Wales and we left for England when I was 11. I only started playing rugby when I was 16. My earliest memory of the All Blacks was them playing the Barbarians when Gareth Edwards scored the try in the corner. The first England–All Blacks game I really took notice of was the 1983 game when a friend of mine, Paul Simpson, who was playing number eight, was put into the hoardings by the All Blacks' centre, Steve Pokere. He actually went through the hoardings on the side of the ground.'

Touring New Zealand:

MS: 'I was the backs' coach for the England "B" team's eight-match tour of New Zealand in 1992. We had some up-and-comers in the backline such as Phil de Glanville, Tony Underwood and an old head in Stuart Barnes as captain. He thought he should have been in the main side ahead of Rob Andrew. In the forwards there was Neil Back, Ben Clarke and Victor Ubogu. Good young players coming through at that time who went on to play a lot higher up.

PdG: 'We saw just how passionate the whole of New Zealand is for their rugby … and how wet it can be! We stayed the first week of the tour on the east coast of the South Island and it rained the whole time. There wasn't a huge amount to do other than train. Remember, this was before satellite sport channels on TV and the internet.'

MS: 'We went everywhere by coach so we were able to see New Zealand as a place. The people were very friendly. We had a great time. We won all our games against the local sides. The only two games we lost were against the New Zealand XV. In the first game we actually scored four tries to their two. On that day, Stu missed seven kicks out of eight and a dropped goal. We lost by six points, which was a bit upsetting. The best player on the field that day was probably Neil Back. He won a hell of a lot of ruck ball. In the second game, New Zealand really sorted us. They made sure that before they moved the ball very far, Neil had made a tackle. They held him on the ground and then moved the ball. That worked.'

PdG: 'The rugby was hard and physical, and though we lost both our matches against the New Zealand XV, they were pretty open and exciting games.'

The 15-9 win at Twickenham, 1993:

NR: 'I always thought the benefit of playing the old-fashioned tours was that you could play against a side three or four times. In 1993, I played against the All Blacks for England 'A' and before that for South-West Division at Redruth, Cornwall. It's a very rural part of England and the pitch has got a famous slope down to one corner. We actually gave them a tough game, losing 15-19.

'Back then, there was no real analysis of teams. So we got to know their game plan by playing against them once or twice before the Test match. I remember someone saying to me very early on that when you play a side like the All Blacks there are always going to be times when you come off the field and think, we could have won that. It's about taking your chances when they come along because the thing about the All Blacks is, if you make a mistake they punish you.'

PdG: 'My experience playing for the South-West against the All Blacks was cut short by that facial injury but we should have won that day if we had our kicking boots on. I think five penalties were missed. So we knew they were beatable.'

NR: 'I played most of my rugby at the middle of the lineout which I was far too short for, at 6ft 3in. Most of the guys in those days were 6ft 7in and above. In the previous two games against the All Blacks

I had jumped at number two in the lineout against Steve Gordon. There was always someone else to cover Ian Jones. I remember when we assembled to train someone asked, who is going to jump in the middle? Martin Johnson turned around and showed what I thought was great leadership. He said, "I've never jumped in the middle so you're going to have to." I'd never played against Jones before but I always welcomed a challenge. I could jump, but with his height advantage over me it was always going to be a physical encounter. It was always about being competitive, standing toe-to-toe and not letting the All Blacks have their own way.

'We used to stay in a hotel in Petersham and we would practise lineouts on the morning of the game in the car park. We were doing our lineouts and there was one stubborn taxi driver who drove right through the middle of our lineout. He had no idea what we were doing and was abused by Brian Moore. The driver just said that he had to because he was doing his job. And it just happened to be a *black* cab. So our pre-match preparation was interrupted by a black-cab driver.'

PdG: 'It was my first starting cap as my previous two caps had been as a replacement for injury, so as you can imagine I was very nervous before the game.'

NR: 'I don't think I've ever said this before but I was incredibly ill the night before the Test. I don't know if I had food poisoning but I was up all night with diarrhoea. It wasn't great preparation but it just made me a little bit more determined.'

PdG: 'The fact the All Blacks had put 50 points on Scotland the week before was very impressive, but in a funny way it just concentrated our minds even more on how to beat them. We definitely knew the midfield would come running at us hard, but that's what All Black backlines do as a given anyway. We put a lot of emphasis on not letting them get momentum and go forward in the game, and that worked quite well across the board in the game.'

NR: 'Because the All Blacks, perhaps surprisingly, didn't get to the final of the RWC in 1991, come 1993 everyone realised the importance of competing against the All Blacks. Most of us had played against most of the players in the Test team, at least once. Geoff Cooke was very progressive as far as coaching was concerned. He was very interested in tactics and game plans and players having a voice. He was very open about the tactics we would use and how we would play the game.

'That 1993 Test was the first one I played in where we had a real game plan. I had been playing for Bath who were dominant and when you are dominant your confidence is high. With England, we weren't that confident. We would win one, lose one. We had a game plan that everyone bought in to, to nullify what they did and allow us to stay in the game.

'New Zealand had a very interesting kicking game where they'd kick it to you, you'd kick it back to them and they'd kick it back to you in the hope that you would attack on foot and New Zealand would put this black wall up. We played them at their own game. We kept kicking it back.

'An interesting thing about New Zealand was that if they lost a key tactical player [*as they did with the withdrawal of injured kicker Matthew Cooper in the days before the Test*] they would lose their way. Also, as we've seen at World Cups, they would win games playing a certain way, but they weren't good at being able to change the way they played. Certainly, on that tour taking them on at their own game seemed to ... I don't know if rattle them is the right phrase because they had some great players ... but it seemed like they didn't always know what to do next.

'The thing about playing a great side is if they start to get momentum you can start to lose confidence and start to think that you need to do something different in order to change the flow of the game. Doing that can start to compound the problem because it's different and not planned. On that day, everyone followed the game plan. When to chase, putting in your tackles, kicking for position, keeping the ball in. The All Blacks probably felt they weren't having as many lineouts as they were hoping because we weren't kicking the ball out. Then when we did have them, they became more important.

'We'd first seen that kicking game from the Australians in 1988. People like Michael Lynagh were keeping the ball in the field. At first, we thought they were bad kicks. We couldn't understand why he was kicking so badly. Our lads were kicking the ball off the field to have a set piece. It took us a while to realise what was happening. It was brilliant. In 1993 we were very mindful of territory which is why we didn't kick the ball into touch much.

'We'd spoken about keeping the mistakes down, keeping the penalties down. Jeff Wilson missed a few kicks at goal and it wasn't a case of us saying, "Crikey that was lucky." It was a case of thinking, right we need to put pressure right back on them. Psychologically, if they missed a kick it had to affect them negatively as well as being a little gain for us. But we needed to put pressure on again. Every time Jon Callard kicked a penalty or Rob Andrew kicked his drop goal, it kept the pressure on them. You take three points, another three points and the pressure starts to mount up. International rugby, I always think, is about keeping your momentum and keeping the board turning.'

PdG: 'Once the game started the concentration levels and pace were so high there was no time to think about where you were and what you were doing. The match went by in a blur for me.'

NR: 'Come the end of the game, I was walking off the field talking to Jon Callard and then someone came up to me and said, "Number five, you're going for drug-testing." So I was taken for drug-testing. I wasn't allowed in the changing room. I went straight to see the drug-testers. It was the first time I'd ever been asked to pee in a pot. I never actually got to celebrate with the team in the changing room. By the time I got there, there was no one left. I showered and bathed and then went along to the Rose Room to see family and friends.

'I remember Sean Fitzpatrick in his after-match dinner speech saying something along the lines of, "Congratulations to England on the win. As an All Black we tend to remember our losses." That indicated to me he was telling us they didn't lose all that much. It was poignant, and in a way a bit arrogant, but he was saying it was very special for England to beat the All Blacks because it doesn't happen all that often.'

The 26-26 draw at Twickenham, 1997:

PdG: 'There was a much more positive attacking mindset going into the second match at Twickenham [*after losing 8-25 at Old Trafford*]. Clive had set us a target to score a minimum of four tries in the match, as he knew that is what it would take to beat New Zealand. As ever, playing at Twickenham is also a big motivator and the crowd were really supportive that day, probably helped by the way we played. I think mentally we were on a much better level that day and our performance reflected that. It was a cracking game, and New Zealand came back so strongly in the second half.

'I think given where we were at half time [*ahead 23-9*] then we should have won, but we stopped attacking and became more passive and New Zealand really stepped it up. I also think we weren't fit enough to keep playing at that intensity and it showed in the second half.'

1999 RWC pool game at Twickenham, won by the All Blacks 30-16:

PdG: 'I have never known such an edge in the air from the supporters going to the game. They were everywhere and it was such an intense environment. Again, it was a cracking game and after New Zealand started so well we managed to get back on a par with them. Then one magical moment from Jonah Lomu was pivotal in the match.

'We had managed to keep him relatively quiet but off the back of a turnover ball it was moved to him. He ran past and through at least three England players including Jeremy Guscott and Austin Healy and scored in the corner. That knocked the stuffing out of us after we had hauled ourselves back. The final result doesn't really show how close the game was as another try in the last minutes from New Zealand closed it out. They played very well in the last 15 minutes and at the same intensity as the rest of the match.'

'Hang on and hope' – tackling Jonah Lomu:

PdG: 'Hang on and hope is right! He came off the top of a lineout straight at me in that 1999 game and the only reason I stopped him was because he tripped on my head as he ran over me! He was a machine. In the match at Old Trafford, he handed me off after he caught an England cross kick to his wing – bad plan – but I did manage to catch him from behind and pull him down. That was probably the easiest way to get him: when he wasn't looking! I haven't played another team when one individual had such an effect and was such a standout player.'

How can England beat the All Blacks more consistently?

MS: 'I think individual New Zealand players know the game better than England players at times. They make better decisions at the right times. Certainly, over the last few years there are times when we've just given away too many penalties. I think also that no matter what the individual position, the New Zealand players all have very good basic skills. Handling wise, I certainly think the All Black forwards are better than the England players. The Premiership has become much more competitive and there are some good young players coming up. But the question is, how do you bring them through? I feel we don't always keep our coaches perhaps as long as we should. I also wonder, are the players having to play too many games? I think they're playing too much, but that's the way it is because it's money.'

NR: 'Every time you play there is enormous pressure on your skill-set, to be able to exercise that under pressure. Good sides like the All Blacks put pressure on you which reduces your time to think and you just have to be in the moment and knowledgeable of the game plan and so on. When to kick it back, when to run into a gap. You need discipline and to be competitive. If you give away penalties you are giving away territory and the ball. If you can be disciplined and competitive, then that's the benchmark for being a good side. Then back that up with skill. The difference in skill level between the top teams can be small margins. That sounds easy but it's not, especially when you have 80,000 people screaming at you and millions watching on television.'

PdG: 'England have had highs and lows in performances, whereas the All Blacks have always been consistently high. We have periods (2000–03) and the start of the Eddie Jones era (2016–17) where we can beat anyone consistently, then we under-perform. I am sure the issue of "hunger" is a challenge, and leadership development of players. Perhaps the professional system in England doesn't develop these characteristics as well as New Zealand. When players are first contracted to academies at the age of 18, they then don't play that many games during the pivotal period up to the age of 21. That is a structural weakness in the England system.'

MATCH 1

Crystal Palace, London, 2 December 1905
ALL BLACKS 15 – ENGLAND 0

'Fifteen points, rather than five tries. It looks better.'
– Vincent Cartwright, England captain

BY the time of the first rugby meeting between England and New Zealand, the former had been playing international rugby for 34 years. Across 84 matches Ireland, Scotland and Wales were the annual opponents in the Home Nations Championship, except for in 1888 when that trio of unions refused to play England on account of the RFU not joining the newly formed IRB. One other 'international' had been played in 1889 against the visiting New Zealand Natives, a predominantly Maori team that played a mind-boggling 74 games in the British Isles. The February match at Blackheath was won by the home side, 7-0.

New Zealand, on the other hand, had only played five (undefeated) internationals since 1903. One of those was by a third-string side against Australia whilst the 'Originals' (as they came to be known) were on the passenger ship bound for 'Home', the first visit to England by a team representing the NZRFU.

On that first tour, before arriving at Crystal Palace the All Blacks had chalked up 23 consecutive wins, including a 12-7 defeat of Scotland and 15-0 triumph over Ireland. Newspaper reporters, almost to a man, were in praise of the All Blacks' try-scoring feats but cried foul over their tactic of having a wing-forward. This uniquely New Zealand positional variation saw the wing-forward feed the ball to scrums, meaning the All Blacks' formation was 2-3-2 as opposed to

3-2-3 or 3-4-1. By keeping one hand on the scrum, the wing-forward could hold his position and block the opposing scrum-half.

Though not the only tourist playing in that position, captain Dave Gallaher was the focus of much vitriol. Crowds jeered at 'That awful man, Gallaher', yelling for him to get onside, even when he wasn't part of the playing XV! He may have been the first All Black loose-forward and captain to earn the ire of the English media and crowds, but he would not be the last.

England hadn't played a match since losing to Scotland eight months earlier. In fact, they had been soundly beaten in all three of their championship matches, conceding a total of 48 points and only getting on the scoreboard once.

The great New Zealand five-eighth and tour vice-captain, Billy Stead, wrote about the interest in the English international in one of the many diary columns he penned for the newspaper of his hometown, *The Southland Times*:

> Seats were at a premium, one Duke even offering £10 for a half-guinea seat, and he would have taken four at that price ... It was the first time that the Crystal Palace Syndicate would allow a rugby match on their beautifully equipped enclosure ... The importance of this last concession to their opponents in football had so wakened up the 'soccer' authorities that they had secured hundreds of the best seats so that they might have an ocular demonstration of how this rugby game, as played by the 'All Blacks' and 'boomed' in every paper, was going to electrify and thrill the mass of spectators. Our appearance was greeted with cheers, and there was an earnest desire and call for our 'war cry', which we never give unless expressly asked for.

A piece of newsreel footage of the match, less than four minutes long, was discovered in New Zealand several years ago, tucked away in an old garage in the South Island.

In the film we see a bleak London December day. Long, bulky coats are the common feature of spectators' clothing. First the England team, which included eight debutants, stand on one goal-line and between the posts. Right-wing Henry Imrie wears a wide belt, while left-wing Alfred Hind (a solicitor who had run the 100 yards in under ten seconds while at Cambridge University) towers above scrum-half Jacky Braithwaite, playing his only Test, and fly-half Dai Gent. Several players warm themselves against the cold and pre-match nerves as the team photo is taken. The skipper, Vincent Cartwright, a product of Rugby School, playfully lobs the noticeably round ball at the cameraman.

Then the New Zealand team appears, confidently led by a ball-carrying Gallaher, his head slightly bowed. Gallaher, who always wore his shin pads outside his stockings, has a few quick words with tour manager George Dixon. The rest of the team follow. A mix of heights and shapes, they look imposing. Two bandsmen standing nearby step back slightly as they pass. Trailing them is the tall, lean George Nicholson, carrying a small flag for his sideline duties during the match. He trudges past the camera puffing on a cigarette.

The All Blacks line up as the English did and the camera moves along the line. It finishes on referee Gil Evans, who wears a cloth cap and knickerbockers. He stands slightly apart from the All Blacks but with a hint of a smile that shows some delight to be part of the auspicious day. The All Blacks then break ranks and Gallaher heads towards the dead-ball line where Evans is now standing. As he goes, he turns and kicks the ball back to his team-mates.

Why has Gallaher run in the opposite direction from his team and why does the referee want to talk to him in front of where the crowd line one of the pitch extremities? It was practice, if not a requirement, for captains to check before kick-off that nothing was intruding onto the field of play.

As the film continues, the England team move up from the opposite end of the field, passing the ball with some aptitude before it becomes more like the lobbing of a beach ball. A day at the seaside this isn't!

We briefly see the finale of the All Blacks' haka before England kick off. We can only imagine the roar from the crowd as the ball left the boot and sailed through the air to begin the game.

Play moves around the field and we see the players in action; scrambling to where a dribbling rush has broken down; a heaving scrum; appeals to the referee; tackles and scrags; players with hands on hips listening to the referee's decision.

The footage is remarkable. Mesmerising. When watching it, one can forget it is only three-and-a-half minutes long, not 80.

While the match on the muddy ground was relatively free-flowing, according to Stead it was a 'tiresome, disappointing one' in which England were spirited in their play but rarely on the attack. It was notable for the haul of four three-point tries by All Black winger, Duncan McGregor.

That match tally would not be equalled by another All Black until the 1987 Rugby World Cup.

The pick of the England players was fullback Edward Jackett, who would tour New Zealand with the 1908 Anglo-Welsh team and the same year win a silver medal with the Cornish team which represented Great Britain in the Olympic rugby tournament. Besides his impressive positional play and punting, he was fearless in making numerous tackles.

At the post-match dinner, Cartwright was most good-humoured in acknowledging that his side had been well beaten and he asked the reporters in the room to record the All Blacks' win as, 'Fifteen points, rather than five tries. It looks better.' Reflecting on the game, Gallaher thought they had encountered a number of other players on tour who deserved to be in the England side.

Under the headline 'A Colonial Triumph', *The Observer* newspaper made much of the temperament of the players:

> It was most strenuously contested from start to finish, and the gay way in which hard knocks were given and received proved the chivalry of the rival champions. Some men got temporarily knocked out, but no serious accident occurred, and the intervals, while the New Zealanders assisted in attending to an injured opponent, or a similar courtesy was exhibited on the other side, only served to display the admirable spirit in which the game was contested.

In *The Times* was the comment that, 'People came to the Palace to see the New Zealanders play and not to see England win.'

The famous C.B. Fry, former sportsman of all-round excellence, politician and writer concluded that, 'The notion that these men beat us because of our physical degeneracy is nonsense. They beat us by organisation and tactics.'

Dai Gent later became well known as a rugby writer for *The Sunday Times*.

During World War I, Cartwright was twice mentioned in dispatches and awarded a DSO and Croix de Guerre. Gallaher and his opposing wing-turned-wing-forward, Belgian-born John Raphael, were both killed in action during 1917; Raphael at Messines and Gallaher at Passchendaele. In all, 27 men who had played international rugby for England and 13 who had played for the All Blacks lost their lives during the Great War.

Referee: G. Evans (Midland Counties)

Attendance: 45,000 (estimate)

Half-time: NZ 9, ENG 0

Scorers: NZ McGregor (4t), Newton (t)

ENGLAND: C.E.L. Hammond (Harlequins), V.H. Cartwright (*Capt.* Nottingham), B.A. Hill (Blackheath), J.L. Mathias (Bristol), E.W. Roberts (Dartmouth), R.F. Russell+ (Leicester), G.E. Summerscale+ (Durham City), J.E. Raphael (Old Merchant Taylors), J. Braithwaite+ (Leicester), D.R. Gent+ (Gloucester), A.E. Hind+ (Leicester), R.E. Godfray+ (Richmond), H.E. Shewring (Bristol), H.M. Imrie+ (Durham City), E.J. Jackett+ (Falmouth)

NEW ZEALAND: S.T. Casey (Otago), G.A. Tyler (Auckland), J.M. O'Sullivan (Taranaki), F. Newton+ (Canterbury), F.T. Glasgow (Taranaki), A. McDonald (Otago), C.E. Seeling (Auckland), D. Gallaher (*Capt.* Auckland), F. Roberts (Wellington), J.W. Stead (Southland), D. McGregor (Wellington), J. Hunter (Taranaki), R.G. Deans (Canterbury), W.J. Wallace (Wellington), G.A. Gillett (Canterbury)

Coach: J. Duncan

MATCH 2
Twickenham, London, 3 January 1925
ALL BLACKS 17 – ENGLAND 11

'You go off!' – Mr. A. Freethy, referee

THE second All Black tour party to England had left New Zealand being pilloried in newspapers as 'the worst team New Zealand ever fielded' and 'a disgrace to its predecessors', following a comprehensive loss to the Auckland provincial team.

Since arriving nearly four months earlier, however, they had won all 27 of their matches.

Johnstone 'Jock' Richardson had become the All Blacks' Test captain following the demotion of tour leader Cliff Porter who on form couldn't hold his place in the side. Richardson took it all in his stride, as one would expect from someone who had enlisted to fight in WWI as a 17-year old and saw active service as a machine-gunner in the Middle East.

From 1921–24, England had won 13 internationals, lost two and drawn one. In 1921–23/24 they had won the Five Nations Championship claiming Grand Slams and Triple Crowns. They were the undisputed champions of northern hemisphere rugby. But, when a Rest (of England) beat the preferred England team in a trial match, the selectors suddenly got the jitters and made seven changes to their original England side.

England lock Ronald Cove-Smith was in the middle of a decade in which he would represent his country in 29 Tests. A physician, he had captained the British team the previous summer on their tour of South Africa.

Captain of England, William Wavell Wakefield (easily identified by the cloth headgear he wore) was an imposing loose forward who helped mould the role of the modern English flanker as a terrier, ball-runner and general nuisance to opposing backs. But he did not hunt alone. Tom Voyce was a tireless competitor and for some years after the duo had hung up their respective boots, they were still revered as the best loose-forwards to have taken the field for England.

Much pre-match comment focused on the merits of the respective forward packs with the home side's 3-4-1 scrum expected to easily dominate the All Blacks' 2-3-2 formation.

By mid-morning on the day of the match, thousands had joined the queues for unreserved tickets and traffic jams clogged the roads surrounding Twickenham. Half an hour before kick-off the ground's gates were closed and a record attendance of 60,000 waited as HRH The Prince of Wales was introduced to the teams. The English players were resplendent in their individual club stockings.

The All Blacks' management had chosen Welsh referee Albert Freethy to whistle his sixth game of their tour. After just eight minutes he made a decision that gave the game an unparalleled infamy. For the first time, a player was sent from the field for foul play in an international match. That player was All Black loose-forward Cyril Brownlie.

Though the biggest man in the All Black touring party at 6ft 3in and weighing 15st, Brownlie was a quiet giant who had seen active service with the Mounted Rifles in Palestine during the Great War. He had the pace to match most of his backs and strength which often saw him loaded down with tacklers as he made his way upfield.

There was much contention about why Brownlie was sent from the field, in a match that had numerous incidents of rough-housing from both sides. Indiscretions named in newspapers included back-chat, stomping a player on the ground and a variety of retaliatory punching scenarios.

The All Blacks expressed some frustration that the alleged initiator of the to-do, Reg Edwards, had no action taken against him. Edwards stood out thanks to his bald pate and had stirred things up a bit during the All Blacks' feisty last-minute win over Newport in October. Interestingly, he never played for England again.

Deathly silence descended over Twickenham as Brownlie left the field. Not even a reported half-time approach to Freethy on behalf of the Prince of Wales would see Brownlie return to play.

The legendary New Zealand fullback, George Nepia, later recounted seeing the despairing Brownlie sitting underneath the stands.

George Nepia (NZ 1924–30): 'He is sitting upon a bench, still in his togs. Brownlie has been a soldier and a farmer, as both he has become inured to the cycle of life and death that governs our lives. He is a big, powerful, mature man. Yet the tears are rolling down his cheeks. You carry the lump in your throat for the rest of your life when you think of him sitting there in his loneliness. Poor Cyril! We did our best to comfort him then, later and for the rest of the life that was cut off far short of his time.'

England were the first to score, some ten minutes after Brownlie's departure. Following a dominant England scrum, Cove-Smith ended a dribbling rush by diving on the ball as it rolled across the in-goal.

Steeled by having to watch his brother depart was Maurice Brownlie, the greatest All Black between the wars and a man the legendary Colin Meads said was probably a better player than he. Maurice played like a man possessed and said to a team-mate after the game that he wouldn't have passed him the ball for £100, so determined was he that the All Blacks would not lose a man *and* the game.

In one charge, Maurice was stopped just short of the try-line – the ball then being swung to the other side of the field where 'Snowy' Svenson scored for the All Blacks – but was not denied a second time. He scooped up a loose ball inside the England 25-yard line and with ten determined strides stormed towards the right-hand corner.

William Wakefield (ENG 1920–27): 'I could see him going straight down the touchline, though it seemed impossible for him to score. Somehow, he went on, giving me the impression of a moving tree-trunk, so solid did he appear to be, and so little effect did various attempted tackles have upon him. He crashed through without swerving right or left, and went over the line for one of the most surprising tries I have ever seen.'

Jim Parker and Jack Steel also scored tries to give the All Blacks a 17-3 lead.

Having to play 72 minutes on a heavy ground with only 14 men (and a gusty breeze in their faces during the second half), the All Blacks noticeably began to tire. Adding further to their struggles was the fact they only had six in the forward pack when loose-forward Parker moved into the backs to cover for the hobbling Steel.

In the absence of Cyril Brownlie, the canny Wakefield called for scrums rather than lineouts to restart play when the ball went out. As a result, there were over 80 scrums in the match, many of which had to be reset. These sapped the legs of the All Black forwards and in the final quarter England's quest for points saw the backs running the ball from everywhere and easily making ground.

Leonard Corbett quickly scored a penalty by drop-kicking the ball between the uprights. Wing Harold Kittermaster then showed his electrifying pace with a try under the posts after a run which began around halfway. The Twickenham stands shook as the crowd's thunderous shouts of 'Go! Go!' urged him to the line.

Eight points in ten minutes for England but they had run out of time. Freethy called 'No side'.

The crowd had witnessed what remains as one of the most dramatic matches in international rugby.

Read Masters (NZ 1923–25): 'England played great football, and territorially had a fair share of the game. Their forwards, whose play was hard and vigorous, worked untiringly all through, adopting bustling tactics that were most effective ... [it] was the hardest and most gruelling game I have ever played in.'

Stan Dean (NZ manager): 'We beat England with a man short and I suppose we should feel triumphant. Instead, we feel sick about the whole show.'

By the end of their unbeaten 32-match tour through Great Britain, Ireland, France and Canada that All Blacks team were labelled 'The Invincibles' and hailed as the greatest team New Zealand had produced. Referee Freethy was asked to submit a report to the RFU the day after the game. He wrote that he had seen Brownlie kick the leg of an English player who was lying on the ground, something Brownlie firmly denied.

In later years he was often asked about that infamous moment.

Albert Freethy (referee): 'Cyril Brownlie was no better and no worse than any of the others. He was unfortunate that he was the player in my line of vision when I made my decision.'

Freethy was also quoted as saying, 'At no point did I see Cyril Brownlie kick an English player.'

Did Brownlie's punishment fit the alleged crime? Certainly, there had been numerous acts of on-field violence in international rugby before that game, and an increasing number in the decades after it. Punching and rucking were 'acceptable' (for want of a better word) parts of the contest, but foul play by a player using the boot was strictly forbidden.

It would be 42 years before another man was sent from the field. Ironically, it was another All Black forward, Colin Meads.

Referee: A. Freethy (Wales)

Attendance: 60,000

Half-time: NZ 9, ENG 3

Scorers: NZ Svenson (t), Steel (t), M. Brownlie (t), Parker (t), Nicholls (c, p)
ENG Cove-Smith (t), Kittermaster (t), Corbett (p), Conway (c)

ENGLAND: R. Edwards (Newport), J.S. Tucker (Bristol), A.F. Blakiston (Northampton), R. Cove-Smith (Old Merchant Taylors), W.W. Wakefield (*Capt.* Harlequins), R.J. Hillard+ (Oxford University), A.T. Voyce (Gloucester), G.S. Conway (Hartlepool Rovers), A.T. Young (Cambridge University), H.J. Kittermaster+ (Oxford University), J.C. Gibbs+ (Harlequins), V.G. Davies (Harlequins), L.J. Corbett (Bristol), R.H. Hamilton-Wickes (Harlequins), J.W. Brough+ (Silloth)

NEW ZEALAND: W.R. Irvine (Hawke's Bay), Q. Donald (Wairarapa), M.J. Brownlie (Hawke's Bay), R.R. Masters (Canterbury), C.J. Brownlie (Hawke's Bay, off 8'-80'), J. Richardson (*Capt.* Southland), A. White (Southland), J.H. Parker (Canterbury), J.J. Mill (Hawke's Bay), N.P. McGregor (Canterbury), K.S. Svenson (Wellington), M.F. Nicholls (Wellington), A.E. Cooke (Auckland), J. Steel (West Coast), G. Nepia (Hawke's Bay)

Manager: S.S.M. Dean

Twickenham, London, 4 January 1936
ENGLAND 13 – ALL BLACKS 0

'So England have beaten New Zealand at last!'
– Daily Mail headline

T
HERE is no greater compliment to the skill or influence of a player than to have a match referred to by his name. This game will forever be Obolensky's.

A Russian prince, Alexander Sergeevich Obolensky was born in Petrograd in 1916 and arrived in England with his family a year later when they fled the revolution in their homeland.

The blond-haired aristocrat was by all accounts an entertaining and lively character. His pre-match fare was often a dozen oysters! The selection on the right wing of 'Obo', as he was known, caused some contention as he was yet to become a naturalised British citizen.

Obolensky was not a complete unknown to the All Blacks. They had seen his youthful flair and confidence when defeating Oxford University 10-9 two months earlier. In dismal weather, the 19-year-old prince had sped down the touchline and around behind the posts for a score. Some of the All Blacks and members of the crowd waited for the touch judge to raise his flag for surely Obolensky had put a foot into touch? The flag stayed down. The privilege of royalty.

Legendary Scottish rugby commentator, Bill McLaren, often recalled seeing Jack Manchester's 1935 All Blacks play the South of Scotland when he was only 11 years old. McLaren was in awe of the men in black as they walked out onto the pitch, describing them as 'prophets of doom'. They may have seemed that way in appearance, but their burdensome efforts to emulate the successes of previous All Blacks tourists came undone when losing to Swansea (3-11) and drawing with Ulster (3-3). Two weeks before meeting England they fell to Wales (12-13) in Cardiff. By the time they arrived in London for their 28th tour game they were a weary team with stale tactics.

A major issue for the tourists was the fact their once favoured 2-3-2 scrum had become outdated thanks to a rule change regarding hooking in the scrum. Players who had grown up using one formation were still adjusting to new scrum positions. The All Blacks' pack had found themselves pushed around by many opponents, so relied on the tactic of clearing the ball from the scrum as quickly as they could.

England captain Bernard Gadney was, for his day, a huge man to be playing halfback, standing 6ft and weighing over 13st. The All Blacks were very impressed by his play. Gadney was the first inductee to Twickenham's Museum of Rugby Wall of Fame and lived to the ripe old age of 91, passing away in 2000.

Two Pathé News cameras filmed the match. As the narrator of the edited match newsreel said about the afternoon of 'rugger':

> Many thought of the All Blacks as unbeatable and their recent whacking by Wales has given England new hope. Today, if they don't put up a good show, His Royal Highness, the Prince of Wales, and 7,000 others will want to know the reason why.

The players were introduced to HRH The Prince of Wales (later King Edward VIII) in the dressing rooms before they walked out onto the slippery field. The *Daily Mail* calculated that the crowd was the equivalent of 1/20th of New Zealand's population. Once the Grenadier Guards' band had played the national anthem, with the teams standing facing each other, the match could begin.

The All Blacks started the match well, dominating the first 20 minutes. Their big, fast lock Ron King came close to scoring but for the next hour, such was the dominance of the large England pack, and the committed defence of the midfield backs, fullback Harold 'Tuppy' Owen-Smith wasn't called on to make one covering tackle.

(Owen-Smith is the only man to have captained both the South African cricket team and the England rugby team. Born in South Africa, he captained their cricket team on the 1929 tour of England.

Whilst studying medicine in England he played ten rugby Tests, captaining the England side three times in 1937.)

The first try of the game came courtesy of Obolensky, who ran with an upright shoulders-back posture, the ball tucked against his chest. Taking a pass inside his own half, he headed for the touchline and was around and away from his opposite Nelson Ball in the blink of an eye. George Gilbert, the All Black fullback, could merely fling himself in faint hope of a tackle as the long-striding prince beat him, then slid on his knees to dot the ball down. Gilbert later confessed that 'Obolensky went so fast I never saw him'. The unsuccessful conversion attempt by number eight 'Pop' Dunkley thudded against the uprights.

Obolensky's second try, just before half-time, was even more of a gem. Taking a pass and almost stopping still, he accelerated on a diagonal run past four All Blacks. It was reported in *The Guardian*:

> Obolensky takes the pass about eight yards from the 25-yard line. The New Zealanders, hopelessly wrong-footed, screechingly pull-up and change direction like cartoon cats. The Russian continues to lance full-pelt and untouched to the line, which he crosses midway between the posts and corner. The try of tries.

In the second half, the All Blacks were chasing the game. Several drop goals were attempted by the visitors to snare quick points, but all failed. Salt was rubbed into that wound when England centre Peter Cranmer (later to captain the Warwickshire cricket team either side of the Second World War) calmly slotted one with his left foot, extending his team's lead to ten points. England left wing Hal Sever put the icing on the cake with an unconverted try.

The *News-Chronicle* trumpeted the win:

> All things must come to an end, even the superiority of the New Zealanders at Rugby. They have suffered the heaviest defeat any New Zealand side has ever experienced in these islands. In all the finer arts of Rugby, save only quick heeling from the scrummages, England surpassed their rivals, whose attempts to batter through the middle of the English defence were frustrated. They seemed to have no alternative method of attack.

This was the first All Black loss in 55 games touring England and only the second time in 88 games in the British Isles that they had failed to register a point. The NZRFU cabled the RFU extending 'hearty congratulations upon your victory'. The Land of the Long White Cloud suddenly had a large black cloud over it. A rugby-obsessed nation was in mourning.

Obolensky played three more internationals but never scored another try. A fortnight after the defeat of the All Blacks, thousands flocked to Twickenham to see him in the flesh. He had a very average game against Scotland, leaving many wondering what all the fuss was about.

At the start of the Second World War, Obolensky declared that he had played for England and now wanted to fight for her. He joined the Royal Air Force and was killed in a landing accident when his Hawker Hurricane crashed at Martlesham, Norfolk, on 29 March 1940. He had just turned 24. Among the many wreaths at his funeral was one from the NZRFU.

Referee: J.W. Faull (Wales)

Attendance: 72,000

Half-time: ENG 6, NZ 0

Scorers: ENG Obolensky (2t), Sever (t), Cranmer (dg)

ENGLAND: R.J. Longland (Northampton), E.S. Nicholson (Leicester), D.A. Kendrew (Leicester), A.J. Clarke (Coventry), C.F.H. Webb (Devonport Services), E.A. Hamilton-Hill+ (Harlequins), W.H. Weston (Northampton), P.E. Dunkley (Harlequins), B.C. Gadney (*Capt.* Leicester), P.L. Candler (St Bartholomew's Hospital), H.S. Sever+ (Sale), P. Cranmer (Richmond), R.A. Gerrard (Bath), A.S. Obolensky+ (Oxford University), H.G. Owen-Smith (St Mary's Hospital)

NEW ZEALAND: J. Hore (Otago), W.E. Hadley (Auckland), A. Lambourn (Wellington), R.R. King (West Coast), S.T. Reid (Hawke's Bay), H.F. McLean (Auckland), J.E. Manchester (*Capt.* Canterbury), A. Mahoney (Bush Districts), M.M.N. Corner (Auckland), E.W.T. Tindill+ (Wellington), N. Ball (Wellington), T.H.C. Caughey (Auckland), C.J. Oliver (Canterbury), N.A. Mitchell (Southland), G.D.M. Gilbert (West Coast)

Manager: V.R.S. Meredith

Twickenham, London, 30 January 1954
ALL BLACKS 5 – ENGLAND 0

'By Jove, chaps, can't you drop your shoulders under my
rump more?' – Bob Stirling, England captain

THOUGH 18 years (and a world war) had passed since the All Blacks were last in Great Britain and Ireland, the results of the tourists led by Canterbury loose-forward Bob Stuart mirrored that of the 1935/36 team. There were draws with Ulster and Swansea and losses to Wales and Cardiff.

England, on the other hand, had been unbeaten for two years, winning seven and drawing one. Twice they had defeated strong Welsh sides, so home expectations were high that they could notch up a second consecutive win over the All Blacks.

All of the English players had experience at international level. In the backline was centre Jeff Butterfield, one of those naturally gifted players who had pace, balance, a deceptive swerve and sure passing. When he retired from Test rugby, he was England's most-capped back with 28 consecutive appearances (as well as four caps for the 1955 Lions). The England international, the All Blacks' 24th tour match, was played in freezing conditions. The Twickenham turf had been covered in 17 tonnes of straw in the days prior to the game to prevent heavy frosts settling on the turf. All Black prop Bill Clark later recalled that the ground had frozen before the stewards had time to spread the straw back on the field after the match.

Possibly because of the cold, both teams threw the ball about and the fact there was only one try in the game belies the fact there was a lot of running play on the firm ground. The backlines of both sides had threatening periods of attack and counter-attack. Frequent barrelling runs by 15st England right-wing Ted Woodward got the crowd to their feet. Invariably it took two or more All Blacks to halt him and rarely had his opposing wing, Ron Jarden, had such a testing day in defence.

Ron Jarden (NZ 1951–56): 'Unfortunately the straw had been laid only to the sidelines and the ground outside was frozen solid. Every time Ted Woodward and I tackled each other we landed on the frozen patches outside the sidelines, with me underneath, it seemed. By the end of the game I was more All Blue than All Black.'

All Black lock, Graham Dalzell (grandfather of 2011 and 2015 World Cup-winning All Black lock, Sam Whitelock) scored the only try of the match. It came at the end of the first quarter after All Black hooker Ron Hemi twice toed the ball on towards the England line. Covering fullback Ian King went down on the ball but lost control of it. Clark scooped the ball up and gave a short pass to Dalzell who stormed through the defence of Woodward and flung his big frame over the line. Bob Scott, who had starred for the NZ Army side in Britain post-war and was famous for his public displays of barefoot place kicking, added the conversion.

Kevin Skinner, the indomitable All Black prop and boxer, often recalled with some amusement English captain Bob Stirling (of the RAF) calling out at a scrum, 'By Jove, chaps, can't you drop your shoulders under my rump more?'

England's number eight, John Kendall-Carpenter, served as president of the Rugby Union in 1980–81 and chaired the international committee that brought about the first Rugby World Cup in 1987.

Referee: I. David (Wales)

Attendance: 72,000

Half-time: NZ 5, ENG 0

Scorers: NZ Dalzell (t), Scott (c)

ENGLAND: D.L. Sanders (Harlequins), E. Evans (Sale), F/Lt. R.V. Stirling (*Capt*. Royal Air Force), L/Cpl. A.R. Higgins (British Army), P.D. Young (Dublin Wanderers), F/Lt. P.G. Yarranton (Royal Air Force), D.S. Wilson

(Metropolitan Police), J.M.K. Kendall-Carpenter (Bath), G. Rimmer (Waterloo), M. Regan (Liverpool), W.P.C. Davies (Harlequins), J.P. Quinn (New Brighton), J. Butterfield (Northampton), J.E. Woodward (Wasps), I. King (Harrogate).

NEW ZEALAND: H.L. White (Auckland), R.C. Hemi (Waikato), K.L. Skinner (Otago), G.N. Dalzell (Canterbury), R.A. White (Poverty Bay), W.H. Clark (Wellington), P.F.H. Jones+ (North Auckland), R.C. Stuart (*Capt.* Canterbury), K. Davis (Auckland), L.S. Haig (Otago), R.A. Jarden (Wellington), D.D. Wilson+ (Canterbury), C.J. Loader (Wellington), M.J. Dixon (Canterbury), R.W.H. Scott (Auckland)

Coach: A.E. Marslin

MATCH 5

Eden Park, Auckland, 25 May 1963
ALL BLACKS 21 – ENGLAND 11

'If it had been 11-all, our fellows might have found a little extra.' – Mike Weston, England captain

IT is amazing to think that the first time England sent a team to New Zealand was as late as 1963, 58 years after the first visit to Britain by the All Blacks. Then Home Nations champions, they were the first of the individual home unions to set foot on the shaky isles. A somewhat wretched itinerary saw the 27 members of the group travelling the length of the country to play five matches in 15 days. They won their opening game, 14-9 against Wellington but then fell to a strong Otago side 9-14.

Tour captain Mike Weston played at centre and fly-half during his nine seasons of international appearances, which included tours with the Lions in 1962 and 1966.

The Bedford loose-forward duo of David Perry and Derek 'Budge' Rogers were fast men who prided themselves on their tackling. The latter set a record of 34 Tests for England and was awarded an OBE in 1969, the first such honour for an English rugby player.

Roger Hosen, one of three debutants for England, had a reputation as one of the longest place-kickers in the game. Thomas Pargetter, a pastry cook by profession, was regarded as the 'giant' of the team, standing 6ft 4in and weighing in at nearly 17st.

All Black winger Ralph Caulton, who had been omitted from the match day team when many expected him to be an automatic selection, was notified the day before the Test match that he had been recalled to replace the originally chosen Rod Heeps. Late in the afternoon, Caulton flew 305 miles north on a special DC3 flight from Wellington to Auckland.

Upon reaching Auckland the airport was closed due to bad weather, so the pilot turned the plane around and flew 246 miles south to Palmerston North. At 6am the next morning, Caulton was supposed to depart on another Auckland-bound flight but bad weather delayed that take-off until 10am. He finally joined the All Blacks at the Station Hotel in downtown Auckland 'just in time to join the team talk'. (A local club player had been placed on standby and must have had an anxious few hours wondering whether he was going to become an All Black.)

After all the weather problems Caulton experienced, it was a fine Auckland afternoon and the surface at Eden Park was in very good condition, due to the fact the match was played early in the New Zealand season.

England tour manager, W. Tom Berry, had told the newsmen following the tour that his side wanted to win the first Test, no question.

The good weather and condition of the ground did not produce a scintillating game for spectators. The first half was more stop than start as the two sets of forwards wrestled and mauled. When the ball was finally released to the backs, both teams' fly-halves (England's Phil Horrocks-Taylor and New Zealand's Bruce Watt) employed the tactic of kicking for touch to gain territory. There were 52 lineouts in the first half alone!

Amidst all this, England were making the most profit, with Hosen kicking two penalties for the visitors to lead at the break by 6-0. A minute after half-time, All Black fullback Don 'The Boot' Clarke kicked a penalty to halve the deficit.

Four minutes later Ranson had a try on debut. England ran the blind-side from a ruck on the All Blacks' 25-yard line. Quick passing saw Ranson with room outside the defenders Clarke and Thomas Wolfe, and he duly scored mid-way between the posts and corner flag. Hosen easily converted, and England were ahead by eight points. An upset was on!

Five minutes later the tide began to turn. Watt put a grubber kick through towards the England line which fullback Clarke ran on to, scoring a try.

Mike Weston (ENG 1960–68): 'We knew their game was to soften us up for about 60 minutes and then apply the pressure, but we were powerless to stop them.'

Clarke kicked the conversion ... on his second attempt. His first shot missed but the referee, Mr Robson, ruled that the England players had been unsportsmanlike in shouting at Clarke in an attempt to put him off. A second attempt was allowed. (Neutral referees were not appointed to internationals in New Zealand until the late 1970s.)

Mike Weston: 'Those two points meant a lot. They took New Zealand from 6-11 to 8-11. At that stage, their forwards were getting on top and when they later went to 13-11, we had no comeback. But if it had been 11-all, our fellows might have found a little extra.'

As play continued, Hosen found himself in the unenviable position of waiting to catch an All Black punt to claim a mark and bearing down on him was the intimidating figure of Colin 'Pinetree' Meads. As he caught the ball, the King Country farmer barrelled the fullback backwards several yards. To his credit, Hosen hung on to the ball as the rest of the home forwards drove over the top of him. He eventually rose from the Eden Park grass somewhat dishevelled and disoriented, but he had protected the England line.

Caulton then came into his own and showed the selectors they had erred in initially overlooking him, scoring two quick tries from moves using the blind-side. Clarke converted both.

Ralph Caulton (NZ 1959–64): 'By half-time I was feeling exhausted. But I could see I had the edge on my opponent, if only I could get the ball. Suddenly the forwards started dominating and the ball began coming my way.' The final points in the match came via a booming drop goal from near halfway by Clarke.

The All Blacks won by ten points, a big margin that didn't seem a true reflection of the efforts of the England side.

The crowd had seen Clarke (who was as tall as a lock and heavy as his brother, a front row forward), become the first All Black to score four different ways in a Test. But they had also seen 92 lineouts and 32 scrums.

Referee: C.F. Robson (New Zealand)

Attendance: 53,000

Half-time: ENG 6, NZ 0

Scorers: NZ D.B. Clarke (t, p, dg, 3c), Caulton (2t)
ENG Ranson (t), Hosen (2p, c)

NEW ZEALAND: W.J. Whineray (*Capt*. Auckland), D. Young (Canterbury), I.J. Clarke (Waikato), A.J. Stewart+ (Canterbury), C.E. Meads (King Country), W.J. Nathan (Auckland), K.R. Tremain (Hawke's Bay), D.J. Graham (Canterbury), D.M. Connor (Auckland), B.A. Watt (Canterbury), R.W. Caulton (Wellington), T.N. Wolfe (Taranaki), I.N. Uttley+ (Wellington), D.W. McKay (Auckland), D.B. Clarke (Waikato)

Coach: N. McPhail

ENGLAND: P.E. Judd (Coventry), H.O. Godwin (Coventry), C.R. Jacobs (Northampton), T. A. Pargetter (Coventry), A.M. Davis (Torquay Athletic), D.P. Rogers (Bedford), V.R. Marriott+ (Harlequins), D.G. Perry (Bedford), S.J.S. Clarke (Cambridge University), J.P. Horrocks-Taylor (Leicester), J.M. Dee (Hartlepool), M.S. Phillips (Fylde), M.P. Weston (*Capt*. Durham City), J.M. Ranson+ (Rosslyn Park), R.W. Hosen+ (Northampton)

Assistant manager: M.R. Steele-Bodger

MATCH 6

Lancaster Park, Christchurch, 1 June 1963
ALL BLACKS 9 – ENGLAND 6

'I was forced to kick a controversial goal from a mark to earn a win.' – Don Clarke, All Black fullback

IN the days after the Eden Park Test, England travelled south to Christchurch via Napier, on the east coast of the North Island. There they played a Hawke's Bay side that were, for only the second time in their history, the dominant side in New Zealand domestic rugby. They were in the middle of a long tenure holding the Ranfurly Shield and dispatched England, as they had local sides, with tremendous interplay between committed forwards and speedy backs. The margin of the 20-5 loss was something of a shock to the England players who had been so competitive in the Test match.

The most talked about change to the England side for the second Test was the recall of 35-year-old wing Frank Sykes, eight years after gaining his only two caps.

The second Test was the 500th game played by the All Blacks and showed the fickle nature of top-level sport. Whereas the week before All Black fullback Don Clarke had scored four different ways, on Lancaster Park he struggled to get on the scoresheet at all.

Early in the match, England lock Mike Davis dislocated his shoulder and, in the days before replacements were allowed, left the field. Later in the half, to the amazement of the crowd – and probably some of his team-mates – he returned to the fray with his shoulder heavily strapped. That he played the rest of the match against one of the strongest forward packs the All Blacks assembled in the 1960s was a testament to his bravery and commitment to the England cause. The doyen of New Zealand rugby writers, T.P. McLean commented that he had, 'never seen greater gallantry in any Rugby man than Davis displayed'.

In the first half, England had a strong, cool wind at their backs. Clarke and Roger Hosen both had admirable but wayward long-range penalty attempts before All Black wing Don McKay sprinted 25 yards to the try-line after taking a short pass from loose-forward Kel Tremain. Clarke's conversion attempt sailed wide.

Six minutes later Hosen kicked a penalty to level the scores.

The All Blacks added another try after a loose ball was toed just over the England line. Davis, with no thought for his injured shoulder, dived to defensively ground the ball but was just beaten to it by All Black second-five, Pat Walsh. Clarke again missed the conversion.

England drew level again when the free-running Budge Rogers put a huge punt in behind the All Blacks' backline. Malcolm Phillips, the fast England inside-centre, was first to the ball, scooping it up and touching down in the corner. A successful conversion from Hosen would have put England in front, but it missed.

With the scores locked at 6-all, the final few minutes were very tense. A first win on New Zealand soil was even nearer to the grasp of the Englishmen than it had been the week before in Auckland.

Arise Don Clarke, who claimed a mark on halfway from a clearing kick. Standing well inside his own half, he lined up a kick at goal.

Don Clarke (NZ 1956–64): 'One [England player] was telling the other to charge the instant I moved towards the ball. They didn't appreciate that they couldn't advance until the ball was placed on the ground and I had [my brother] Ian holding it six inches above the ground. So, I took one step forward and paused. The three of them charged, and I protested to the referee who correctly awarded me a free kick.'

Clarke's kick – at which the England players were not allowed to charge – was successful, the only goal from a mark in matches between the two countries.

The Christchurch crowd held their breath as Hosen had a late chance to draw the game. Kicking into the wind, his long-distance penalty attempt was blown wide.

It's fair to say the English side could have won the match. Few All Blacks supporters would not have regarded them as deserved victors.

Don Clarke: 'There were clear signs in the match of what might have been, of growing strength in the [England] pack, and enterprise in the backs, but by then the tour was over.'

So, England departed after a fortnight in New Zealand with a one win-four and four losses from their whirlwind tour.

Don Clarke: 'They were hardly here before they were gone again. We had no opportunity to see them at their best and they must have gone away with little impression of New Zealand other than the toughness of our forwards, the interior of our hotels, and our transport system. This was disappointing because some great players made the trip.'

Hosen, who had scored 30 of the team's 45 tour points, had been the pick of the England backs. Perry consistently impressed, being very hard to stop when his 16st frame had some steam up. Davis was respected by the All Blacks, both for his toughness and skills as a versatile forward. Halfback Simon Clarke also earned the typically understated Kiwi epithet of 'a good player'.

A mere three days later, of which one was taken up with crossing the Tasman by air, England played Australia at the Sydney Cricket Ground, losing 9-18. To think that some coaches of today are heard to say their teams play too many matches in a short space of time.

Referee: J.P. Murphy (New Zealand)

Attendance: 40,000

Half-time: NZ 6, ENG 3

Scorers: NZ McKay (t), Walsh (t), Clarke (gfm)
ENG Phillips (t), Hosen (p)

NEW ZEALAND: W.J. Whineray (*Capt.* Auckland), D. Young (Canterbury), I.J. Clarke (Waikato), A.J. Stewart (Canterbury), C.E. Meads (King Country), W.J. Nathan (Auckland), K.R. Tremain (Hawke's Bay), D.J. Graham (Canterbury), D.M. Connor (Auckland), B.A. Watt (Canterbury), R.W. Caulton (Wellington), P.T. Walsh (Counties), I.N. Uttley (Wellington), D.W. McKay (Auckland), D.B. Clarke (Waikato)

Coach: N. McPhail

ENGLAND: P.E. Judd (Coventry), H.O. Godwin (Coventry), C.R. Jacobs (Northampton), D.G. Perry (Bedford), A.M. Davis (Torquay Athletic), D.P.

Rogers (Bedford), V.R. Marriott (Harlequins), B.J. Wightman (Coventry), S.J.S. Clarke (Cambridge University), J.P. Horrocks-Taylor (Leicester), J.M. Ranson (Rosslyn Park), M.S. Phillips (Fylde), M.P. Weston (*Capt.* Durham City), F.D. Sykes (Northampton), R.W. Hosen (Northampton)

Assistant manager: M.R. Steele-Bodger

MATCH 7

Twickenham, London, 4 January 1964
ALL BLACKS 14 – ENGLAND 0

'More fire in the mauls, chaps!'
– Nicholas Drake-Lee, England prop

FOR the third time in eight months England faced the All Blacks, only this time they were back on home soil on a misty, cold afternoon.

Both teams had one international debutant. For England, centre Roger Sangwin came in for the injured Peter Jackson while number eight Brian Lochore got a call-up to the top visitors' XV. He replaced Waka Nathan whose jaw had been broken in the tour match against Llanelli.

Brian Lochore (NZ 1963–71): 'I was still coming to terms with my first Test selection while they were playing the anthems. It was a strange mixture. Emotion, anticipation, some trepidation, pride, awe. The experience did not stop because the last whistle went. The experience that day, my first Test, had no use-by date. It influenced my rugby to the day I played my last game.'

Both backlines were accused of stretching the offside laws. Very flat defensive lines, used by both the All Blacks and their opponents, had been an issue all tour. On attack, the All Blacks tried to counter it by having forwards run from mauls with the ball before releasing it to the backs. In this match, the defensive speed with which the All Blacks were up on halfback Simon Clarke and fly-half Phil Horrocks-Taylor meant they shared a somewhat nightmarish afternoon trying to clear the ball.

Don Clarke, who hadn't enjoyed his usual success with the boot on tour, kicked penalties for the All Blacks in the fifth and 22nd minutes. After half an hour of play, All Black loose-forward Kel Tremain broke from a maul and inter-passed with his captain, prop Wilson Whineray. Ball in hand again, Tremain linked with wing Ralph Caulton who scored out wide. Clarke missed the conversion, but the All Blacks led at the break by 9-0.

As the players devoured their respective oranges at half-time, Whineray addressed his team. 'Lads, I'd like us to get a try in the first five minutes after half-time,' he said.

That instruction was fortuitously carried out two minutes after the restart when Caulton intercepted a long floating pass Horrocks-Taylor had intended for Malcolm Phillips. Instead, Caulton raced towards the English line. As the desperate cover defence reached him, he passed to supporting flanker John Graham who strode on before feeding Colin Meads. Unstoppable, he thumped the ball down under the posts in the tackles of two Englishmen. Clarke easily converted.

Try as they might – Phillips created an overlap, but Roger Sangwin couldn't hold the pass and a long-range penalty attempt by captain and fullback John Willcox bounced away off the woodwork – the home side just could not get on the scoreboard. Their 14-point defeat was the largest losing margin by an England team at Twickenham.

Don Clarke (NZ 1956–64): 'The easiest Test of the tour, the match against England, was a peculiar delight and disappointment. We were pleased to win as we did, but some of us were surprised too that English players we met on the earlier short tour of New Zealand had absorbed so little from those matches.'

Some rugby historians have pointed to this period as being one of the low points of English rugby. Certainly, it was part of a frustrating decade in which the team won only 16 of 46 internationals and drew ten others.

Post-match, as the All Blacks left the field to a standing ovation from the crowd, one RFU official was heard to say it was, 'Perhaps the most magnificent period of rugger ever seen at Twickenham.'

If the All Blacks' play was considered that good, there was even better to come.

Referee: D.C.J. McMahon (Scotland)

Attendance: 65,000

Half-time: NZ 9, ENG 0

Scorers: NZ Caulton (t), Meads (t), Clarke (con, 2 pen)

ENGLAND: N.J. Drake-Lee (Cambridge University), H.O. Godwin (Coventry), P.E. Judd (Coventry), A.M. Davis (Torquay Athletic), J.E. Owen (Coventry), V.R. Marriott (Harlequins), D.P. Rogers (Bedford), D.G. Perry (Bedford), S.J.S. Clarke (Cambridge University), J.P. Horrocks-Taylor (Middlesbrough), J. Roberts (Sale), M.P. Weston (Durham City), R.D. Sangwin+ (Hull & East Riding), M.S. Phillips (Fylde), J.G. Willcox (*Capt.* Harlequins)

NEW ZEALAND: W.J. Whineray (*Capt.* Auckland), D. Young (Canterbury), K.F. Gray (Wellington), A.J. Stewart (Canterbury), C.E. Meads (King Country), K.R. Tremain (Hawke's Bay), D.J. Graham (Canterbury), B.J. Lochore+ (Wairarapa), K.C. Briscoe (Taranaki), B.A. Watt (Canterbury), R.W. Caulton (Wellington), D.A. Arnold (Canterbury), P.F. Little (Auckland), M.J. Dick (Auckland), D.B. Clarke (Waikato)

Coach: N. McPhail

Twickenham, London, 4 November 1967
ALL BLACKS 23 – ENGLAND 11

*'You scored five tries to England's two because you
executed the basics of rugby better than they did.'*
– Fred Allen, All Blacks coach

I F those who saw the All Blacks' win in 1964 thought the men from
the southern hemisphere couldn't play any better, they had a big
surprise when Brian Lochore's 1967 team visited Twickenham in
the NZRFU's 75th Jubilee year.

The All Blacks' end-of-year tour of the British Isles, France and
Canada came about after a planned visit to South Africa was called
off. An increasing percentage of the New Zealand public did not
accept the South African Rugby Union policy of 'whites-only' teams
and put unsurmountable pressure on the NZRFU to cancel the trip.
The 'short' 17-match tour replaced it.

Coached by Fred 'The Needle' Allen, who had been a ball-running
star of the 1945/46 'Kiwis' army side that played in Britain and later
captain of the All Blacks, the side had won their first five games (two
of which were easy 'shake-downs' in Canada) with an exciting brand
of running rugby, reminiscent of the 1905 and 1924 tourists.

When the squad for the tour had first been named in New Zealand,
Allen had a public announcement to players, pressmen and public
alike.

Fred Allen (NZ coach 1966–68): 'This will be one hell of a team,
but it won't be playing the type of football you're used to seeing these

past few years. This team will run with the ball at every opportunity and it will win by scoring tries – not by kicking goals. Rugby is basically a running, passing game so our number one priority will be to attack at all times from all parts of the field. And if we get it right, the game will benefit immensely because wherever we go spectators will come to watch.'

When the team assembled in Wellington for a training run prior to their departure, and the style of play was reiterated, Colin Meads reportedly said, 'You mean we're going to run the ball all the time?'

Members of the England forward pack had already come up against the All Blacks when playing for the county selection Midlands, London and Home Counties who had been defeated the previous week, 3-15. In that game, centre Danny Hearn, who had played seven internationals for England, suffered a shocking injury when he dislocated his neck making a tackle.

England captain, Phil 'Juddy' Judd was nearing the end of his playing career, having made his debut for Coventry way back in the 1952/53 season. Referee McMahon had controlled the All Blacks' previous visit to Twickenham and thus became the first man to officiate two Tests between the sides.

For the second tour of Britain in a row, All Black flanker Waka Nathan missed the England match due to a broken jaw, courtesy this time of a punch from Budge Rogers in the Home Counties game. New Zealand rugby commentator and writer Winston McCarthy likened it to 'as fine a punch as Jack Dempsey ever threw'. That the English pressmen following the tour made no detailed mention of the incident, which had even caused a reaction from sideline spectators, was an annoyance to some of the tourists.

On the field before the match, Queen Elizabeth and the Duke of Edinburgh were introduced to each player, the first time an English monarch had undertaken this duty.

Earle Kirton (NZ 1963–70): 'Charlie Saxton [1938 All Black and captain of the 'Kiwis'], our manager, said spin the ball at all costs. He wanted every back to have a run in the first five minutes. Why let wingers get cold and apprehensive, he asked. So we ran it.'

The All Blacks' ambition was to be tested by the slippery conditions under foot, thanks to several days of constant rain. However, in the first few minutes of the game England debutant William Gittings threw a nervous pass that went to ground. The All Blacks claimed the ball and Meads drove into the England 25. The ball was fed to the backs and second-five Bill Davis stepped twice off his left foot to elude England defenders. It looked as though he would make it to the line himself, but he lost his balance. As he tumbled to the ground he passed to Kirton who scored in his first international.

The All Blacks' second try came after Kirton dropped a pass inside his own half. England's forwards couldn't grasp it and All Black loose-forward Graham Williams came away with it. He ran upfield before making a left-footed kick ahead which was partially charged by experienced England fullback, Don Rutherford, who had first played for his country in 1960. The ball then pinballed around between defending England players and the boots of All Blacks Ian McRae and Meads before wing Bill Birtwhistle picked it up and dived over the line in the left-hand corner.

Williams was the next to score after a superb cross-field kick from McRae inside the All Blacks' half bounced kindly for Birtwhistle who, with a jink and a couple of swerves, all but made it to the England line. The trailing Davis tried to pick the ball up but knocked on. At the ensuing scrum on the England line, pressure from the All Blacks slowed the home side's heel and Williams reached through the legs of England forwards to force the ball for a try.

Kirton had a second try when he took a pass from Laidlaw just outside the England 25 and scythed through a gap, running towards the left-hand corner flag where he dived over. Referee McMahon consulted his touch judge as to whether Kirton had stayed in the field of play before awarding the try, which didn't please all of the nearby spectators.

Late in the half, England produced their own scintillating piece of running rugby. Keith Savage and Colin McFadyean combined midway inside the All Blacks' half to put Bob Lloyd into space and he raced away to score, leaving three All Blacks in his wake.

All Black prop Jack Hazlett, who had captained Southland to a win over the 1966 Lions, had looked a picture of gentility and courtesy when shaking the hand of the Queen pre-match, but once the game was on, he was looking for a chance to get some retribution for the injury to Nathan. As the players left a lineout he clobbered Rogers. There was nothing subtle about it and, being on halfway, a better spot for everyone to see it couldn't have been found. Allen's final words to the team before they took to the field had been, 'No rough stuff'. It was to be Hazlett's last Test match for the All Blacks.

When McMahon blew his whistle for half-time, there was genuine applause from the crowd who had seen 40 minutes of almost perfect play and execution from the All Blacks.

In the second half, England made changes to their defensive patterns and their forwards drew the All Blacks into more rucks and mauls.

Colin Meads (NZ 1957–71): 'Suddenly we were in the middle of a hell of a battle. Where it had been all advance before, now it was all hold because these English, just as they had done in 1963, were fighting. It was unfortunate for them that again, as in 1963, the match was out of their reach by the time they pulled themselves together.'

The final All Black try, from a set piece, was again exceptional. After captain Lochore had tapped the ball back to Laidlaw from a lineout, Davis ran straight in midfield, breaking two tackles. He then passed to right-wing Malcolm Dick who sped away to score.

In the final minute of the match, with light fading, England broke downfield. John Finlan made a huge centring kick which wasn't controlled by the All Blacks. The England forwards regathered it 15 yards from the New Zealand line. McFadyean passed left to Lloyd who, as Davis had done in the first half, twice stepped back off his left foot and ran untouched for a score by the left-hand upright. A second try on debut, matching Prince Obolensky's deeds 31 years prior.

It was appropriate that this was the first Test match televised in colour, as this All Black side had thrown off the drab shroud of slow, grinding, forwards-dominated rugby and shone a new light on how to play 15-man football at pace.

It was a glimpse into the future, too. While similar play would be used by the victorious 1971 Lions in New Zealand, it wouldn't really be seen by All Black teams for another 20 years.

After the obligatory soak in the Twickenham bath tubs, the teams and 300 invited guests attended a formal dinner at the Park Lane Hilton.

Bob Lloyd, then a 24-year-old civil engineer, went on to face the All Blacks again, as part of the Barbarians side that played their part in a magnificent game at Twickenham five weeks later. The All Blacks won 11-6 but Lloyd, who had also dotted down against the tourists for Midlands, London and Home Counties, scored his fourth try against the All Blacks.

The All Blacks were denied the opportunity to complete their first Grand Slam when an outbreak of foot and mouth disease in England saw the Republic of Ireland close her borders and the Dublin Test was cancelled.

Fred Allen coached the All Blacks in 14 undefeated internationals from 1966–68. He remains the only All Black coach not to have lost a Test match.

Referee: D.C.J. McMahon (Scotland)

Attendance: 74,000

Half-time: NZ 18, ENG 5

Scorers: NZ Kirton (2t), Birtwhistle (t), Laidlaw (t), Dick (t), McCormick (4c)
ENG Lloyd (2t), Rutherford (c), Larter (p)

ENGLAND: P.E. Judd (*Capt.* Coventry), H.O. Godwin (Coventry), A.J. Horton (Blackheath), P.J. Larter (Northampton), J.E. Owen (Coventry), R.B. Taylor (Northampton), D.P. Rogers (Bedford), G.A. Sherriff (Saracens), W.J. Gittings+ (Coventry), J.F. Finlan (Moseley), R.E. Webb (Coventry), C.W. McFadyean (Moseley), R.H. Lloyd+ (Harlequins), K.F. Savage (Northampton), D. Rutherford (Gloucester)

NEW ZEALAND: E.J. Hazlett (Southland), B.E. McLeod (Counties), B.L. Muller (Taranaki), S.C. Strahan (Manawatu), C.E. Meads (King Country), K.R. Tremain (Hawke's Bay), B.J. Lochore (*Capt.* Wairarapa Bush), C.R. Laidlaw (Otago), E.W. Kirton+ (Otago), W.M. Birtwhistle (Waikato), W.L. Davis (Hawke's Bay), I.R. MacRae (Hawke's Bay), M.J. Dick (Auckland), W.F. McCormick (Canterbury)

Coach: F. Allen

MATCH 9

Twickenham, London, 6 January 1973
ALL BLACKS 9 – ENGLAND 0

*'Can England rise to the challenge of today's All
Blacks as they did to the challenge of the Springboks?'
– David Frost, rugby writer*

WHILE the mid-to-late 1960s was a golden period for the
All Blacks, the early-to-mid 1970s were days of relative
gloom for the NZRFU. The highly fancied All Blacks lost
the brutal 1970 Test series in South Africa 1-3 and the following year
the British and Irish Lions won their first series in New Zealand with
brilliant running rugby. England wing David Duckham became a
favourite with the New Zealand crowds, who were thrilled by his
speed and skill.

Controversy then enveloped the All Blacks' 32-match tour of Great
Britain, Ireland, France and North America. Hulking prop Keith
Murdoch was sent home six weeks into the tour after a late-night
dust-up with a doorman at a Welsh hotel the team were staying at.
In the shadow of that distraction, three days later the All Blacks lost
8-16 to Midland Counties West, who had in their line-up England
Test players Duckham (who captained the side), centre Peter Preece
and fly-half John Finlan.

England hadn't started the decade too well, either, winning only a
quarter of their Test matches and suffering heavy defeats to rampant
French and Scottish teams along the way. This despite having a
formally appointed coach for the first time, former international
forward Don White.

A change of fortune came on England's 1972 tour to South Africa. It was the first time an England team had visited the Republic and, much like their first trip to New Zealand almost a decade earlier, the schedule was a punishing one for captain John Pullin and his 25 players. There were seven games between May 17 and the single Test match on June 3. Add in that three of the fixtures were at altitude, and the side's record of remaining undefeated – drawing 13-all with Northern Transvaal and convincingly defeating the Springboks 18-9 at Ellis Park – was all the more remarkable.

So, as David Frost wrote in the matchday programme:

> Can they do it again? Was it a once-in-a-lifetime performance? Can England rise to the challenge of today's All Blacks as they did to the challenge of the Springboks? It is indeed a tantalising question.

Unfortunately, after 80 minutes on very soft ground, the answer was no.

Grant Batty (NZ 1972–77): 'I cannot recall us making fewer mistakes in any of the other 55 games I played for New Zealand ... It was like performing a play where every actor was right on cue and gave of his best.'

Notable among them was halfback Sid Going, whose runs from behind the pack kept his big men moving forward, and second-five Mike Parkinson made 16 tackles – a staggering amount for the times – which illustrated where England had concentrated much of their attack.

After just eight minutes, flanker and captain Ian Kirkpatrick became the All Blacks' greatest Test try-scorer when he picked the ball up from behind a disintegrating maul and scrambled over the line by the right-hand upright. Kirkpatrick's 11th Test try broke a record that had stood since before World War I. Fullback Joe Karam converted.

Kirkpatrick nearly had a second try close to fulltime but lost the ball as he went to put it down in the in-goal, having charged to the line from near the 22.

Ian Kirkpatrick (NZ 1967–77): 'It was my own silly fault. I tried to force the ball with one hand.'

Sam Doble, the towering 6ft 4in England fullback, who had kicked four penalties and a superb sideline conversion in the Johannesburg victory, had five penalty shots at goal and just could not get the ball to fly through the uprights. Sadly, the young schoolmaster died of cancer just four years later.

Preece (whose father Ivor had captained England in the 1950s) and debutant Peter Warfield did create their side's best try-scoring opportunity in midfield but were called back for a forward pass.

To complete the scoring for the All Blacks, wing Bryan 'Beegee' Williams knocked over what would be his only drop goal in 113 matches for the All Blacks.

In his match report for *The Evening News*, Doug Ibbotson wrote:

> England produced most of the good football and showed tremendous spirit, but even the smallest errors were seized upon by the fates (not to mention the referee), and they were denied the glory they so richly deserved.

David Frost's post-match report in *The Guardian* saw the match as one where:

> There seemed to be a corporate discipline that had been lacking earlier in the tour ... the [All Blacks'] style of play was moulded to fit the individual performance of Sid Going, and he responded with one of the greatest displays of running and intelligent defence.

England prop William Anderson was the first player from the Orrell club to play for his country and, in another first, New Zealand fans had been able to see the match live via satellite.

Referee: J. Young (Scotland)
Attendance: 72,000
Half-time: NZ 6, ENG 0
Scorers: NZ Kirkpatrick (t), Karam (c), Williams (dg)
ENGLAND: C.B. Stevens (Penryn), J.V. Pullin (*Capt.* Bristol), W.F. Anderson+ (Orrell), P.J. Larter (Northampton), C.W. Ralston (Richmond), J.A. Watkins

(Gloucester), A. Neary (Broughton Park), A.G. Ripley (Rosslyn Park), J.G. Webster (Moseley), J.F. Finlan (Moseley), D.J. Duckham (Coventry), P.J. Warfield+ (Rosslyn Park), P.S. Preece (Coventry), A.J. Morley (Bristol), S.A. Doble (Moseley)

Coach: J. Elders

NEW ZEALAND: G.J. Whiting (King Country), R.W. Norton (Canterbury), K.K. Lambert (Manawatu), H.H. Macdonald (Canterbury), P.J. Whiting (Auckland), A.J. Wyllie (Canterbury), I.A. Kirkpatrick (*Capt*. Poverty Bay), A.R. Sutherland (Marlborough), S.M. Going (North Auckland), I.N. Stevens (Wellington), G.B. Batty (Wellington), R.M. Parkinson (Poverty Bay), B.J. Robertson (Counties), B.G. Williams (Auckland), J.F. Karam (Wellington)

Coach: B. Duff

Eden Park, Auckland, 15 September 1973
ENGLAND 16 – ALL BLACKS 10

'We have plucked the crown jewel of rugby.'
– Sandy Sanders, England manager

ENGLAND'S second visit to New Zealand, a decade after the first, was against a backdrop of international political turmoil. Their tour had been hastily arranged in July when the RFU cancelled the planned tour of Argentina, due to a volatile political situation and reported threats against the team.

The All Blacks had again been scheduled to tour South Africa but the NZRFU postponed it after receiving a letter from Prime Minister Norman Kirk 'asking' that the tour be deferred, in part due to the unrest it caused in the Republic and New Zealand.

The NZRFU openly objected to the mix of sport and politics, but the whole affair just added to a shambolic time for the sporting body still struggling to deal with the fall-out from the sending home at the end of the previous year of Keith Murdoch.

With South Africa no longer a destination for the season, Scotland were approached to tour New Zealand but declined on account of player availability. England agreed to a four-match visit, following a stop-over in Fiji. There they scraped home 13-12 against the home side thanks to a last-minute Peter Squire try.

Before their arrival, the All Blacks had a disastrous four-match internal tour in which they lost to the New Zealand Juniors and a President's XV captained by the 'retired' Colin Meads. Wags were known to joke that the consolation was that New Zealand teams had won both games. When the All Blacks assembled for the Test, they stayed in the same hotel as when England had toured ten years prior. But, it had now lost most of its earlier grandeur.

J.J. Stewart (NZ coach 1974–76): 'We were in rooms no longer used because they did not meet the statutory standards. Two All Blacks to each little room, no individual room facilities, a bathroom toilet at the end of the passage. It was pre-war facilities.'

Little was expected of the England side in the Test match after they had struggled to topple Fiji and then lost their three provincial matches against Taranaki (3-6), Wellington (16-25) and Canterbury (12-19).

England could have won the Canterbury game. They had played well but their kickers – fly-half Alan Old and fullback Peter Rossborough – failed with all nine shots at goal and a pass from Rossborough to Squires was intercepted, giving Canterbury the winning try.

In the days before the Test match the England team travelled to the Bay of Islands, in the north of New Zealand. There a mixed diet of skills work, running, set piece drills, rounds of golf and fishing trips put the under-rated team in the right frame of mind heading to Auckland.

Roger Uttley (ENG 1973–80): 'Some people were even surprised that we bothered to appear. But as John Pullin had said at the after-match dinner following the Irish game [in February, lost 9-18 after suffering a 9-25 defeat to Wales the previous week]: "We might not be much good, but we do at least turn up."'

In the team-talk before the match, in changing rooms Uttley described as 'among the most cold and miserable in the world', England felt that the All Blacks were prepared for them to constantly run the ball. The England plan, however, was that their loose-forwards (Andy Ripley, Tony Neary and John Watkins) were the winning of the match if they could disrupt the All Blacks and defuse the threat seen at Twickenham at the start of the year, that of a running Sid Going.

The hookers, England captain John Pullin and former All Black captain Tane Norton, were opposing each other for the ninth time in provincial and international matches.

Chosen by the England management group to referee the match was former 11-Test All Black wing, Frank McMullen.

In the first half England played into the prevailing westerly wind. New Zealand had the first points when an 8- (Alex 'Grizz' Wyllie) 9- (Sid Going) 14- (Grant Batty) blind-side move from a scrum on the England line resulted in an unconverted try. If used again almost immediately, the same move could have brought another try to Batty.

Grant Batty (NZ 1972–77): '[They] hadn't reinforced their blind-side defence, so I called for the same move. If I hadn't scored, Sid would have. But Grizz said no. He switched play to the open side, and the chance was lost.'

Three minutes later, England replied in fantastic fashion when, from a scrum near the middle of the pitch, halfback Jan 'Sprat' Webster – who played the game of his life – Watkins and the long-haired, head-band-wearing Ripley passed among themselves to make quick ground upfield. Finding himself with the ball again, Webster arced a pass to Squires. A contracted professional cricketer with Yorkshire, Squires usually had a safe pair of hands but, in the words of the New Zealand commentator Keith Quinn, 'he had it, lost control of it and gathered it again' to score in the corner.

Rossborough, with a kicking style which saw him keep his head bowed long after he'd booted the ball, converted. Things were going England's way, 6-4.

With 13 minutes still to play in the first half, All Black centre Ian Hurst scored untouched thanks to a long pass from Going. The conversion gave the home side a 10-6 lead at the break.

'More problems for Pullin, who hasn't had a happy time of it in New Zealand,' remarked Quinn.

In the second half, thanks to pressure from England and moments of hesitation in a reshuffled All Black backline, due to first-five Mike Parkinson leaving the field injured, the home side's play became very disjointed. With eight minutes gone, fullback Bob Lendrum failed to find touch with a defensive clearance that was partially charged. Webster claimed it and in-passed to prop Brian 'Stack' Stevens. He gave a short pass to the charging Chris Ralston who then threw the ball back to Stevens. The 32-year old Cornwall farmer, who had begun his first-class rugby career as a wing but was having a dominant day in the scrum, ran the remaining ten metres to score his first Test try. Watkins was all smiles as he lifted Stevens from the Eden Park turf.

Rossborough knocked over the easy conversion. England in front again, 12-10, and increasingly looking the dominant side.

'Now, Ian Kirkpatrick, the problems belong to you,' said Quinn.

Bryan Williams (NZ 1970–78): 'That can happen so easily in rugby, when two evenly-matched sides are opposing each other. The tide will turn, and you are helpless to do anything about it.'

Fran Cotton (ENG 1971–81): 'What we hadn't reckoned on was our domination of the set pieces where we pushed New Zealand all over the field.'

The score remained the same until there were only nine minutes left to play.

'It seems the word has gone out from Ian Kirkpatrick that New Zealand must try everything and anything to win this game,' said Quinn.

Chants of 'Black, Black, Black!' went up from sections of the crowd, urging their players on.

Lendrum had a close-range penalty chance to put the All Blacks in front but the kick was a poor one, barely reaching the height of the crossbar and curling away from the posts sharply like a hooked golf shot.

As the scoreboard clock ticked on, a long high box kick from Webster kept blowing away from Lendrum as he tried to claim it. All he could do was smother it as it hit the ground. Who was there to claim it? Webster. Metres from the All Black line he sent a pass to Old who gave it to Neary. The Lancashire lawyer, playing his 17th consecutive international for England, dived across the line leaving Rossborough a relatively easy conversion. 16-10.

The All Blacks finally started to play with some cohesion and spirit but there was no way England were going to give up their lead. The final minute of play summed up the difference between the two teams. Rather than maul and close the game down, prop Fran Cotton burst into the open and threw not one but two outrageously slow dummy passes, one to his left then to his right. They completely bamboozled Going.

Fran Cotton: 'He was in the third row of the stands before he realised I still had the ball. This was followed by a dainty little side-step past John Dougan, the fly-half, and then an enormous welly downfield ... Immediately after the game I had my Front Row Union card torn up by Mickey Burton who never forgave me.'

Roger Uttley: 'For a visiting prop to commit such a crime in New Zealand only served to emphasise our superiority.'

Cotton's 'welly downfield' ran all the way to the All Blacks' in-goal. Such was the day he was having, Lendrum had great difficulty controlling the ball but was judged to have forced it a millisecond before the chasing Ripley put his hand on it.

Then the final whistle blew. Pullin's men had made history! The Eden Park crowd acknowledged the momentousness of the occasion and gave the men in white a standing ovation.

Interviewed on the field in the minutes after the final whistle, Pullin – who was the first England captain to lead sides to wins over South Africa, Australia and New Zealand – was both ecstatic and exhausted.

John Pullin (ENG 1966–76): 'I thought I'd never surpass Ellis Park, but this is even better because we didn't have too good a record up until now. I can't say thank you enough to the lads for what they did for me this afternoon. They really pulled out everything.'

England's loose forwards had been the winning of the match. They were superb, as was halfback Webster. They deservedly humbled the All Blacks at home for the first time. The result brought John Watkins to tears.

Ian Kirkpatrick (NZ 1967–77): 'Full credit to them. The England forwards, especially, played well ... We were flat and just couldn't get motivated ... Frankly, I didn't care all that much at the time. I'd had a gutsful. My own form had been terrible, easily the worst of my career. I didn't tell anyone but actually at the end of that 1973 season I came very, very close to retiring.'

Alex Wyllie (NZ 1970–73): 'That was a game better forgotten, like the whole season.'

Frank McMullen (referee): 'It was an easy game to referee. As I came off J.J. Stewart [All Black coach] said, "Thanks, Frank, we've got no complaints," which heartened me.'

England celebrated long into the night. After the post-match function, on their return to their central city lodgings (which were much more salubrious than where the All Blacks were holed-up), the Royal International Hotel resounded with the high-spirited party singing a victory song which had been appropriated from that chanted on football terraces:

'I went down to Auckland swinging my chain,
I met an All Black on the train,
I kneed him in the balls and kicked him in the head
Now that All Black is dead.
Na-na-na-na-na-na-na-na-na
Na-na-na-na-na-na-na-na-na
We are the England boot boys!'

Referee: R.F. McMullen (Auckland, New Zealand)

Attendance: 56,000

Half time: NZ 10, ENG 6

Scorers: ENG Squires (t), Stevens (t), Neary (t), Rossborough (2c)
NZ Batty (t), Hirst (t), Lendrum (c)

NEW ZEALAND: M.G. Jones+ (North Auckland), R.W. Norton (Canterbury), K.K. Lambert (Manawatu), H.H. MacDonald (Canterbury), S.C. Strahan Manawatu), K.W. Stewart+ (Southland), I.A. Kirkpatrick (*Capt*. Poverty Bay), A.J. Wyllie (Canterbury), S.M. Going (North Auckland), J.P. Dougan (Wellington), G.B. Batty (Wellington), R.M. Parkinson (Poverty Bay), I.A. Hurst (Canterbury), B.G. Williams (Auckland), R.N. Lendrum+ (Counties)

From the reserves' bench: T. Morrison+ (Otago)

Coach: J.J. Stewart

ENGLAND: C.B. Stevens (Penryn), J.V. Pullin (*Capt*. Bristol), F.E. Cotton (Coventry), R.M. Uttley (Gosford), C.W. Ralston (Richmond), J.A. Watkins (Gloucester), A. Neary (Broughton Park), A.G. Ripley (Rosslyn Park), J.G. Webster (Moseley), A.G.B. Old (Leicester), D.J. Duckham (Coventry), G.W. Evans (Cooper), P.S. Preece (Coventry), P.J. Squires (Harrogate), P.A. Rossborough (Coventry)

From the reserves' bench: M.J. Cooper (Moseley)

Coach: J. Elders

MATCH 11

Twickenham, London, 25 November 1978
ALL BLACKS 16 – ENGLAND 6

'We were thumped.' – Bill Beaumont, England captain

THE 18-match tour of Great Britain and Ireland for Graham Mourie's 1978 All Blacks is remembered as much for a famous loss as for becoming the first New Zealand team to complete the Grand Slam. In the fifth match of the tour they were defeated by Munster at Limerick, 0-12. All Blacks who played that day have quipped that their side was so out-gunned by the fevered tackling of the Munstermen they were lucky to get 0! A few days later, a try with two minutes remaining gave them a 10-6 Test win over Ireland in Dublin.

The England selectors' plan was to match the All Blacks forwards, particularly in the loose. Their devised pack saw specialist loose-head prop Barry Nelmes at tight-head and usual number eight John Scott moved into the second row, in essence giving their side a fourth loose-forward. (Scott was never selected to play in that position again.) Even at the time these were baffling selections, given that the All Black pack had also been commanding at scrum time, most notably against a well-drilled, muscular Midlands pack.

Peter Wheeler (ENG 1975–84): 'It was the sort of experiment which [the selectors] might just have toyed with against the Americans; to do it against the All Blacks was asking for trouble and we got it.'

Andy Haden (NZ 1972–85): 'Chris Ralston was always respected by [All Black lock] Peter Whiting as a world-class middle-of-the-lineout man. By the time I encountered him, in England in 1978, he was considered past his best and was no longer selected at international level ... but he should have been. He would have been a far better bet than John Scott, who never really had a chance in the lineout against the All Blacks. [The selections were] a classic example of the folly of fielding players out of position at Test level. England handed us that international on a plate.'

Bill Beaumont (ENG 1975–82): 'Given this lop-sided pack, we were on a hiding to nothing.'

Adding to the poor preparation was the fact the England team had only come together at Bisham Abbey for training two days before the Test. Then, the night before the game the squad went into central London to the theatre, not returning by coach to their base until very late in the evening. No early to bed for those lads.

Brian McKechnie (NZ 1977–81): 'To get to Twickenham on time on matchday we had to leave the hotel in the morning and have lunch near the ground. It was interesting to note the number of people who had set up picnic and bar areas out the back of the ground – it had a country-style atmosphere to it.'

The day dawned clear and cold with a cool wind, but the turf was dry and firm. Spectators who had paid what was then regarded by some as an exorbitant price for stand tickets – £7.50 – had a not unreasonable expectation that there would be some exciting running rugby, from the tourists at least. There was, but there was no great cohesion to it as both sides made mistake after mistake after mistake.

England fullback Dusty Hare gave his side the first points when he dropped a goal, having been awarded a free kick. Though his kicking was largely on song, Hare's catching of the high ball wasn't, and he spilled three attempted catches. Planned moves by the England backline invariably broke down due to poor passing.

Chances for the All Blacks went begging, too, when centre Bill Osborne cut back towards the midfield rather than use an overlap 15 metres from the England line. Halfback Mark Donaldson sent a long pass to wing Stu Wilson with the line beckoning, but he couldn't hold the ball.

Graham Mourie (NZ 1977–82): 'Against a side that was poorly selected and played as though they knew it, we threw away scoring opportunities which would have made our win much more convincing and emphatic ... We faltered because the forwards played well and the backs poorly in their appreciation of attacking play.'

The All Blacks' first points came after a scrum near the England line twisted, turned and collapsed.

Through the tangle of bodies, All Black lock Frank Oliver picked up the ball and scored.

Fullback McKechnie, who had kicked the match-winning penalty two weeks earlier when the All Blacks beat Wales 13-12, did not have a great first half, missing several shots at goal, including that conversion. At one point he was asked by Mourie if Bryan Williams should take over the kicking.

Hare added another penalty to give England the lead. Williams (who had led the pre-match haka and has often said that Twickenham was his favourite ground), attempted a penalty goal from ten metres inside his own half, without success.

It was a very stop-start game witnessed by the fact referee Norman Sanson awarded 36 penalties – 17 to England, 19 to the All Blacks – and there were 45 lineouts.

From one of those lineouts, five minutes before half-time and right on the England line, All Black prop Brad Johnstone scored.

Brad Johnstone (NZ 1976–80): 'The throw-in had gone high to Scott in the middle of the lineout and he tapped down, straight to me at the front. I thought it was a bit early for a Christmas present, but I gladly accepted it and only had to drop down over the line.'

In the second half, one penalty shot from McKechnie hit a post and went through between the tall uprights while another had less troubled passage over the crossbar. Hare also hit the woodwork with a penalty attempt.

Bill Beaumont: 'We were thumped ... They could easily have doubled their score if they had not decided to coast through the second half and they made our pack look thoroughly inadequate.'

Brian McKechnie: 'We thought England would have the toughest forward pack, but our forwards held control throughout the game. I never felt we could lose the game ... The game was one of those matches you felt you could win by 25 or 30 points.'

The English pack looked decidedly disjointed, especially in comparison to the Welsh forwards who had exerted enormous scrum pressure on the All Blacks at Cardiff. All Black hooker Andy Dalton struck two tight-heads.

Andy Dalton (NZ 1977–85): 'In other games in Britain the scrummaging exhausted us. Against England we had reserve power to do our share in the loose.'

At the dinner after the match, Beaumont began to notice an evasiveness from members of the RFU.

Bill Beaumont: 'It soon dawned on me that I was going to be made the scapegoat for all the howlers that the selectors had made and, sure enough, I was relieved of the captaincy. To me it was like putting Jackie Stewart in a Mini Metro and, when he failed to win the British Grand Prix, sacking Stewart rather than changing the car.'

It was the seventh match in a row on tour that the All Blacks had not conceded a try, but it is not being unfair to say that England never looked like scoring one.

Two weeks later, Mourie's All Blacks beat Scotland 18-9 and became the first New Zealand side to complete the Grand Slam.

Peter Wheeler: 'The best overseas captain during my career was Graham Mourie ... He himself was a clever captain and great player with certain physical attributes that set him apart from others: tremendous stamina and speed of reaction.'

McKechnie also played cricket for New Zealand and was the man on strike when Australian Trevor Chappell bowled the infamous underarm delivery at the Melbourne Cricket Ground in 1981.

Referee: N.R. Sanson (Scotland)

Attendance: 67,750

Half-time: NZ 10, ENG 6

Scorers: NZ Johnstone (t), Oliver (t), McKechnie (2p, c)
       ENG Hare (p, dg)

ENGLAND: R.J. Cowling (Leicester), P.J. Wheeler (Leicester), B.G. Nelmes (Cardiff), W.B. Beaumont (*Capt.* Fylde), J.P. Scott (Cardiff), M.J. Rafter (Bristol), P.J. Dixon (Gosforth), R.M. Uttley (Gosforth), M. Young (Gosforth), J.P. Horton (Bath), M.A.C. Slemen (Liverpool), A.M. Bond+ (Sale), P.W. Dodge (Leicester), P.J. Squires (Harrogate), W.H. Hare (Leicester)

Coach: P. Colston

NEW ZEALAND: B.R. Johnstone (Auckland), A.G. Dalton (Counties), G.A. Knight (Manawatu), A.M. Haden (Auckland), F.J. Oliver (Otago), G.N.K.

Mourie (*Capt.*, Taranaki), L.M. Rutledge (Southland), G.A. Seear (Otago), M.W. Donaldson (Manawatu), O.D. Bruce (Canterbury), B.G. Williams (Auckland), W.M. Osborne (Wanganui), B.J. Robertson (Counties), S.S. Wilson (Wellington), B.J. McKechnie (Southland)

Coach: J. Gleeson

Twickenham, London, 24 November 1979
ALL BLACKS 10 – ENGLAND 9

'If we had picked the right team we might well have won.'
– Bill Beaumont, England captain

E NGLAND were determined that after their limp effort the previous autumn they would be much more competitive at the next meeting. With Mike Davis – he who had battled on with a damaged shoulder against the All Blacks in 1963 – as head coach, assisted by Budge Rogers, an England side went away on a May tour to Japan, Fiji and Tonga.

The All Blacks returned to Britain on an 11-game tour of Scotland, England and Italy with their squad missing a number of players who had featured during the New Zealand winter. They had either declared themselves unavailable or were unwanted by the selectors. Andy Haden, whose All Black career spanned 14 seasons, later described it as the weakest team he had toured with.

In the fourth tour match, the All Blacks were themselves thumped by the Beaumont-captained Northern Division, a side full of current and former internationals. They completely dominated a shadow All Black Test side and won by 21-9. This not only delighted the 11,000 who had been at the match at Otley, but also former All Blacks player and coach Fred Allen who passed the comment that he had seen no greater performance by any side against the All Blacks. England fans and those in the North XV had high hopes for their national team to secure another victory. But, once again, selectorial decisions were to disadvantage England.

Bill Beaumont (ENG 1975–82): 'The first name on our team sheet should have been Alan Old, specially [sic] as Mike Davis intended to play the same style as the North had done. Incredibly, he was left out in favour of Les Cusworth, a very talented individual but at that stage very much a running fly-half. It was an unbelievable decision that was to cost us the match.'

Roger Uttley (ENG 1973–80): 'The promise of Otley had disappeared in a stroke; not through the fault of the players, but because the selectors – as they had done through the seventies – had failed to realise the strength of the regions and to use this to England's advantage.'

The selection of Cusworth meant that the crucial 9-10 combination of him and Steve Smith had never played together. Their first training together wasn't until 72 hours before the match. It was the 16th 9-10 combination England's selectors had chosen in just 27 games.

Peter Wheeler (ENG 1975–84): 'Maybe [England's selectors] thought they could beat New Zealand playing a running game, hence the selection of Les and Richmond's Nick Preston at centre. The overall plan was not entirely clear to the players.'

Scotsman Norman Sanson was in charge of the match, as he had been the year before.

Graham Mourie (NZ 1977–82): '[Sanson was] easily the best referee I encountered in my career. He not only knew the rules, the game and what the players and public expected, but he also had the courage to make his own decisions irrespective of those expectations.'

While the All Blacks were doing the Stu Wilson-led haka, a man ran onto the pitch, dropped his trousers and 'mooned' the New Zealanders. Mourie apparently said to his team, 'That's what they think of us.' Motivation enough.

Despite the All Blacks having four players originally selected as wings for the tour in the backline, the only try of the game came in the 27th minute when a high kick from All Black halfback Dave Loveridge couldn't be taken by England wing, John Carleton. As the ball bobbled away from his grasp it was picked up by All Blacks' lock John Fleming who crashed over the line for an unconverted try. Wing Bernie Fraser later had a golden opportunity to score after he kicked through and Hare fumbled, knocking the ball infield. Fraser grabbed at the ball with the line open but knocked on.

Dusty Hare kicked three penalties for England and Richard Wilson two for New Zealand, but both also missed chances for more points.

The critical difference between the two sides was the dominance of the All Blacks' forwards and tactical play of halfback Dave Loveridge in the final 20 minutes of the game. Though the All Blacks were kept scoreless in the second half, once Hare had reduced his side's deficit to a single point England found themselves pinned down deep in their half for long periods. Their defence was stout, but their attempts to break out with ball in hand were quickly stymied by an All Black backline that would herd England ball-runners towards the touchline.

The final whistle came as a relief to both sets of exhausted forward packs. Though a close encounter, one Mourie regarded as the most enjoyable Test win of his career, there had been mistakes aplenty from both sides.

Phil de Glanville (ENG 1992–99): 'My father took me to Twickenham to watch that match. I was 11 years old. I remember being behind the posts and seeing the trajectory of one of Dusty Hare's penalties as he kicked it over. The game was very close and England just lost, but it was a gripping match, and the atmosphere at Twickenham was spectacular.'

A few months later, thanks to a last-gasp penalty kick by Dusty Hare, Bill Beaumont's England defeated Wales at Twickenham to win the Home Championship, the Triple Crown and claim their first Grand Slam in 23 years.

Referee: N.R. Sanson (Scotland)

Attendance: 70,000

Half-time: NZ 10, ENG 3

Scorers: NZ Fleming (t), R.G. Wilson (2p)
ENG Hare (3p)

ENGLAND: C.E. Smart (Newport), P.J. Wheeler (Leicester), F.E. Cotton (Sale), W.B. Beaumont (*Capt.* Fylde), M.J. Colclough (Angouleme), A. Neary (Broughton Park), M.J. Rafter (Bristol), J.P. Scott (Cardiff), S.J. Smith (Sale), L. Cusworth+ (Leicester), M.A.C. Slemen (Liverpool), A.M. Bond (Sale), N.J. Preston+ (Richmond), J. Carleton+ (Orrell), W.H. Hare (Leicester)

Coach: M. Davis

NEW ZEALAND: J.E. Spiers (Counties), P.H. Sloane (North Auckland), B.R. Johnstone (Auckland), J.K. Fleming (Wellington), A.M. Haden (Auckland), K.W. Stewart (Southland), G.N.K. Mourie (*Capt.* Taranaki), M.G. Mexted (Wellington), D.S. Loveridge (Taranaki), M.B. Taylor (Waikato), B.G. Fraser (Wellington), G.R. Cunningham (Auckland), S.S. Wilson (Wellington), B.R. Ford (Southland), R.G. Wilson (Canterbury)

Coach: E. Watson

MATCH 13

Twickenham, London, 19 November 1983
ENGLAND 15 – ALL BLACKS 9

*'New Zealand are feeling the pressure that so many
England sides have felt from them in the past.'*
– Nigel Starmer-Smith, TV commentator

ALL Black lock Andy Haden had said that the 1979 team to Britain was the weakest he toured with. His unavailability for the 1983 tour, along with six other players – four of them tight forward – who had featured in the 4-0 win over the Lions the previous summer meant the team he wasn't part of was even weaker. For the first time in history the All Blacks' tour captain was a wing, Stu Wilson, the All Blacks' record try scorer in tests.

Craig Green (NZ 1983–87): 'Nothing against Stu but expecting anyone to captain from the wing was stupid.'

The All Blacks' eight-match tour – again replacing a visit to Argentina – was not a happy one, as players old and new struggled with the appointments and direction of coach Bryce Rope and manager Paul Mitchell. The week before the England game the All Blacks drew 25-all with Scotland, a performance notable for the All Blacks' lack of discipline and the Scots' rousing dominance at scrum time.

Dusty Hare, England's record point scorer made his 19th Test appearance to equal Bob Hiller's record for an English fullback. Les Cusworth, who had refused to swap jerseys after the 1979 game against the All Blacks because he thought he was unlikely to win another cap, had returned to the England side the previous year. He

77

was one of five backs from the Peter Wheeler-captained Midland Division side who, 11 days earlier, had beaten the All Blacks 19-13.

Wheeler was a week off turning 35 and playing with a fractured finger. Fellow front-rower Chris White was making his Test debut at the ripe old age of 34. With a tight five who had a total of 75 caps to their opposites' 13, England were going into the Test as favourites. The All Blacks' game plan made things easier for them.

Murray Mexted (NZ 1979–85): 'After Peter Wheeler's Midlands team had devised tactics at Leicester to disrupt our drives, Rope decided that ... we wouldn't drive at all. Can you believe it – an All Black team abandoning the drive? Suddenly we were a team not to be feared.'

Interestingly, when the All Blacks performed their haka at the Midlands match, Wheeler had taken his side down to the goalposts behind the All Blacks so his players wouldn't be distracted by the challenge. At Twickenham, he took his team off to the side of the pitch as the haka was performed.

While Cusworth may not have had the best debut when facing the All Blacks in 1979, four years on he was a much more mature and astute player. His high punting and the accompanying chases by wing Mike Slemen drew numerous errors from the All Blacks' backs, which included Robbie Deans, the grand-nephew of 1905 tourist, Bob Deans.

Stu Wilson (NZ 1977–83): 'England played the Test to a plan and had the character and guts to stay with it. They won quality ball, they kicked for position to play the game in our half.'

Halfback Nick Youngs was a ball-running threat but more often than not his passes would be back to his forwards rather than feeding his backline.

The All Blacks' 9-10 combination of the long-passing Andrew Donald and the tactically adept Wayne Smith were the pick of a side that continued to make handling errors or break the offside line without any real pressure put upon them by England. They were justifiably caned with penalty after penalty, eventually conceding 12 and receiving only three from referee Hosie.

The collective power and confidence of the England forwards, although surprisingly beaten in the lineouts 15-25, brought the increasingly vocal crowd into the game.

Hare had two successful penalties to Deans' one as half-time neared. The All Blacks were feeling the pressure.

All Black wing Bernie Fraser sprinted after a high kick and with kamikaze ferocity took John Carleton's legs out from under him. Such was the force of the collision, Carleton had to leave the field. A penalty was awarded against Fraser who had chants of 'Off! Off! Off!' directed at him by sections of the crowd.

England lock Steve Bainbridge, the 6ft 7in former England students' decathlon champion, stomped on the leg of All Black flanker Mark Shaw, a player renowned for his enforcer status. As Shaw rose from the long Twickenham grass, he was also given a verbal spray by the big England lock. That use of the boot did not draw the ire of referee Hosie (who had great control of a free-flowing game) but minutes later All Black prop Brian McGrattan was penalised for the same offence.

Early in the second half, the first try by an Englishman at Twickenham against the All Blacks since 1967 was scored when lock Maurice Colclough claimed a lineout and his team-mates drove him several metres to score under a heap of bodies. Hare converted for a 12-3 lead.

Peter Wheeler (ENG 1975–84): 'Maybe now we have laid to rest the folk tales of Prince Obolensky's 1936 try. Forget the Russian prince, let us promote the legend of the Marquis Maurice de Colclough.'

A drive at the line by the All Black forwards brought about a try to prop Murray Davie, who had come on as a replacement for his only Test appearance. Deans converted.

With England's lead reduced to three points, the All Blacks gave away another needless penalty which Hare unerringly kicked.

As England's fans willed the clock to tick faster, there was one final scare. All Black second-five Craig Green had a chance to go in for a try under the posts following a break by number eight Murray Mexted but the England defence weathered the desperate attack and the final whistle blew.

Murray Mexted: 'I felt as low as I ever have. We failed to switch tactics when the state of the game screamed for it.'

England's second win over the All Blacks at home had been hard-fought and bruising. Gary Pearce played for almost the whole match with a broken nose; John Scott needed eight stitches in a head wound; debutant Paul Simpson ended up with a gashed forehead; and New Zealand prop Scott Crichton had to leave the field after damaging a rib.

Clive Woodward (ENG 1980–84): 'It was not a great game. I hardly saw the ball all match ... Don't get me wrong, it was good to win, great to be part of a winning team, but that win was just a one-off and it was not exactly a memorable match ... And there certainly was not a sense that we had taken part in creating a bit of history.'

Referee: A.M. Hosie (Scotland)

Attendance: 60,000

Half-time: ENG 6, NZ 3

Scorers: ENG Colclough (t), Hare (3p, c)
NZ Davie (t), Deans (c, p)

ENGLAND: C. White+ (Gosforth), P.J. Wheeler (*Capt.* Leicester), G.S. Pearce (Northampton), M.J. Colclough (Wasps), S.J. Bainbridge (Gosforth), P.D. Simpson+ (Bath), P.J. Winterbottom (Headingley), J.P. Scott (Cardiff), N.G. Youngs (Leicester), L. Cusworth (Leicester), M.A.C. Slemen (Liverpool), P.W. Dodge (Leicester), C.R. Woodward (Leicester), J. Carleton (Orrell), W.H. Hare (Leicester)

Reserve: N.C. Stringer (Wasps)

Coach: M. Davis

NEW ZEALAND: B. McGrattan (Wellington), H.R. Reid (Bay of Plenty), S. Crichton (Wellington), G.J. Braid (Bay of Plenty), A. Anderson (Canterbury), M.W. Shaw (Manawatu), M.J.B. Hobbs (Canterbury), M.G. Mexted (Wellington), A.J. Donald (Wanganui), W.R. Smith (Canterbury), B.G. Fraser (Wellington), C.I. Green (Canterbury), S.T. Pokere (Southland), S.S. Wilson (*Capt.* Wellington), R.M. Deans (Canterbury)

Reserve: M.G. Davie (Canterbury)

Coach: B. Rope

Lancaster Park, Christchurch, 1 June 1985
ALL BLACKS 18 – ENGLAND 13

*'We were six points behind and having to claw our way
back into the game.' – Andy Dalton, All Black captain*

PAUL Dodge had twice tasted victory over the All Blacks –
for Midland Division and England in 1983 – but the side he
captained to New Zealand in 1985 was very light on experience.
A notable inclusion in the party of 26 was the Hong Kong-born inside-
centre James Lionel Broome Salmon who became the first – and only
– player to appear in Tests for both England and New Zealand. As a
teenager, he had moved to Wellington with his family and progressed
through the rugby ranks, culminating in playing six games, including
Three Tests, on the All Blacks' 1980/81 tour of France and Romania.
He had played for Wellington against the Lions in 1983, one of his
64 games for the province, before moving to England and turning
out for Harlequins.

As had been the case on England's previous New Zealand tour
12 years earlier, the volatile subject of a scheduled All Blacks visit to
South Africa was again in the news. Legal proceedings were being
prepared to halt the tour and anti-tour protestors were making their
opposition known during the All Blacks' time in Christchurch. So
much so, some of the players were apparently reluctant to be seen
wearing their All Blacks blazers. Coaching the All Blacks was Brian
Lochore, whose international debut against England in 1964 had
been the start of a stellar career as player and captain of the national
side.

Brian Lochore (NZ coach 1985–87): 'There were bomb scares in the middle of the night, people were chanting outside the hotel all night ... after training one day at Rugby Park there were no buses and we had to get taxis back to the hotel. While we waited we just had to stand there in the face of unrelenting abuse. The language was appalling, especially from the women. We couldn't do anything, say anything, just stand there and let it wash over us.'

The esteem in which the England side were, or rather weren't, held in the eyes of the New Zealand rugby public was reflected by the fact a crowd of only 25,000 made their way to the ground on a showery, overcast afternoon. It perhaps showed that absence did not always make the heart grow fonder when it came to amateur international rugby. Plus, the price for seats in the grandstand had risen from $12 the season before to $16.

England had notched up wins against North Auckland, Poverty Bay and Otago, but they were soundly beaten by Auckland. There was much post-match comment on what were deemed to be overly defensive tactics by the England backline.

For the Test match, a trio of debutants turned out in white: wing Mike Harrison (who would captain England at the inaugural RWC two years later), prop Paul Huntsman and Salmon.

Making their debuts for New Zealand were three players who would have long careers in the black jersey, including being in the World Cup-winning squad two years later: lock Murray Pierce, halfback David Kirk and fullback Kieran Crowley.

The All Blacks had established a pattern over a number of years of performing poorly in the first home Test match of the season. It was certainly the case in Christchurch, on a muddy field that had been cut up needlessly by the playing of a curtain-raiser between two club sides. Lochore later said that he found it hard to motivate his players for this game.

England, though, had to be applauded for taking the opportunities that presented themselves in the first 40 minutes. To get proceedings underway, Harrison had a try on debut thanks to an intercept.

Andy Dalton (NZ 1977–85): 'The guys were just starting to move the ball confidently when bang, suddenly, we were six points behind and having to claw our way back into the game.'

Rugged England number eight Mike Teague, in only his second Test, thundered after a deft kick from halfback Nigel Melville and came up with the ball over the line, the first of his three tries in internationals. Stuart Barnes converted, to go with an early penalty, and England – playing with great gusto but unable to win a lineout in the first 25 minutes – led 13-12 at the break.

All the All Blacks' points had come from Crowley penalty kicks. It looked like a repeat of the 1963 game at the same ground; England scoring tries, New Zealand relying on kicks.

Unfortunately, the second half was a tedious 40 minutes of rugby. The All Blacks continued to play in a disjointed fashion while England seemed committed to try and defend their lead rather than extend it. After all their enterprise in the first stanza, they did not trouble the scoreboard attendants further but did hold their lead until midway through the half.

Then referee Kerry Fitzgerald harshly penalised Dodge for being just inside the ten metres at a lineout. Crowley goaled and the All Blacks were in front.

Barnes had the chance for his side to regain the lead but his 40-metre attempt flew wide. Crowley then landed another penalty to conclude the scoring.

The All Blacks' greatest territorial gains in the match were from Crowley's penalty touch-finders, long spiral punts of the black-tipped Adidas ball. His haul of six penalties (from eight attempts) mirrored the great Don Clarke's 1959 tally when the All Blacks beat the Lions (who had scored four tries) 18-17.

Referee: K.V.J. Fitzgerald (Australia)

Attendance: 25,000

Half-time: ENG 13, NZ 12

Scorers: NZ Crowley (6p)
ENG Harrison (t), Teague (t), Barnes (c, p)

NEW ZEALAND: J.C. Ashworth (Hawke's Bay), A.G. Dalton (*Capt.* Counties), G.A. Knight (Manawatu), M.J. Pierce (Wellington), G.W. Whetton (Auckland), M.W. Shaw (Manawatu), M.J.B. Hobbs (Canterbury), M.G. Mexted (Wellington), D.E. Kirk (Auckland), W.R. Smith (Canterbury), C.I. Green (Canterbury), W.T. Taylor (Canterbury), S.T. Pokere (Auckland), J.J. Kirwan (Auckland), K.J. Crowley (Taranaki)

Coach: B.J. Lochore

ENGLAND: R.P. Huntsman+ (Headingley), S.E. Brain (Coventry), G.S. Pearce (Northampton), S.J. Bainbridge (Gosforth), J. Orwin (Gloucester), D.H. Cooke (Harlequins), J.P. Hall (Bath), M.C. Teague (Gloucester), N.D. Melville (Wasps), S. Barnes (Bristol), M.E. Harrison+ (Wakefield), J.L.B. Salmon+ (Harlequins), P.W. Dodge (*Capt.* Leicester), S.T. Smith (Wasps), G.H. Davies (Wasps)

Coach: M.J. Green

Athletic Park, Wellington, 8 June 1985
ALL BLACKS 42 – ENGLAND 15

'That game was the first time I'd played for the All Blacks when we really fired and blew away the opposition.'
– John Kirwan, All Black wing

WHEN the teams for the second Test were named it came as a surprise to most pundits that neither team had made any changes. Five times capped 6ft 8in lock Wade 'Blackpool Tower' Dooley was still not in the English starting XV, which was good news for the All Blacks who to a man were determined to put on a better performance than the week before.

Despite it being a cool, sunny afternoon, the ground was again well short of a capacity crowd at kick-off.

All Black skipper Andy Dalton joked with media during the week that when the team had watched a video of the first Test match he had nearly fallen asleep. The team resolved to speed up all aspects of their play. But in the opening minutes it was England who had the better start, thanks to All Black halfback David Kirk being unable to initially gather the ball from a forceful lineout tap-back and then his clearing kick was charged down. A variety of boots and hands tried to secure the ball before it spilled back over the All Black goal line where Jon Hall dived on it for the opening try. With Stuart Barnes converting, the crowd was stunned.

The All Blacks were stung into action and minutes later John Kirwan had the first of his 35 Test tries after a towering centre kick from Wayne Smith was reclaimed by the All Blacks and sent wide.

Smith and Barnes traded drop goals and with two Crowley penalties the All Blacks led 13-9.

All Blacks loose forwards Jock Hobbs (a Canterbury lawyer who later captained the side and was a key figure in New Zealand rugby administration at the advent of professionalism) and Murray Mexted both scored from scrums near the England line. Wing Craig Green added another after one of his many breaks when joining the backline. All afternoon the All Blacks made great territorial profit from forwards running straight with ball in hand and cut-out passes in their midfield.

Brian Lochore (NZ coach 1985–87): 'We recognised that they were vulnerable to us driving straight through the middle because they tended to fan their defence. At Christchurch we'd tried to go around them, and repeatedly been knocked down behind the advantage line.'

Much of the second 40 minutes was played in the England half, which was by then in the cold shadow of the large, wooden Millard Stand.

Mike Harrison had his second intercept try in as many Tests, running 70 metres to score but the All Blacks struck back with Mark Shaw dotting down after a powerful All Black drive from a lineout. A scything run from Crowley set up Green for a second try.

With only minutes to go an ugly fracas broke out after the diminutive All Black centre Steve Pokere bundled the lanky Harrison into touch. The latter went after his tackler, throwing a punch. Unsurprisingly, like a moth to a flame, Shaw came in with a punch aimed at Harrison. He had just finished the arc of his blow when England hooker Steve Brain launched at him. More players arrived, all of whom were yapped at by referee Fitzgerald who, like a farmer to his sheepdogs, repeatedly told them to 'Get out of it!'

It was at the scrum where England most tested the All Blacks but in broken play flanker David Cooke was prone to concentrate too much on being disruptive off the ball and the England backs' defence, which had been stout in Christchurch, wilted. The cause was not helped by being reduced to 14 men in the final quarter when winger Simon Smith had to go off injured. England had already used two replacements, Dooley and scrum-half Richard Hill. The arrival of the former certainly added impetus to England's set pieces, by fair means and foul.

Mark Shaw (NZ 1980–86): 'He had only been on the field a few minutes when he whacked me in the face. He started winning lineout ball, and then he clobbered Gary Knight. I don't know how they ever left him out of the original selection.'

The All Blacks' 42 points was the highest number conceded by an England team, their highest losing margin and the most points scored by New Zealand in a Test.

Referee: K.V.J. Fitzgerald (Australia)

Attendance: 20,000

Half-time: NZ 13, ENG 9

Scorers: NZ Green (2t), Kirwan (t), Mexted (t), Hobbs (t), Shaw (t), Crowley (3p, 3c), Smith (dg)
ENG Harrison (t), Hall (t), Barnes (dg, 2c)

NEW ZEALAND: J.C. Ashworth (Hawke's Bay), A.G. Dalton (*Capt.* Counties), G.A. Knight (Manawatu), M.J. Pierce (Wellington), G.W. Whetton (Auckland), M.W. Shaw (Manawatu), M.J.B. Hobbs (Canterbury), M.G. Mexted (Wellington), D.E. Kirk (Auckland), W.R. Smith (Canterbury), C.I. Green (Canterbury), W.T. Taylor (Canterbury), S.T. Pokere (Auckland), J.J. Kirwan (Auckland), K.J. Crowley (Taranaki)

Coach: B.J. Lochore

ENGLAND: R.P. Huntsman (Headingley), S.E. Brain (Coventry), G.S. Pearce (Northampton), S.J. Bainbridge (Gosforth), J. Orwin (Gloucester), J.P. Hall (Bath), D.H. Cooke (Harlequins), M.C. Teague (Gloucester), N.D. Melville (Wasps), S. Barnes (Bristol), M.E. Harrison (Wakefield), J.L.B. Salmon (Harlequins), P.W. Dodge (*Capt.* Leicester), S.T. Smith (Wasps), G.H. Davies (Wasps)

Reserves: R. Hill (Bath), W. Dooley (Preston Grasshoppers)

Coach: M.J. Green

Twickenham, London, 3 October 1991 (RWC)
ALL BLACKS 18 – ENGLAND 12

'Heck, at half-time I felt I hadn't done anything.'
– Michael Jones, All Black loose forward

SIX years had passed since the last meeting between England and the All Blacks and the rugby landscape had become very different in that time. The inaugural RWC had been played in Australia and New Zealand. The All Blacks, playing with pace, skill and power throughout the tournament, defeated France 29-9 in the final at Eden Park.

England, on the other hand, had to pack their bags for home after a 3-16 quarter-final loss to Wales in Brisbane. Looking back at the score-line and seeing that the men in red had scored three tries, one could be forgiven for thinking the emphasis of the Welsh was on attack. It was only part of the story. Their relentless tactic to kill the ball when England had possession saw them penalised 25 times (to England's 9) and it made for a frustrating game to watch. English coach Martin Green seemed to have his head in his hands for much of the match.

England's early exit from the tournament saw Geoff Cooke appointed as the new coach, which reflected the need for the England players to match the cardio-intensity of the antipodean teams if they were to be competitive for the full 80 minutes. Cooke, who had lectured in Physical Education, changed well-worn training methods but also freshened up his squad. There was no better example of this than his appointment of Will Carling as captain. The young centre was only 22 and had taken the field for England a mere six times.

Of the players that had met six years earlier in New Zealand, Mike Teague, Wade Dooley and Richard Hill again started for England while John Kirwan (who was still only 26) and Gary Whetton ran out for New Zealand.

The defending champions and hosts opposed each other in game 1A of the 1991 RWC which was played on a Thursday afternoon, the only time the teams have played each other on a weekday.

Pre-match expectation was that the match would be a suitable spectacle to begin the tournament, as well as answering the increasingly loud media banter as to which was the better team. The All Blacks had enjoyed an extraordinary unbeaten sequence of 50 games from 1987–90, including 23 Tests without a loss – one draw – but there was widespread unease that the ageing team was on the wane.

English fans saw their team as one of the tournament favourites after a winning Five Nations campaign, Grand Slam and Triple Crown. A 15-40 loss to Australia at the Sydney Football Stadium in July was best not mentioned.

Following the singing of the special anthem 'No More Steps to Climb' by theatre star Michael Ball, and the arrival of the fibreglass RWC Message ball (which had travelled through the five host countries in the three months prior to the tournament), HRH Prince Edward declared the tournament open.

The match was a tight, tense, dour one, with Scottish referee Jim Fleming blowing 26 penalties and being particularly vigilant when it came to players diving over the ball at rucks. Both sides grew frustrated with the constant whistling.

Nigel Redman (ENG 1984–97): 'I think both sides were nervous. It was one of those archetypal matches where both sides spent more time figuring each out rather than actually playing the game.'

The All Blacks dominated possession, won the scrum battle and just had the better of the lineouts (19-16), especially when they utilised quick throws. But they were also guilty of making an array of errors.

Va'aiga Tuigamala (NZ 1989–93): 'We knew we needed 150 per cent effort from everyone, including the reserves. It was an incredibly nerve-wracking time, not helped by my sitting in front of [coach] Grizz Wyllie who kept going "Grrrrrrrr!"'

Penalties (and missed kicks) were traded by Grant Fox and Jonathan Webb for set-piece infringements, a high tackle (Gary Whetton) and punching (Peter Winterbottom winding up at a ruck to clobber All Black lock Ian Jones but only landing on Dean Richards' thigh, right in front of the referee).

A wobbly Rob Andrew drop goal from a tap-penalty just before half-time saw England ahead, 12-9.

Jason Leonard (ENG 1990–2004): 'After half-time, the All Blacks turned up the power and started varying everything until they had thrown us off course and they could muscle over for the only try of the game.'

That try was scored in the 51st minute, just as the sun broke through, by the mercurial All Black open-side flanker, Michael Jones. Playing his only Test against England, the softly spoken devout Christian, who never played on Sundays, had the hands and pace of a midfield back, was as spring-heeled as a basketballer and tackled with the power of a pile-driver. John Mason of the *Daily Telegraph* wrote of Jones as 'the personification of athletic power'.

The score came from All Black halfback Graeme Bachop doubling round from a scrum to take a pass from centre Craig Innes before sending a long pass to John Kirwan. In trademark fashion he swerved and fended off the flailing Chris Oti until stopped by Webb. In support was Jones who took Kirwan's inside pass and crossed the line untouched, breaking the hearts not only of England fans but also bookmakers who had him at 20/1 to score the first try of the tournament. Remarkably, he had also scored the opening try of the 1987 tournament.

Grant Fox, whose slow steps back and across from the ball when lining up his kicks drew louder and louder whistles from the crowd, converted to give the All Blacks the 18-12 win.

The second global rugby tournament was underway, but this Test match had been more of a traditional All Blacks' visit to Twickenham.

Jeremy Guscott (ENG 1989–1999): 'It was a flop, a poor, penalty-strewn match and we were rarely in the hunt.'

Grant Fox (NZ 1985–93): 'England had a fine tight-five with the best ball-winning ability by far of the five nations. There was, however, a lack of mobility in the loose forwards ... Most of the backline were talented players but playing to such a taught, restrictive recipe that there was little, we felt, to fear from them. So it proved.'

Referee: J.M. Fleming (Scotland)

Touch Judges: J. Anderson (Scotland), R. Hourquet (France)

Attendance: 70,000

Half-time: ENG 12, NZ 9

Scorers: NZ M. Jones (t) G. Fox (4p, 1c)
ENG Webb (3p), Andrew (dg)

ENGLAND: J. Leonard (Saracens), B.C. Moore (Harlequins), J.A. Probyn (Askeans), P.J. Ackford (Harlequins), W.A. Dooley (Preston Grasshoppers), M.C. Teague (Gloucester), P.J. Winterbottom (Harlequins), D. Richards (Leicester), R.J. Hill (Bath), C.R. Andrew (Wasps), C. Oti (Wasps), J.C. Guscott (Bath), W.D.C. Carling (*Capt*. Harlequins), R. Underwood (Leicester & RAF), J.M. Webb (Bath)

Coach: G. Cooke

NEW ZEALAND: S.C. McDowall (Auckland), S.B.T. Fitzpatrick (Auckland), R.W. Loe (Waikato), I.D. Jones (North Auckland), G.W. Whetton (*Capt*. Auckland), A.J. Whetton (Auckland), M.N. Jones (Auckland), Z.V. Brooke (Auckland), G.T.M. Bachop (Canterbury), G.J. Fox (Auckland), J.K.R. Timu (Otago), B.J. McCahill (Auckland), C.R. Innes (Auckland), J.J. Kirwan (Auckland), T.J. Wright (Auckland)

Coach: G. Wyllie

Twickenham, London, 27 November 1993
ENGLAND 15 – ALL BLACKS 9

'We deserved to lose. We never fired a shot all day.'
– Sean Fitzpatrick, All Black captain

JOHN Reason of the *Daily Telegraph* wrote in the match programme that it had been 'eight years since England's last tour of New Zealand, an absurdly long gap in that some very good players in either country have missed out on an experience of a rugby lifetime'.

That didn't mean, however, that there had been no New Zealand visits by England players. In 1992, Jeremy Guscott had played in the World XV team that helped celebrate the NZRU's centenary. Will Carling, Richard Hill, Wade Dooley and Dean Richards were among those who withdrew from the series. A couple of months later Stuart Barnes captained 30 England 'B' players on an eight-match tour of the New Zealand provinces.

Come 1993 and the Lions toured New Zealand for the first time in ten years, with the Test series reduced from the traditional four matches to three. There were 16 Englishmen in the group captained by Scotland's Gavin Hastings. The tourists convincingly won the second Test in Wellington (20-7).

Several of the provincial games were particularly spiteful. In the match against North Harbour, Lions and England number eight Dean Richards rucked the head of North Harbour centre Frank Bunce, who required 11 stitches. To the dismay of a number of All Blacks and local media, this incident escaped mention in many of the overseas pressmen's daily reports.

There was also increasing friction between the two rugby hemispheres when it came to perceived definitions of the word 'amateur'. League scouts were hard at work trying to lure players to clubs in England and Australia. There was constant talk of a professional rugby union circuit, ever since the entrepreneur David Lord had begun door-knocking with contracts for a rebel international rugby competition in the 1980s. Players in New Zealand felt that the IRB was preventing players from accepting income from commercial opportunities at the same time as allowing top English players to make large amounts of money from speaking engagements or stints with European clubs at which they were paid in 'brown envelopes'. Conversely, English players on the Lions tour believed some of their opponents were receiving questionable payments as 'sales representatives' for large companies.

These undercurrents aside, the All Blacks had been unbeaten in ten tour games, including a 51-15 demolition of Scotland, but controversy had reared its head on the field in the close-fought 19-15 win against England South-West when Phil de Glanville suffered a severe gash on his cheek that required 15 stitches. The much-replayed incident pointed the finger at either Ian Jones or Sean Fitzpatrick as being the owner of the 'stray' All Black boot that did the damage. The media, who had been decrying some of the All Blacks tactics as 'cheating' all tour, were now in a frenzy.

Phil de Glanville (ENG 1992–99): 'I was phoned by the New Zealand manager, who apologised on behalf of the All Blacks. I have hardly looked back at it, but it was pretty much a case of players jumping into a mass of bodies and rucking whoever was there, and my face happened to be in the wrong place. There was a lot of media storm at the time, but by the time the Test came round, it was hardly mentioned. The best way to respond was on the pitch, and that's what we did.'

The All Blacks remained the bookies' favourite even when key backline member and reliable goal-kicker, Matthew Cooper, was ruled out with a groin strain and replaced by Eroni Clarke.

There were milestones for both captains. Will Carling equalled Nick Farr-Jones' record for the most Tests as captain (36) while All Blacks' captain Sean Fitzpatrick, whose father Brian had played for the All Blacks on their 1953/54 tour, was playing his 54th consecutive Test, overtaking Welsh great Gareth Edwards' record for most international caps.

At the other end of the experience scale was England lock, Martin Johnson. Though he had played in two Tests for the Lions in New Zealand, this was only his second game for England. Several years earlier, Johnson had spent time playing and working in New Zealand in the heartland of rugby, Te Kuiti. The small, rural town in the middle of the North Island was home to Colin Meads and that legend of All Black rugby was sad to see Johnson return to England, as he considered he could have made the All Blacks.

Jason Leonard (ENG 1990–2004): 'We wanted revenge on the All Blacks for beating us in the opening game of the [1991] World Cup. And so it was – from start to finish it was our day. The Twickenham crowd was louder, sang more vociferously and seemed more animated and alive throughout the match than I've ever heard them before.'

On the quarter-hour mark Eroni Clarke was penalised for a late tackle. Jonathan Callard, on debut at fullback, was given the kicking responsibilities over Rob Andrew. While his wayward efforts for the South-West Division may have cost them the chance of an upset against the tourists, he had no problem with his first penalty kick in international rugby and added another ten minutes later. Right on half-time, 20-year-old All Black wing Jeff Wilson missed his third penalty attempt. All had been from comfortable distances and angles.

England wing Tony Underwood should have scored after a run from the All Blacks' 10-metre line which saw him in space with only the covering fullback John Timu to beat. Timu steered him closer and closer to the touchline and, carrying the ball in the wrong hand, Underwood was put into touch a metre or so from the corner flag. Nine times out of ten he would have scored from such an opportunity.

In the second half, England rolled on. When they didn't have the ball, their forwards were disrupting the All Blacks' rucks, mauls and lineouts. When they did have it, they made large amounts of territory through mauling, punts off the left and right feet by Rob Andrew and quick backline passing.

Nigel Redman (ENG 1984–97): 'For me personally, now, I almost find Twickenham to be too big because you can be so far back from the pitch. I liked the old Twickenham when you could actually see the people right behind the hooker's arm. You could sense in '93 from the reactions of the crowd that something special was happening.'

Wilson finally found his direction with a penalty but that was negated by another to Callard barely 60 seconds later. Wilson added two more penalties, Callard one and Andrew snapped a drop goal. England were still ahead but by only three points.

Then prop Victor Ubogu saved the game for England. With Timu looking set to score in the corner, Ubogu bounced the flying fullback towards the touchline. Timu's boot just crossed the white stripe before he dived over the line.

Nigel Redman: 'I remember when Victor tackled Timu into touch. Now, when your tight-head prop tackles one of their outside backs, it gives you a lift. There were little gains during the match, to keep us in the game.'

With 15 minutes to play, Callard added another penalty and England increased the tempo of their game. De Glanville made a break following a lovely short pass from loose-forward Ben Clarke (who had a better day distributing the ball than the All Black first-five Marc Ellis) but couldn't find his supporting runners when tackled.

At the final whistle it was England winners by 15-9, the same score as their previous win against the All Blacks, at the same venue, ten years and eight days earlier. Choruses of 'Swing low, sweet chariot' broke out in the ecstatic crowd along with prolonged chants of 'England! England!'

Sean Fitzpatrick (NZ 1986–97): 'The good news about losing to England 9-15 was that we didn't concede a try. There wasn't any other good news. What's worse, we deserved to lose. There are no sour grapes: we never fired a shot all day.'

Frank Bunce (NZ 1992–97): 'The fundamental backline weakness we fielded against England was that no one from first five to centre could kick under pressure ... Marc kicked poorly and neither Eroni nor I could kick at all. So, we had a huge problem when our forwards were being beaten.'

The All Black forwards were well beaten, and de Glanville and Carling tackled like tyros in midfield but a change of tactics from the visitors never came. As the game wore on, England were able to smother virtually all the All Black attempts at getting over the advantage line because their play had become so predictable.

Ian Jones (NZ 1989–99): 'We were given a game plan which we followed to the letter. You didn't have to be a genius to see that particular game plan was going nowhere. We were beaten in the lineouts and beaten in the loose ... we ran too often and people like [Tim] Rodber gobbled us up.'

Indiscretions by England had presented the All Blacks with chances for points, but Wilson missed four penalty attempts.

Jeff Wilson (NZ 1993–2001): 'We may have won if I'd had a better success rate with my kicking, but we'll never know that. The fact is we lost and I felt it more than most. I was bitterly disappointed afterwards and sat in the dressing room and cried. Some of the players attempted to cheer me up, to tell me that it's teams that lose Tests, not individuals, but Mike Brewer told them to leave me alone, that I had to learn to lose. It was a valuable, if painful, lesson.'

With the win in the bag, Carling had also equalled Nick Farr-Jones' record of leading sides to wins over all senior IRB nations. Geoff Cooke became the first England coach to guide sides to wins over Australia, New Zealand and South Africa.

While the after-match dinner was good-natured, the next morning the relationship between the two sides soured somewhat.

Early in the game All Black blind-side flanker Jamie Joseph had deliberately stomped on the ankle of debutant Kyran Bracken, but only the television cameras picked it up at the time. In the words of de Glanville, 'Kyran did amazingly well to get through the game' but was then on the sidelines for several months. There was great coverage of the act in the media. One veteran New Zealand rugby journalist referred to it as 'witless'. Joseph was stood down by All Blacks management for the final tour match against the Barbarians.

It must be said, however, that there was a lot of rucking away from the ball by both teams. In the run up to Callard's third penalty goal – awarded after Joseph entered a ruck from the side – both Leonard and Moore used their sprigs freely a number of times on All Blacks' ankles that were well away from the ball. Ben Clarke also stomped on the back of Aaron Pene, who had made a tackle on Tim Rodber, and was instantly penalised.

Then, in his *Sunday Times* newspaper column, England hooker Brian Moore alleged that Fitzpatrick had made a racist slur against Ubogu. When asked about the allegation, Ubogu said he didn't hear any such comment directed at him.

Fitzpatrick may have publicly said there were no sour grapes but just how much this loss stung the All Blacks would be abundantly apparent when the teams next met.

Referee: F. Burger (South Africa)

Touch Judges: S.R. Hilditch (Ireland), G. Black (Ireland).

Attendance: 68,000

Half-time: ENG 6, NZ 0

Scorers: ENG Callard (4p), Andrew (dg)
          NZ Wilson (3p)

ENGLAND: J. Leonard (Harlequins), B.C. Moore (Harlequins), V.E. Ubogu (Bath), M.O. Johnson (Leicester), N.C. Redman (Bath), T.A.K. Rodber (Northampton), B.B. Clarke (Bath), D. Richards (Leicester), K.P.P. Bracken+ (Bristol), C.R. Andrew (Wasps), T. Underwood (Leicester), P.R. de Glanville (Bath), W.D.C. Carling (*Capt.* Harlequins), R. Underwood (RAF & Leicester), J.E.B. Callard+ (Bath)

Coach: G. Cooke

NEW ZEALAND: C.W. Dowd (Auckland), S.B.T. Fitzpatrick (*Capt.* Auckland), O.M. Brown (Auckland), I.D. Jones (North Auckland), S.B. Gordon (Waikato), Z.V. Brooke (Auckland), J.W. Joseph (Otago), A.R.B. Pene (Otago), S.T. Forster (Otago), M.C.G. Ellis (Otago), V.L. Tuigamala (Auckland), E. Clarke (Auckland), F.E. Bunce (North Harbour), J.W. Wilson (Otago), J.K.R. Timu (Otago)

Coach: L. Mains

Newlands, Cape Town, 18 June 1995
(RWC semi-final)
ALL BLACKS 45 – ENGLAND 29

*'I suspect Jonah Lomu won't get the chance to run at me
because we'll have him under so much pressure.'*
– Mike Catt, pre-match diary entry

TO this day, the first meeting between the two teams on neutral territory can be summed up in two words: Jonah Lomu.

The giant wing, standing 6ft 5in and weighing over 18st, had just turned 20 and the game had never seen anyone like him. As Prince Obolensky's family had fled the Russian revolution for England, Lomu's parents had left Tonga for a better life in New Zealand, one where hard-earned wages were used to support family members, both in their adopted country and in their homeland, and children could benefit from better education and health systems.

(At the time of writing, there had been 1,173 All Blacks. Of those, only 38 were born in American Samoa, Samoa, Fiji or Tonga and the first to wear the silver fern was way back in 1928. Those who subscribe to the myth of the All Blacks 'player-poaching' from the Pacific Islands (PI) ignore or fail to understand the administrative and legislative relationships that New Zealand has had with PI nations. It is a bit like suggesting England's Olympic track and field programme is built on poaching athletes from Africa and the Caribbean.)

Lomu had been told by his mentor Phil Kingsley-Jones that the 1995 RWC was going to be *his* stage. Thus, on a sunny, warm afternoon Lomu stunned everybody but himself with a performance that left England's players struggling to lay a hand on him and the world's rugby press equally floundering for superlatives to describe his four-try haul. Will Carling's England had made their way into the last four of the 1995 tournament with a 25-22 quarter-final win over their RWC nemesis, and cup-holders, Australia. A last-minute, long distance Rob Andrew drop goal won the game for England. As part of their build-up to the semi-final, the team holidayed at the Sun City resort for three days. The beer flowed.

The All Blacks had powered past Scotland 48-30 in the quarter-finals. They were the form team, seemingly scoring at will, but leaking a lot of points. Minnows Japan had scored 17 points in their encounter, though they conceded 148!

Sean Fitzpatrick (NZ 1986–97): 'We were very concerned about the size of the England pack and thought they would definitely nullify us at lineout time ... We had some real doubts about whether we'd be good enough to beat them.'

The 1993 loss at Twickenham was still fresh in the minds of the All Blacks who had suffered it, but the media were solely focused on Lomu, and how to stop him. England wing Tony Underwood turned things around by reportedly saying that Lomu had never had to mark a player like him before.

Josh Kronfeld (NZ 1995–2000): 'The intensity of the desire to win, the furious determination to atone for the Twickenham defeat in 1993, was astonishing to behold and experience ... I sensed something truly epic was up, but even so I was unprepared for the outburst from Zinny [Zinzan Brooke]. He began to shout at us, and he was incredibly insistent and animated ... I looked at him and thought, "Jesus, you're hysterical." ... If he'd started foaming at the mouth I wouldn't have been surprised.'

Martin Johnson (ENG 1993–2003): 'Carling's team talk ahead of the match ... was a typical Will speech, along the lines of, "Let's get the ball out to Jerry and the wingers and we'll rip these boys to pieces."'

Jason Leonard (ENG 1990–2004): 'We decided that we would play our own game, making sure that we defended well all over the park. I think that with hindsight (what a great thing that is!) we simply underestimated the impact that Lomu would have.'

Will Carling (ENG 1988–97): 'We watched Lomu on video and analysed him. We thought, "Yeah, he's a big guy, he's fast," and everything else, but we felt we could deal with him. When I saw him on the pitch it was completely different. I said he was a freak, and I meant it as a compliment. I've never seen anything like him in rugby.'

The media had done a bit of bear-baiting during the week with reported comments from Rory Underwood that he would put his money on brother Tony if he was running at Jonah in a one-on-one. Lomu put the newspaper clippings on the mirror of his hotel room and looked at them every day. Then, on the night before the match, he was so wound up and ready to play, rather than nervous, he was awake all night walking around the team hotel and car park, visualising the approaching game.

Jonah Lomu (NZ 1994–2002): 'As the teams lined up before kick-off I looked over at Tony Underwood. Nothing was said – but at the end of our haka he gave me a little wink. I was furious. When I'm doing the haka I'm issuing a challenge. At the time, I thought Tony was being disrespectful in the way he took it up. I didn't say anything, but I was thinking plenty – *I'm gonna wipe that wink off your face ...*'

Frank Bunce (NZ 1992–97): 'I think I probably watched the video of the England–Australia game eight times. We felt we had all the England players tagged. We recognised the Underwoods as dangerously fast but not great defenders, we saw Will Carling as the strong setter-upper with Jeremy Guscott the runner and one player who could initiate counter-attacks. Andrew, we knew, tended to kick first and run second from fly-half while Mike Catt didn't appear the bravest of tacklers at fullback.'

Catt's bravery was tested within two minutes. From the kick-off, all eyes were on Lomu, even those of Carling and Underwood who collided when both tried to field Andrew Mehrtens' switch kick which had the All Black number 11 thundering towards the descending ball.

Several plays later, a long pass left from halfback Graham Bachop floated over the head of Lomu. He turned, picked up the ball and found himself in space midway inside the England half. Tony Underwood was swatted away with ease. The covering Carling ankle-tapped the giant who staggered but didn't fall to the turf.

Mike Catt (ENG 1994–2007): 'I thought I only had to go low and he would crash to earth. I first felt his left knee knocking me backwards off my feet. Next came his right and I went from my backside onto my back with the force of the collision. I grasped for something to hold on to, my arms flailing. But he was over the top of me, those tree-trunk legs pumping like pistons. And then it was over ... I lay sprawled on the Newlands turf, shell-shocked at what had just happened.'

Lomu strode on and dived over the line, pounding the ball into the turf as he scored. When he got up he allowed himself a little smile.

While the main telecast camera angle was from behind Lomu, the more astonishing pictures were from front on. Then one could see the determination and aggression on Lomu's face, the thundering god dismissing the mere mortals who hoped to bring him to earth.

Jonah Lomu: 'After I scored, it was like a huge release of emotions ... My body had been in overload all week and suddenly I had this amazing amount of energy – a huge surge like I was buzzing on 20 shots of coffee. Everything just poured out. I was running on pure adrenaline for the whole match.'

No greater statement of the power of one man had ever been seen on a rugby field. The crowd could not believe what they had seen. But there was more to come.

Two minutes later, the All Blacks ran the ball from inside their 22. Second-five Walter Little picked up another bouncing pass from Bachop.

Jeremy Guscott (ENG 1989–99): 'There are few images that have stuck in my mind from playing rugby, but that one of me sliding down Little's thigh, his shin and his rugby boots and then watching him sprint 50 metres to tee up Josh Kronfeld for their second try was one of them. It was the biggest slap in the face I've ever had on a rugby field.'

Ten points behind after six minutes, Andrew tried a dropped goal which sailed wide then shanked a penalty attempt. Mehrtens made no such mistake in slotting a penalty a few minutes later.

The audaciousness of the All Blacks' play reached new heights when lock Robin Brooke fielded a hacked kick from Catt and, near the sideline inside his own half, kicked deep into the England 22. Carling returned with a kick that was intended for the touchline, but it only found Robin's brother, Zinzan, just inside his own half. The number eight ran five paces into England territory and let fly with a drop kick that sailed over the crossbar. (Had he really told Lomu at lunch that day he wanted to kick a drop goal in a Test match?)

Andrew's bad kicking day continued when he muffed another penalty, then he found himself between Lomu and open space on the England 22. Andrew barely touched the accelerating Lomu who sailed past and then strode around behind the posts to score.

Will Carling: 'They tore us to pieces. We were in shock. I could see it on the faces of the players ... New Zealand's power and pace was phenomenal. We did not so much as sniff the ball ... New Zealand were touched by genius that day.'

Martin Johnson: 'I have never felt so powerless, so impotent, on a rugby field. It was humiliating.'

England then enjoyed a couple of minutes on attack, building some pressure. But, when an overlap had been created 15 metres out, Andrew dropped the first pass. Chance gone.

Finally, in the 37th minute, Andrew was successful with a penalty. England were on the board, but still 22 points behind.

A minute later, Carling sprinted with ball in hand from just outside his 22. With Tony Underwood to his right they had a two-on-one with a turning Lomu the man to beat. Taking the pass, Underwood was quickly caught by Lomu who threw him like a rag doll into touch.

There is a story that just after Carling released the ball to Underwood, he was tackled by his ultra-competitive opposite, Frank Bunce. Apparently, as Carling lay winded on the ground, Bunce pushed his face into the grass and said, 'That's from New Zealand!'

The half-time whistle sounded, and the teams went to their respective rooms under the stands. The All Blacks at that point probably wished they could keep playing. For England, it was a welcome break in a place where Jonah could not be seen. Coach Jack Rowell, whose record in charge of England from 1994–97 would stand at 21 wins from 29 games, simply told his men that they were now playing for personal pride.

Jack Rowell: 'I have not seen any international team play with the ease, the power and the pace that they did. We planned that there would always be someone right up on Lomu before he got into stride. But it did not work. We allowed him too much room.'

The start of the second half continued the nightmare for England. With just over a minute gone, Lomu plunged across in the left-hand corner.

The All Blacks' fifth try came five minutes later when Bachop ran across to score, in a way that was much more sedate than the crowd were used to seeing. Fortunately for England, Mehrtens was missing kicks at that end in the way Andrew had in the first half.

England's forwards started to come into their own with Tim Rodber, Victor Ubogu and Ben Clarke fearlessly hitting the ball up. All Black prop Craig Dowd received a stern warning from referee Hilditch about rucking a player well away from the ball.

After 56 minutes, England finally got across the All Blacks' line only to be held up. Mike Catt then went close before Rory Underwood crossed in the tackle of Glen Osborne, though not before at least one of his legs went into touch. Despite protestations from Fitzpatrick, Hilditch awarded the try. Andrew's sideline conversion made the scores 35-10.

With 15 minutes to go, England were really throwing the ball around but not all the passes were going to hand. An All Black counter-attack from a spilled ball saw Catt put Osborne into touch a metre short of the try-line.

Play then swung to the other end of the field where the tireless Carling ran down the side line ten metres from the All Blacks' line and tried to chip the ball over Lomu. The big man rose high to block the ball but merely tipped it down into the hands of Carling who dived over in the corner. Fortuitous, yes, but good reward for a captain who prior to the tournament had been sacked and then reinstated after describing the RFU general committee as '57 old farts'.

Lomu made amends almost immediately, storming down the left-hand touch to dot down again.

With nine minutes to play, Carling took a pass from Clarke following a tap penalty and weaved past two defending forwards for his second try. Mehrtens added a dropped goal to bring up 100 points in Test rugby, a milestone achieved faster than any other player, in just his fifth Test.

The final try, in the final minute of the game, came to Rory Underwood (with a suggestion of shepherding by Guscott on two All Black defenders). Andrew converted.

In any other game, you would expect that two England backs scoring a brace of tries each would see them on the winning side. Not that day. England definitely had the better of the game in the final quarter, as the All Blacks forwards became a bit ragged but that was not surprising given the score and the way they had played the first 40 minutes in such destructive fashion.

Jeremy Guscott: 'I joined all the other players in the dressing room holding my head in my hands, staring at the floor. From time to time I had a little peep to see if everyone was maintaining the same grieving posture. Almost to a man they were, with the exception of Jason Leonard, who caught my eye, winked, and raised his hand to his mouth indicating he was ready for a beer. Like me, Jason despised losing but knew shedding a few tears was not going to make any difference.'

Tony Underwood (ENG 1992–98): 'The only saving grace I can take from the whole thing is that I wasn't steamrollered by Jonah for his four tries. I was one of the few Jonah actually ran around rather than through.'

Writing in *The Telegraph*, John Mason's appraisal of the match was:

> It was a hair-raising marvel of a performance from this 6ft 5in giant of a man, blessed with a strength and physical presence way beyond his 20 years. From the kick-off at a full house Newlands it was: 'Good afternoon, Tony Underwood. Here I am to make your life a misery for the next 79 minutes 50 seconds.'

Rob Andrew (ENG 1985–1997): 'I'd never seen any player make such an impact before our meeting with New Zealand, and I don't think for a moment that I'll see anything like it again. In that sense, if no other, it was a privilege to be on the same pitch.'

Lomu later wrote that in the years after the match he felt a bit sorry for Catt and had tired somewhat of seeing that particular try replayed over and over, especially at RWC time.

As for Catt, he became a household name as part of one of rugby's most memorable and extraordinary moments.

Mike Catt: 'I look back on the day with great fondness ... I defy anyone to have made that tackle ... I love talking about it. I love telling the story.'

There was further satisfaction for the All Blacks the next day when both teams boarded a flight for Johannesburg. The victors were ushered to seats at the front of the plane and then watched the losers file past to their assigned seats at the back of the aircraft.

Referee: S.R. Hilditch (Ireland)

Touch Judges: J. Dume (France), S. Neethling (South Africa)

Attendance: 51,000

Half-time: NZ 25, ENG 3

Scorers: NZ Lomu (4t), Kronfeld (t), Bachop (t), Mehrtens (3c, p, dg),
Z. Brooke (dg)
ENG Carling (2t), R. Underwood (2t), Andrew (3c, pg)

ENGLAND: J. Leonard (Harlequins), B.C. Moore (Harlequins), V.E. Ubogu (Bath), M.O. Johnson (Leicester), M.C. Bayfield (Northampton), T.A.K. Rodber (Northampton), B.B. Clarke (Bath), D. Richards (Leicester), C.D. Morris (Orrell), C.R. Andrew (Wasps), R. Underwood (Leicester), J.C. Guscott (Bath), W.D.C. Carling (*Capt.* Harlequins), T. Underwood (Leicester), M.J. Catt (Bath)

Coach: J. Rowell

NEW ZEALAND: C.W. Dowd (Auckland), S.B.T. Fitzpatrick (*Capt.* Auckland), O.M. Brown (Auckland), R.M. Brooke (Auckland), I.D. Jones (North Harbour), M.R. Brewer (Canterbury), J.A. Kronfeld (Otago), Z.V. Brooke (Auckland), G.T.M. Bachop (Canterbury), A.P. Mehrtens (Canterbury), J.T. Lomu (Counties), W.K. Little (North Harbour), F.E. Bunce (North Harbour), J.W. Wilson (Otago), G.M. Osborne (North Harbour)

Reserve: B. P. Larsen

Coach: L. Mains

The Professional Era

MATCH 19

Old Trafford, Manchester, 22 November 1997
ALL BLACKS 25 – ENGLAND 8

'A bit of red mist and a bit of aggression and let's take it to them.' – Richard Cockerill, England hooker

THIS was the first game between the two sides in the professional age, but when the All Blacks first arrived in London to start their nine-match tour, which included visits to Llanelli and Dublin, there was a real throwback to the amateur days as several of the players constructed bespoke scrum machines out of timber.

The match itself seems best remembered for two incidents that book-ended the clash, but there was much more to the game.

Firstly, it was a return to Manchester, stronghold of rugby league, for the first time by the England rugby union side in a century. Secondly, the venue was the home ground of arguably the most famous club football team in the world, Manchester United, and players from both sides were awestruck and full of nervous excitement to be playing at such a venue.

Norm Hewitt (NZ 1993–98): 'We went for our usual pre-match stroll and I just shivered the whole time ... It was stunning – like being inside one of those amazing English cathedrals. Which, I suppose, it was – because soccer is Britain's only true religion ... I knew that whatever else I did in rugby, nothing would match how I felt as I walked over Old Trafford that morning. It was like I was on holy ground.'

It was also the first time former England and Lions player Clive Woodward coached an England side against New Zealand. In fact, it was only his second game in charge, his first being a 15-15 draw with Australia the week before. Woodward had succeeded Jack Rowell as coach, his appointment coming after the RFU unsuccessfully courted New Zealander Graham Henry, coach of the Super Rugby champions, the Auckland Blues.

On his appointment, Woodward secured former England loose-forward Roger Uttley in a managerial role and former All Black loose-forward John Mitchell (who had been a midweek captain on the 1993 tour and was coaching Sale) as a part-time assistant coach. In the England backline was Will Greenwood, son of former England coach, Dick.

The 1997 All Blacks were being acclaimed in English rugby circles as one of the greatest sides of all time. They had played some exhilarating rugby in the southern winter, had some all-time greats in their squad and the chance to go through the year unbeaten.

John Mitchell (ENG assistant coach 1997–2000): 'I've never seen a team as nervous and scared as England were … It quickly became apparent to me that they had no intention of playing to win. They just wanted to hang in there and not prove an embarrassment.'

Phil de Glanville (ENG 1992–99): 'I think we *were* nervous before that match – the noise and the fans were so much louder than normal, and they were so close to the pitch that you could see faces when the anthems were playing. I have never gone out to play with no intention to win, but yes, we were nervous before that game and our mental state didn't help us perform well. New Zealand had scored two tries before we even got going!'

England hooker Richard Cockerill, making his first run-on appearance in his fourth Test, was visibly fired up as he left the players' tunnel and quickly showed he wouldn't be shrinking back from any physical confrontation. As his opposite, Hewitt, led the All Blacks' haka, Cockerill sought him out and stood in front of him, so close that both were nose to nose. In Maori culture this is usually a warm way of greeting friends or newcomers, but in this case Hewitt was shouting his challenge into the face of Cockerill, while Cockerill offered some choice colloquialisms of his own. Referee Peter Marshall briefly tried to separate the two but then thought better of it and the haka ended with a bit of pushing and shoving.

Richard Cockerill (ENG 1997–99): 'I was obviously quite excitable. A bit of red mist and a bit of aggression and let's take it to them … It's a war dance after all, isn't it? It's a challenge. They want to smash you, you want to smash them. Right, you want to take us on, let's have a crack. We turned back for the kick-off and Jonno [Martin Johnson] said to me, "What the f*** have you done?"'

Norm Hewitt: 'I just wanted to slug him [Cockerill]. But I knew I couldn't. Not in front of that many people and an international TV audience … And yet, I didn't think he or the English players were disrespecting the haka. People who say that miss the point of what the haka is about. It's a challenge – a challenge to war. And the Poms had exactly the right answer to it – you accept the challenge and you throw it back. But, I'll tell you this – I was one motivated Maori boy that afternoon! And I made sure Cockerill knew it too.'

Six minutes into the match, Martin Johnson (according to his recollection) 'slapped' the All Black captain, Justin Marshall.

Martin Johnson (ENG 1993–2003): '[Marshall] had come offside to compete for the ball a couple of times. The third time, as he got the ball away, I caught him with a stiff arm – not even a proper punch – around the back of the head. He would hardly have felt it.'

Justin Marshall (NZ 1995–2005): 'I'd just cleared the ball from a ruck and was ready to follow the pass and he just king-hit me. I was in a bit of trouble there for a while [with blurred vision and impaired hearing].'

All Black coach, John Hart (who had coached Johnson in 1990 when he played for the New Zealand Colts whilst living and working in New Zealand), described the whack as 'an act of thuggery'. As the incident hadn't been seen by referee Marshall, Woodward and Uttley suspended Johnson for a week, which saved him from the citing commissioner who may have suspended him for the usual penalty period of 30 days.

While post-match the media made much of that punch, English rugby writers wondered why Johnson should have to miss a Test while

All Black centre Frank Bunce, who had fired a jab to the face of Neil Back and been formally warned by the referee with a yellow card, was free to play? (Under the evolving card and citation protocols, a yellow card didn't mean time in the sin-bin.)

What, then, of the game itself?

England had no shortage of ball, something that occasionally seemed to catch them by surprise and once or twice open running in the backs ended with the unopposed player in space slowing or turning the ball back inside as if they were still on the training field. Matt Perry made a memorable break, but the movement broke down. Both sides did play some great running rugby that thrilled the northerners but were also guilty of a plethora of errors.

Mike Catt – who never shirked his role as kicker despite reaching a point where he wished he didn't have that duty – had an off-day with his place-kicking, missing five from five. He also punted straight to Jonah Lomu who set about creating a try for Ian Jones. As some consolation, he did produce a lovely cross kick which brought about a try to Phil de Glanville.

The other All Black tries were to Jeff Wilson, from broken play, while Taine Randell's came from a scrum on the England line.

The 17-point margin was England's largest defeat at home and as the disappointed home players entered the tunnel, they were herded back onto the field by an RFU official. He told them to acknowledge the Old Trafford crowd.

As the England team walked up and down the field clapping in appreciation of their supporters, who in turn gave them a standing ovation, over the speaker system came a symphonic rendition of 'Land of Hope and Glory'.

Providing comments on the New Zealand broadcast was former All Black Grant Fox who said, 'This is unusual to see. I'm cynical by nature. They're applauding themselves and they still lost.' Half a minute later, with the All Blacks having already disappeared under the stands, it was acknowledged that the England players were indeed thanking the crowd.

So, from a confrontational haka to a 'victory lap', there was much for fractious fans on both sides to needle each other about.

Referee: P.L. Marshall (Australia)

Touch Judges: W.J. Erickson (Australia), A.J. Cole (Australia)

Attendance: 55,243

Half-time: NZ 15, ENG 3

Scorers: NZ I.D. Jones (t), J.W. Wilson (t), T.C. Randell (t), A.P. Mehrtens (2c, 2p)
ENG P.R. de Glanville (t), M.J. Catt (p)

ENGLAND: J. Leonard (Harlequins), R. Cockerill (Leicester), D.J. Garforth (Leicester), M.O. Johnson (Leicester), G.S. Archer (Newcastle), L.B.N. Dallaglio (*Capt.* Wasps), R.A. Hill (Saracens), A.J. Diprose (Saracens), K.P.P. Bracken (Saracens), M.J. Catt (Bath), A.A. Adebayo (Bath), P.R. de Glanville (Bath), W.J.H. Greenwood (Leicester), D. Rees (Sale), M.B. Perry (Bath)

Reserves: N.A. Back (Leicester, 40'), A.S. Healey (Leicester, 55'), P. Grayson (Northampton), D. Grewcock (Saracens), A. Long (Bath), G. Rowntree (Leicester)

Coach: C. Woodward

NEW ZEALAND: C.W. Dowd (Auckland), N.J. Hewitt (Southland), O.M. Brown (Auckland) I.D. Jones (North Harbour), R.M. Brooke (Auckland), T.C. Randell (Otago), J.A. Kronfeld (Otago), Z.V. Brooke (Auckland), J.W. Marshall (*Capt.* Canterbury), A.P. Mehrtens (Canterbury), J.T. Lomu (Counties Manukau), A. Ieremia (Wellington), F.E. Bunce (North Harbour), J.W. Wilson (Otago), C.M. Cullen (Manawatu)

Reserves: A.F. Blowers (Auckland, 52'), S.J. McLeod (Waikato, 59') J.P. Preston (Wellington, 79'), M. Allen (Manawatu), C.C. Riechelmann (Auckland), A.D. Oliver (Otago)

Coach: J. Hart

Twickenham, London, 6 December 1997
ENGLAND 26 – ALL BLACKS 26

*'When I went in to speak to the forwards it was clear
they were blowing bubbles and gasping for oxygen.'
– John Mitchell, England assistant coach*

IN the fortnight since the Old Trafford match, England had lost 11-29 to the Springboks while the All Blacks had beaten an England Rugby Partnership XV in Bristol, Wales (at Wembley Stadium, due to the construction of the Millennium Stadium in Cardiff) and England 'A' in Leicester.

New protocol requiring teams to be separated by the halfway line were introduced for the haka to avoid a repeat of the Cockerill–Hewitt machismo, great theatre though it was.

Zinzan Brooke was playing his 100th (and last) match for New Zealand while it was also to be Frank Bunce's last international.

John Mitchell (ENG assistant coach 1997–2000): 'The whole mindset changed overnight and suddenly we were heading to the Twickenham Test with a degree of confidence. England took on an attacking mindset and started off at 100 miles an hour.'

Apparently Clive Woodward said to his players pre-match, 'Let's just have a f****** go at this f****** New Zealand team. Let's just tap everything. We don't have much to lose, so let's absolutely go for it.'

Clive Woodward (ENG coach 1997–2004): 'I set the guys a target of 35 points because that's what I felt would be needed to beat this New Zealand team. What did I say to them at half-time? Simple. I told them that we had 23 of the 35 and that there were a dozen more to find.'

England made an extraordinary start after four minutes when, for some unknown reason, from a free kick inside his 22, Andrew Mehrtens kicked long downfield to where it was caught by David Rees on his ten-metre line. With acres of space in front of him, he sprinted upfield, chipped over Jonah Lomu, regathered, beat the flailing Zinzan Brooke and crossed the line – just – in the tackle of Bunce. It was an utterly electrifying solo try!

'Swing low, sweet chariot...'

Four minutes later, the home side dotted down again. England fans were on their feet. From halfway, England ran down the left-hand side of the field. Austin Healey fed Will Greenwood who swerved and side-stepped to beat two defenders before being brought down by Justin Marshall just short of the line. He lobbed a pass to his left where it was picked up by Richard Hill who simply had to fall over the line for the try.

Richard Hill (ENG 1997–2008): '[After] grounding the ball a defender picked me up and held me up in the air. Worried the referee hadn't spotted my touchdown I was left hanging there, trying to get the ball down again. It was real Tom and Jerry stuff.'

'Swing low, sweet chariot' got louder still.

Paul Grayson missed both conversions, but England were up 10-0.

In response, the All Blacks put their foot on the accelerator, using a charging Lomu near the rucks, where it would take three or four players to bring him to the ground. Mehrtens got the visitors on the board with a penalty as England did their best to slow down the All Blacks' ruck ball.

Then, when the All Blacks tried to run the ball out of their half, Bunce had no support as he was tackled. The ball rolled loose, and England captain Lawrence Dallaglio toed it towards the All Blacks' line, beating Lomu and Marshall to the score. Grayson converted.

17-3! In the stands, Woodward could not contain himself.

Referee Fleming pinged the All Blacks' midfield for being offside on their 22, though at the previous ruck Bracken looked to have clearly knocked the ball on. Grayson slotted the easy penalty.

Mehrtens kicked penalties after England were penalised for holding on to the ball in the tackle and using hands in the ruck. That was all good and well, but what his side needed was tries.

England had a reprieve just before half-time when Jeff Wilson looked to have scored the first try for his team after breaks by Christian Cullen and Taine Randell. Fleming adjudged the final pass forward, something of a rough call given that the touch judge who was running in line with the play had no concerns about it.

The rugby gods again smiled on England right on half-time when Fleming ruled that Matt Perry had been taken out of play by Walter Little, who had jumped to block a chip kick. The crowd's boos as Perry hit the turf turned to cheers as Grayson knocked over the 40-metre penalty and England ended the pulsating half 14 points ahead.

While the fans in the stands were basking in the jubilation of what they had just seen, for the England players under the stands it was a very different story.

Lawrence Dallaglio (ENG 1995–2007): 'I felt sick and was retching … It was carnage in the changing room. No one could speak. Players were sprawled on the floor, others were vomiting into the bins.'

The All Blacks started the second half as England had the first. After a couple of minutes, Mehrtens had a try following a sustained attack where Wilson was brought down short of the line and then Hewitt and Robin Brooke went on the pick and drive from successive penalties for England offences at the ruck.

All Black captain Marshall (one of the leading exponents of the 'albatross' arm-waving to attract the attention of the referee to infringements) was marched 20 metres by Fleming for back-chat.

Justin Marshall (NZ 1995-2005): 'I was bitterly disappointed with the way Fleming reffed that day and particularly the way he wouldn't listen to any genuine feedback that we wanted to give him … My forwards were saying to me, "They're lying all over the place. Get him to sort it out or we will." But I couldn't communicate with him all day.'

England again transgressed at a ruck, using their hands, and Mehrtens had another three points. The gap was narrowing.

Another All Black pass went to ground and was hacked through by an England player. From the goal-line ruck, England came up with the ball and had an overlap to the right. A great scoring chance. To the dismay of many, Perry took the first pass and ran back towards a wall of All Black forwards and the ball was lost forward.

The All Blacks didn't bottle their next scoring opportunity. Following a sideline run by Lomu, Mehrtens followed up his own bomb and tapped the ball back. Prop Mark 'Bull' Allen grabbed it and made a few metres before Marshall sent the ball left to Little who beat two weak tackles to score. For the first time in the match, the All Blacks were in the lead and with Mehrtens chipping over the conversion, the All Blacks were ahead by three.

Roger Uttley (ENG manager 1997–99): 'The sides were like two punch-drunk boxers. They'd worn each other out and you could see the strength draining away from them, but they were still trying things, still seeking the killer blow.'

England summoned all their remaining energy to attack the All Blacks' line and looked to have the numbers to score on the left-hand side but once again Perry took the ball into contact and a chance for a try was lost. Fortunately for England, Fleming ruled the All Blacks offside and Grayson kicked a simple penalty from near the left-hand post.

The scores were even. 26-26.

Mehrtens had a long-range drop-goal attempt to win the match but it sailed to the left of the posts.

When Fleming blew the whistle for full time, there were standing ovations for the players who had put on one of the finest spectacles of pulsating rugby Twickenham had seen.

For the players, most of whom were out on their feet, there were very mixed feelings.

Lawrence Dallaglio: 'Even though we had drawn … it felt like a defeat because we had been in such a strong winning position.'

Norm Hewitt (NZ 1993–98): 'We slackened off again and lost the intensity and that allowed them to get the 26-all draw. I don't know what it is, but last Tests of the year always seem to trip the All Blacks up … They had recalled Neil Back so he gave them some added zip at the breakdown. Dallaglio had a great game that day – he's a real tough bastard and tends to play a bit like a Bok loosie. All elbows and knees.'

Referee: J.M. Fleming (Scotland)

Touch Judges: C. Muir (Scotland), K.W. McCartney (Scotland)

Attendance: 75,000

Half-time: ENG 23, NZ 9

Scorers: ENG Rees (t), Hill (t), Dallaglio (t), Grayson (3p, c)
NZ Little (t), Mehrtens (t, 4p, 2c)

ENGLAND: J. Leonard (Harlequins), R. Cockerill (Leicester), D.J. Garforth (Leicester), M.O. Johnson (Leicester), G.S. Archer (Newcastle), L.B.N. Dallaglio (*Capt.* Wasps), N.A. Back (Leicester), R.A. Hill (Saracens), K.P.P. Bracken (Saracens), P.J. Grayson (Northampton), A.S. Healey (Leicester), P.R. de Glanville (Bath), W.J.H. Greenwood (Leicester), D. Rees (Sale), M.B. Perry (Bath)

Reserves: M.J.S. Dawson (Northampton, 59'), T.R.G. Stimpson (Newcastle, 59'), M.P. Regan (Bath, 62'), C.M.A. Sheasby (Wasps, temp), D.J. Grewcock (Saracens), K. Yates (Bath)

Coach: C. Woodward

NEW ZEALAND: M.R. Allen (Manawatu), N.J. Hewitt (Southland), O.M. Brown (Auckland), I.D. Jones (North Harbour), R.M. Brooke (Auckland), T.C. Randell (Otago), J.A. Kronfeld (Otago), Z.V. Brooke (Auckland), J.W. Marshall (*Capt.* Canterbury), A.P. Mehrtens (Canterbury), J.T. Lomu (Counties Manukau), W.K. Little (North Harbour), F.E. Bunce (North Harbour), J.W. Wilson (Otago), C.M. Cullen (Manawatu)

Reserves: C.J. Spencer (Auckland, 63'), S.J. McLeod (Waikato, 73'), C.C. Riechelmann (temp sub), C.K. Barrell (Canterbury), A.D. Oliver (Otago), J.P. Preston (Wellington)

Coach: J. Hart

MATCH 21

Carisbrook, Dunedin, 20 June 1998
ALL BLACKS 64 – ENGLAND 22

The 'tour from Hell'

AFTER the 26-all draw at Twickenham the previous December, Clive Woodward would have been hoping that his seven-match summer tour to Australia, New Zealand and South Africa would have shown continued improvement from his squad and close matches, if not a win or two. It was not to be.

A frustrating aspect of the still-fledgling professional rugby scene came to the fore as a number of English clubs refused to release players contracted to them. Others withdrew with a mix of injuries, both certified and not. As such, 17 of the 37 touring players were uncapped (a number of which weren't chosen for their country again). Only Gareth Archer, Neil Back, Richard Cockerill, Austin Healey and Matt Perry remained from the Twickenham draw.

Thus, before even leaving England, the 'weak' party was roundly criticised by rugby writers, especially in Australia and New Zealand, as making a mockery of the trips to the southern hemisphere, especially when there was always an expectation that sides travelling north would bring their best players.

Being walloped by a record 76-0 in Australia, and then falling to New Zealand 'A' and New Zealand Rugby Academy sides did little to stop New Zealand rugby officials from grinding their molars at the prospect of a very lopsided two-match series.

The relationship between visitors and hosts soured further when Woodward announced, on the Thursday before the match, that he wouldn't name his playing XV until an hour before kick-off. As a result, the match programmes carried the names of the entire England squad as:

> that was all that was available from English management at the time of printing. We have supplied boxes beside players' names so that you can tick the box of the final 15 to take the field.

On a cool, clear afternoon, New Zealand fans got their first sighting of England's much-touted 19-year-old fly-half, Jonny Wilkinson. An age-group star with less than an hour of senior club rugby under his belt before he made his international debut as a replacement during the Five Nations tournament at the start of the year, he had been the youngest player to turn out for England in 71 years.

For the first half an hour of the match, any thoughts that the All Blacks would be able to better the score posted by the Wallabies soon faded as England ably contested every facet of the game. The scoreboard only climbed in increments of three, thanks to penalties by Andrew Mehrtens and Tim Stimpson. All Blacks 9, England 3.

Then came the turning point in the match. While England were on attack in the All Blacks' 22, a scrum collapsed and a minor scuffle broke out. All Black vice-captain Robin Brooke could be heard through an onfield microphone saying, 'You're off.' Referee Erickson then pointed to England lock Danny Grewcock and sent him for an early shower. His indiscretion was a kick to the head of the prone All Black hooker, Anton Oliver. Grewcock became only the second England player sent off in an international. Mike Burton had been the first, in 1975 versus Australia.

With England a man down, the All Blacks' backline stars Christian Cullen and Jonah Lomu began to run riot. The latter had already enjoyed a number of runs close to the forwards, targeting the defence of Wilkinson. The young fly-half may not have always had the best tackling technique, but he could never be accused of not giving it his all.

Jonny Wilkinson (ENG 1998–2011): 'This first time, I hit [Lomu] full on with all I've got, fairly high on the ball, just enough to halt him for a second for everyone else to dive in. On the second occasion, I have no time to prepare myself and am not so successful. We're five metres from our line and I know that if I go high, he'll carry me over and score anyway, and then probably toss me into the crowd, so I sink down low to try to get round his legs and I just get smashed. He knocks me on to my back and runs over my chest.'

England conceded three quick tries in the ten minutes before half-time but clawed one back thanks to the efforts of Richard Cockerill. The score had leapt to 26-8, in favour of the All Blacks.

There was a lot of niggle in the scrums once Grewcock was sent off. This resulted in All Black coach John Hart suggesting to referee Erickson at half-time that Golden Oldies scrums be used. This approach to the referee incurred the wrath of Woodward when he later found out.

The interval only prolonged the inevitable as the All Blacks ran in try after try to lead by 57-8. England captain Matt Dawson (who had spent time playing club rugby in New Zealand for the Te Awamutu club in Waikato prior to establishing himself as a top-level player) was doing his utmost to keep his players positive. With great resolve he and Tom Biem (a former Welsh hockey representative and professional polo player who had replaced Wilkinson when the second half was barely underway) scored tries. The final score of 64-22 was the All Blacks' highest total and winning margin against England.

The drama did not end at the final whistle. In the hours after the match, All Black lock Ian Jones was cited for allegedly stomping on England prop Graham Rowntree but was cleared of the charge. Then Woodward learnt that his father, Ronald, had passed away. The next day Woodward flew back to England for the funeral.

As the night wore on, the student town's inner-city pubs and flats were heaving with partying rugby fans, and a number of players who had been involved in the match.

Outside the Bowling Green Tavern, the oldest and most infamous 'scarfie' haunt, Cockerill and Hewitt came to blows after the latter was invited to join England players out on the town. Banter about hakas and splinters in backsides due to time spent on reserves' benches eventually led to a bit of fisticuffs.

Norm Hewitt (NZ 1993–98): 'Two big hookers rolling around the mini-van trying to get a headlock on each other ... it wasn't pretty.

Anyway, when we got into town, we poured out of the mini-van and exchanged a few blows. It wasn't anything major – we were too pissed to do each other any real harm.'

While the Carisbrook ground was colloquially known as 'The House of Pain', Dunedin was very much the 'Town of Pain' for the 1998 England team.

Referee: W.J. Erickson (Australia)

Touch Judges: P.L. Marshall (Australia), S.M. Young (Australia)

Attendance: 36,576

Half-time: NZ 26, ENG 8

Scorers: NZ Cullen (2t), Randell (2t), Wilson (2t), Lomu (t), Mayerhofler (t) Kronfeld (t), Mehrtens (3p, 5c).
ENG Cockerill (t), Dawson (t) Biem (t), Stimpson (p, 2c)

NEW ZEALAND: C.W. Dowd (Auckland), A.D. Oliver (Otago), O.M. Brown (Auckland), I.D. Jones (North Harbour), R.M. Brooke (Auckland), M.N. Jones (Auckland), J.A. Kronfeld (Otago), T.C. Randell (*Capt.* Otago), O.F.J. Tonu'u (Auckland), A.P. Mehrtens (Canterbury), J.T. Lomu (Counties-Manukau), W.K. Little (North Harbour), M.A. Mayerhofler+ (Canterbury), J.W. Wilson (Otago), C.M. Cullen (Wellington)

Reserves: T.J. Blackadder (Canterbury, 20'), M.D. Robinson (North Harbour, 62'), M.P. Carter (Auckland), N.J. Hewitt (Southland), C.H. Hoeft (Otago), C.J. Spencer (Auckland), C.S. Ralph (Auckland)

Coach: J. Hart

ENGLAND: G.C. Rowntree (Leicester), R. Cockerill (Leicester), P.J. Vickery (Gloucester), D.J. Grewcock (Saracens, R 30'-80'), G.S. Archer (Newcastle), B.B. Clarke (Richmond), P.H. Sanderson* (Sale), S.O. Ojomoh (Gloucester), M.J.S. Dawson (*Capt.* Northampton), J.P. Wilkinson (Newcastle), T.R.G. Stimpson (Newcastle), O.J. Lewsey* (Bristol), N.D. Beal (Northampton), A.S. Healey (Leicester), M.B. Perry (Bath)

Reserves: W.R. Green (Wasps, temp 11', sub 58'), B. Sturnham (Saracens, temp 36'), T.D. Biem* (Sale, 42'), P.B.T. Greening (Gloucester, 57'), D. Sims* (Gloucester, 77'), S. Benton (Bradford), A.J. Diprose (Saracens)

Coach: C. Woodward

MATCH 22

Eden Park, Auckland, 27 June 1998
ALL BLACKS 40 – ENGLAND 10

'The two Tests were meaningless mismatches.'
– Jeff Wilson, All Black wing

WHILE Clive Woodward was away on the whirlwind five-day trip to attend the funeral of his father in England, England had suffered further humiliation at the hands of the New Zealand Maori, losing 62-14 in Rotorua.

Lewis Moody (ENG 1998–2011): 'I had never – never – played in such a heavy defeat as 62-14 in my life – not at school, nor for my country, and definitely not for Leicester. I was embarrassed.'

There were changes to both Test sides but most notably Jonny Wilkinson hadn't recovered from his injury, so Josh Lewsey wore the England number ten jersey. Steve Ravenscroft, who had lived in Auckland for a time and turned out for the North Harbour Under-21s, was included on the England bench.

Prior to kick-off there was a public acknowledgement of All Black great Sean Fitzpatrick who had retired due to an ongoing knee problem. He left the game as the most-capped international forward with 93 Test appearances.

After the drama of the previous Saturday, the final score of 40-10 is somewhat misrepresentative of the All Blacks' domination of the game. They began strongly with wing Jeff Wilson scoring after only four minutes. But as the match progressed, the home side were playing more like a collection of individuals than a cohesive unit. This wasn't helped by coach John Hart making five substitutions in the first hour.

England, certainly with pride at stake – and 15 men on the paddock – played with a John Mitchell-enthused 'controlled fury'.

Clive Woodward (ENG coach 1997–2004): 'Matt Dawson captained brilliantly and his example enabled England to show some spirit in their best performance of the tour.'

Dawson certainly did lead by example, scoring all his side's points.

All Black flanker Josh Kronfeld wrote in his diary that he felt the All Blacks were losing their way and forgetting how to play the game simply. He believed four try-scoring opportunities had been missed in the match, simply because the team weren't doing the basics like using the ball to beat the man.

Jeff Wilson (NZ 1993–2001): 'We knew ... that all they would be trying to do would be to minimise the scores against them and that if we didn't beat them comprehensively, we'd be criticised. The two Tests were meaningless mismatches and didn't feel like proper Tests. I didn't take much satisfaction from either one of them and the sooner they're forgotten, the better.'

England players felt exactly the same way about their month-long nightmare, which ended with a 0-18 loss to South Africa.

This Test was the last time the All Blacks played a home fixture against England during an afternoon. Due to the terms of lucrative broadcasting deals, stadia were replaced or rebuilt and lights for night matches installed. The kick-off time for the majority of their home matches is now 7.35pm.

Referee: P.L. Marshall (Australia)

Touch Judges: W.J. Erickson (Australia), S.M. Young (Australia)

Attendance: 45,000

Half-time: NZ 14, ENG 7

Scorers: NZ Wilson (2t), Mayerhofler (t), Vidiri (t), Maka (t), Randell (t), Spencer (3c), Mehrtens (2c)
ENG Dawson (t, c, p)

NEW ZEALAND: C.W. Dowd (Auckland), A.D. Oliver (Otago), O.M. Brown (Auckland), I.D. Jones (North Harbour), R.M. Brooke (Auckland), T.J. Blackadder (Canterbury), J.A. Kronfeld (Otago), T.C. Randell (*Capt.* Otago), O.F.J. Tonu'u (Auckland), A.P. Mehrtens (Canterbury), J.T. Lomu (Counties Manukau), M.A. Mayerhofler (Canterbury), C.S. Ralph (Auckland), J.W. Wilson (Otago), C.M. Cullen (Wellington)

Reserves: C.H. Hoeft (Otago, temp 5', 68'), N.J. Hewitt (Wellington, 40'), C.J. Spencer (Auckland, 40'), I. Maka (Otago, 49'), J. Vidiri (Counties Manukau, 58'), M.P. Carter (Auckland, 61'), M. D. Robinson (Canterbury)

Coach: J. Hart

ENGLAND: G.C. Rowntree (Leicester), R. Cockerill (Leicester), P.J. Vickery (Gloucester), R.J. Fidler+ (Gloucester), D. Sims (Gloucester), B.B. Clarke (Richmond), P.H. Sanderson (Sale), A.J. Diprose (Saracens), M.J.S. Dawson (*Capt.* Northampton), O.J. Lewsey (Bristol), T.D. Biem (Sale), J.J.N. Baxendell+ (Sale), N.D. Beal (Northampton), A.S. Healey (Leicester), M.B. Perry (Bath)

Reserves: B. Sturnham (Saracens, temp 16'), T.R.G. Stimpson (Newcastle, 28'), S.C.W. Ravenscroft (Saracens, 68'), P.B.T. Greening (Gloucester, 71'), S. Benton (Gloucester), W.R. Green (Wasps), S.O. Ojomoh (Gloucester).

Coach: C. Woodward

Twickenham, London, 9 October 1999 (RWC)
ALL BLACKS 30 – ENGLAND 16

'It was a bruising, highly physical game
and I was physically shattered the next day.'
– Anton Oliver, All Black hooker

CLIVE Woodward (ENG coach 1997–2004): 'I had never been more confident going into a match of such importance as I was on that day ... Basically we bottled it. Not physically, where everyone gave their all, but mentally. Our mindset let us down badly, and under the pressure of the game we reverted to type and played a very typical English game.'

The 15th match of the 1999 RWC was the third match in Pool B and followed comfortable wins for England over Italy and the All Blacks against Tonga.

In his usual match-eve motivational talk, Woodward had written the names of the players from both sides on a whiteboard. He then told his charges that there was not one member of the All Blacks he thought would be good enough to get into his England team.

Matt Perry (ENG 1997–2001): 'It certainly made you puff your chest out a little knowing Clive thought so highly of us ... However, there was one comparison we were all drawn to and it was left to Jason Leonard, who was sitting in front of me and next to Lawrence Dallaglio, to verbalise what every player in the room was thinking. He leaned over to Lawrence and in a stage whisper everyone could hear, said, "I don't know about you, Lol, but that 6ft 5in, 19st winger [Jonah Lomu] would get into my f****** side every day of the week."'

The All Blacks had a police escort to the match and arrived about 90 minutes earlier than was necessary. There was time to kill. The players wandered around the ground and, in the case of hooker Anton Oliver, had a sleep for nearly an hour on the floor of the changing room.

There was nothing soporific about the start of the much-hyped match. An oft-used adjective by those who were on the field that day is 'intense'. Jonny Wilkinson, still only 20 years old at the time, recalled that the match began at an incredible pace, with players reacting purely on instinct and adrenaline in the early stages.

Martin Johnson (ENG 1993–2003): 'We had a plan to try and play away from their strengths and we considered [Josh] Kronfeld a major threat. We went out to try to minimise the impact he would have on the game, but he was a real nuisance and we just couldn't get the better of him.'

The All Blacks had to contend with an England pack that was tearing into everything, albeit sometimes with a bit too much exuberance, which resulted in errors. Nonetheless, they were dominating the exchanges and thus possession and territory.

The issue for England was how to break down the All Black defence which was committed and cohesive. At no time did any panic set in when the men in black went long periods without the ball. It seemed as though they were content to defend and defend and wait for their turn with the ball.

Andrew Mehrtens had the first points after 11 minutes when England were penalised for not rolling away at a ruck ten metres from their line.

The first All Black try came after Perry had put a huge punt out on the full. Having won the lineout just outside the England 22, Lomu came in on the crash. Three England players stalled his progress, but the ball went to Christian Cullen, playing at centre. He glided through between Phil de Glanville and Dan Luger before passing to Tana Umaga. Austin Healey brought him down a metre short of the line but as he was falling Umaga got a pass away to Jeff Wilson who scored. Mehrtens' sideline conversion made it 10-0.

After two uncharacteristic early misses, Wilkinson put the first points on the board for England with a penalty kick.

Following a succession of All Black forward drives up the middle of the field, Richard Hill was penalised at a ruck. Mehrtens added three more points.

From the kick-off, Kronfeld claimed the ball but was turned by Dallaglio. Referee Marshall penalised the All Black for not releasing the ball and Wilkinson notched up another three points.

At that, the half-time whistle blew. There was some booing from sections of the crowd as the players left the field, perhaps frustrated that their much-hyped England side had done so little with so much ball.

As he had done in the first half, Mehrtens opened the scoring in the second with a long-range penalty.

Lomu made a barnstorming run up the centre of the field but lost the ball to de Glanville on the England 22. The England centre then set off in the other direction. He made it to halfway. From there Neil Back ran another 30 metres deep into All Black territory. England went left then right before Jeremy Guscott drilled the ball along the ground towards the All Blacks' posts. Neither Matt Perry nor Justin Marshall could control it, leaving de Glanville to collect the ball in a slide against the left-hand upright, scoring a great counter-attacking try.

Wilkinson converted and then added another penalty. The scores were level, 16-16. Was this going to be the 1997 draw all over again?

Jonah Lomu (NZ 1994–2002): 'The English are great talkers on the field. It was especially noticeable in the second half. As they closed the gap on us and eventually levelled at 16-16, the chatter was upbeat, and it was non-stop. For us, the talking was all about our defensive lines and the need to keep digging it in.'

A great ball-and-all tackle by Cullen on Perry saw the All Blacks with quick ball. Lock Robin Brooke sent the ball left. Cullen threw a skip-pass to Lomu.

Jonny Wilkinson (ENG 1998–2011): 'Lomu finally gets away. I sprint across the pitch, too far away to make any impression, watching him on the outside, looking unstoppable, going through one, two, three and then a fourth tackler. It is almost like I am 16 years old again, sitting in front of the TV watching the semi-final of the 1995 World Cup.'

The crowd rose to their feet as Lomu thundered downfield from inside his own half. He left Guscott, Healey and Matt Dawson in his wake. A hesitant-looking Luger wrapped his arms around the big man as he plunged over the line.

Austin Healey (ENG 1997–2003): 'I put everything I had into hitting him low and just squeezing my arms. Even if I only got one leg, I was determined to hold onto it. I hit him as hard as I could around his right thigh, got my arms linked, which usually means you're going to drag your man down, squeezed as hard as I could and thought to myself *"Job done! I've got him."* Next thing I know, his heel hits me in the chin and he's gone.'

A melee then broke out on the try-line after Dallaglio, who had been following play holding the jersey of Cullen from about 30 metres out, then put his forearm into the face of the prone Lomu as he flopped to the ground, claiming to have been pushed from behind.

Replacement All Black halfback Byron Kelleher added another try, sniping over in the left-hand corner after a quick 22 restart backfired on England.

Jeff Wilson (NZ 1993–2001): 'The problems of us being an uncreative team did not really surface because it was our defence that was most crucial in winning that game, not our attack. England had so much of the possession that they should have won the game twice over, and would have against any lesser team.

'I was proud of the way the All Blacks defended in that game and of the way we were able to take the few scoring opportunities available to us.'

Jonah Lomu: 'We were absolutely knackered when we came off the field.'

According to the final match statistics, England had over 60% of both territory and possession. An inconsolable Wilkinson sat in the English changing room after the match, punishing himself for his four missed kicks.

Jeremy Guscott (ENG 1989–99): 'Did we take too many easy decisions along the way rather than opting for the tough one that might have reaped a reward? I know that I chipped for the corner early on when I might have been better backing myself to make some yardage with ball in hand. What might have been ...'

Lawrence Dallaglio (ENG 1995–2007): 'That day we were in the Rose Room at Twickenham and none of them was interested in any sort of conversation. Maybe they just didn't like us, I don't know. I found it strange, though.'

Remarkably, England and the All Blacks didn't face each other in any of the next four RWC tournaments. New Zealand are (at the time of writing) the only nation of the 16 who have opposed England in the various events not to have been beaten by the men in white.

Referee: P. Marshall (Australia)

Touch Judges: D. Bevan (Wales), D. Méné (France)

Attendance: 72,000

Half-time: NZ 13, ENG 6

Scorers: NZ: J.W. Wilson (t), J.T. Lomu (t), B.T. Kelleher (t), A.P. Mehrtens (3p, 3c)

ENG: P.R. de Glanville (t), J.P. Wilkinson (3p, c)

ENGLAND: J. Leonard (Harlequins), R. Cockerill (Leicester), P.J. Vickery (Gloucester), M.O. Johnson (*Capt.* Leicester), D.J. Grewcock (Saracens), N.A. Back (Leicester), R.A. Hill (Saracens), L.B.N. Dallaglio (Wasps), M.J.S. Dawson (Northampton), J.P. Wilkinson (Newcastle), A.S. Healey (Leicester), J.C. Guscott (Bath), P.R. de Glanville (Bath), D. Luger (Saracens), M.B. Perry (Bath)

Reserves: M.J. Corry (Leicester, temp 12', 75'), D.J. Garforth (Leicester, 53'), T.A.K. Rodber (Northampton, 62'), P.B.T. Greening (Sale, 70'), P.J. Grayson (Northampton, 70'), N. Beal (Northampton), W. Greenwood (Leicester)

Coach: C. Woodward

NEW ZEALAND: C.H. Hoeft (Otago), A.D. Oliver (Otago), C.W. Dowd (Auckland), N.M.C. Maxwell (Northland), R.M. Brooke (Auckland), R.D. Thorne (Canterbury), J.A. Kronfeld (Otago), T.C. Randell (*Capt.* Otago), J.W. Marshall (Canterbury), A.P. Mehrtens (Canterbury), J.T. Lomu (Counties Manukau), A. Ieremia (Wellington), C.M. Cullen (Wellington), T.J.F. Umaga (Wellington), J.W. Wilson (Otago)

Reserves: G.E. Feek (Canterbury, temp 29', 37'), B.T. Kelleher (Otago, 64'), R.K. Willis (Waikato, 65'), D.P.E. Gibson (Canterbury, 68'), T.E. Brown (Otago, 75'), M.G. Hammett (Canterbury), D.G. Mika (Auckland)

Coach: J. Hart

MATCH 24

Twickenham, London, 9 November 2002
ENGLAND 31 – ALL BLACKS 28

*'If I'd missed [that tackle] I would have gone and packed
my bags, got into my car and never played for England
again.' – Ben Cohen, England wing*

C OACHING the All Blacks on this end-of-year tour was John
Mitchell, former assistant to Clive Woodward. Previous All
Blacks coach Wayne Smith had lost confidence in his own
abilities and stepped down from the role. Mitchell, by contrast, had
the air of a man who dared anybody to disagree with him. His over-
used term for the All Blacks' preparation for the 2003 World Cup,
with fellow former All Black Robbie Deans as his assistant, was it
being a 'journey'.

Mitchell decided to 'rest' about 20 players for the trip north
meaning there were 12 uncapped players in the group and seven
debutants in his matchday squad to face the best team in the northern
hemisphere at their home ground. The All Blacks' locking combination
of Ali Williams and Keith Robinson didn't have a Test appearance
between them, while Martin Johnson and Danny Grewcock had a
combined 100 caps. Somewhat remarkably, given it was only three
years since the sides last met, only Johnson and Jason Leonard had
played the All Blacks previously.

In attendance to see if England could make it 16 Twickenham
wins in a row was England's then oldest former international, Hal
Sever, the man who was the scorer of the third try in the 1936
'Obolensky match'.

The All Blacks and England line up before their first ever encounter, Crystal Palace, 1905. *Daily Graphic/ Toby Goodman collection*

All Black forward Cyril Brownlie suffers the ignominy of being the first player sent off in a rugby international, Twickenham, 1925. *Illustrated London News/ author's collection*

Coverage of England's first win over the All Blacks, 1936. Bernard Gadney, England captain and scrum-half, passes the ball. Star of the game Prince Obolensky (bottom right) discusses the match with All Blacks Hart and Corner.
Sir George Grey Special Collections, Auckland Libraries.

The 1963 All Blacks during a training run in London's Green Park.
New Zealand Newspapers Ltd / author's collection

Programme from the first Test played by
England in New Zealand, 1963.
Author's collection

Programme from England's historic first win in
New Zealand, 1973. *Author's collection*

England prop Brian 'Stack' Stevens scores at Eden Park, 1973. All Blacks Bryan Williams, Ian Hurst and Sid Going arrive too late.
Auckland Rugby Union

The programme template of which minor variations were used by the RFU for the All Blacks' visits from 1953–83.
Author's collection

RUGBY FOOTBALL UNION

ENGLAND

v

NEW ZEALAND

TWICKENHAM
SATURDAY 19th NOVEMBER
1983
Official Programme
Fifty Pence

Secretary R.F.U.

England players celebrate as lock Maurice Colclough (unseen) scores the vital try to give England their second home win over the All Blacks, 1983. *Getty Images*

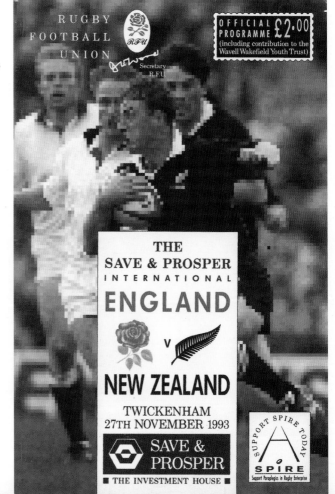

The curiously pixilated programme cover from the 1993 England win at Twickenham. *Author's collection*

RUGBY
FOOTBALL
UNION

Secretary
R.F.U

OFFICIAL
PROGRAMME £2·00
(including contribution to the
Wavell Wakefield Youth Trust)

THE
SAVE & PROSPER
INTERNATIONAL

ENGLAND

v

NEW ZEALAND

TWICKENHAM
27TH NOVEMBER 1993

SAVE &
PROSPER
■ THE INVESTMENT HOUSE ■

SUPPORT SPIRE TODAY
SPIRE
Support Paraplegics in Rugby Enterprise

Rob Andrew and Brian Moore celebrate the 1993 win at Twickenham. The memory of such celebrations would be motivation for the All Blacks two years later. *Getty Images*

Seconds before impact! Twenty-year-old Jonah Lomu about to become rugby's first global superstar, at the 1995 RWC. *Getty Images*

Programme from England's first international at Old Trafford in 100 years.
Author's collection

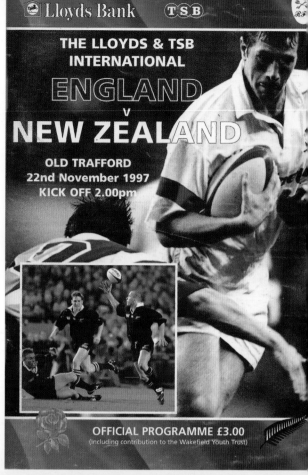

Richard Cockerill takes up the challenge of the Norm Hewitt-led haka, Old Trafford, 1997.
Getty Images.

When things go from bad to worse. Danny Grewcock sent off at Carisbrook on the 'Tour from Hell', 1998.
Getty Images

Wilkinson, Healey, Dallaglio and de Glanville faced with bringing down the unique and extraordinary Jonah Lomu, 1999 RWC.
Getty Images

Ben Cohen's match-saving tackle on All Black fullback Ben Blair, Twickenham, 2002.
Getty Images

England coaches Clive Woodward, Andy Robinson and Phil Larder deep in thought a day before the 'six-man scrum' victory in Wellington, 2003. Jonny Wilkinson (third left) would give a masterclass in place- and tactical kicking.
Getty Images

The knee from Simon Shaw that saw him red-carded, Eden Park, 2004.
Getty Images

Dan Carter and Richie McCaw, two key players in the All Blacks' nine straight wins from 2004–2010, were helpless to stop Manu Tuilagi and a rampant England, Twickenham, 2012.
Getty Images

On an overcast day, referee Jonathan Kaplan was in charge of his first Test at Twickenham.

Wilkinson kicked the first points after four minutes, the All Blacks penalised for flopping over the ball and five minutes later he had another three points as the All Blacks didn't release in a smothering tackle from Richard Hill, who was playing his 50th Test.

The All Blacks' Australian-born halfback Steve Devine, who had only been declared eligible to play in the hours before the game, made a break into the England 22 and his grubber kick saw Jason Robinson carry the ball back over the line.

The All Blacks had a five-metre scrum and a series of rucks under the England posts. Finally, an offside penalty came, back near the touchline. Captain Taine Randell opted for a lineout rather than scrum or kick. From the ensuing lineout win, Jonah Lomu barged over in the far corner. There were repeated viewings by the TMO as to whether Mike Tindall had dislodged the ball from the bulk of Lomu's bent arm, but the try was awarded. Fullback Ben Blair converted from the sideline.

Superb running and passing from an unlikely trio of black-glove-wearing hooker Steve Thompson, prop Trevor Woodman and Hill saw England sweep 70 metres downfield to where a drop goal attempt by Wilkinson was charged down.

England continued to press in the All Blacks' half and were gaining scrum dominance. In the 25th minute, after several surges towards the try-line, England were awarded a penalty in the right-hand corner. Matt Dawson's ploy was a chip kick over the line of defenders. It was easily caught by Lomu.

In chasing the kick, Will Greenwood charged at the line of All Blacks, noticeably picking out one of the smaller players, Spencer (rather than lock Williams or Lomu flanking him), who held his line. The collision saw Spencer knocked backwards and Greenwood crumpled to the turf.

Will Greenwood (ENG 1997–2004): 'As I hit the ground I couldn't breathe. As I lay there doubled up in agony gasping for air and waiting for the physio to appear, a handful of All Blacks leaned over me and gave me a tirade of abuse: "What's wrong with you, you big f***ing p****. Are you a f***ing little fag or what?"'

After a solid Lewis Moody charge from a scrum, which left the tackling Devine prone on the ground, Wilkinson snapped a left-foot drop goal to put England ahead, 9-7. England were making the play, including confidently running the ball out from their 22.

A long pass from Randell was intercepted by Hill and then his pass to Greenwood was intercepted by Tana Umaga who fed Doug Howlett, just inside the England half. There was no better example of Howlett's exhilarating speed than in the way he left the covering Jason Robinson unable to even lay a finger on him. Howlett (who ended his playing career in 2007 as the All Blacks' top Test try-scorer with 49) ran around behind the posts to dot down. Blair converted.

Blair then had the chance to make the lead for his side eight points with a long-range penalty attempt – only the second awarded to the visitors by Kaplan in the half – but the ball swung wide.

In the 39th minute, Wilkinson nailed a penalty from 42 metres out but missed another from inside his half in injury time.

Kaplan had a developing reputation for playing exceedingly long periods of injury time, but the All Blacks showed no inclination to put the ball out. They suffered for that. In the 45th minute, after Thompson barged into the All Blacks' 22, the ball went right to James Simpson-Daniel who, with a clever shimmy, turned a 4-3 overlap into a 3-1 player advantage. He passed to Wilkinson and on to Moody who slid over right in the corner, under the legs of the arriving Howlett and Randell. Rather than being able to indulge in a planned try celebration, he lay winded on the ground.

The All Blacks had surrendered their lead.

Four minutes into the second half, Moody took a pass in the tramlines from Mike Tindall and made good metres. Ben Cohen, racing up in support, overran the inside pass. From the ruck, Simpson-Daniel went on a curving run into space. A pass should have gone to Robinson, but Simpson-Daniel cut inside and lost his footing. Hill looked to have knocked the ball on, wrestling for it at the next ruck but as play progressed towards the All Blacks' 22, Kaplan signalled advantage to England.

Wilkinson then produced a piece of magic that proved his standing as the best player in the world. In a split-second, standing on the 22, he looked to cross kick to his left but saw an array of black jerseys. He then feigned as if to snap a drop goal, saw that fullback Blair was well out of position and chipped over the line of All Black defenders. The bounce was perfect, and, in the tackle of debutant All Black halfback Danny Lee, he scored just outside the right-hand upright. Wonderful play. With the simplest of conversions, England were ahead by ten.

After a dominant All Black maul, replacement centre Ben Johnston flew up on Mehrtens who was standing on halfway. The All Black first-five lost the ball in the tackle. Wilkinson scooped it up and flicked a back pass that bounced into the hands of Cohen. The big man could see a clear channel to the All Black line between three defenders and scooted away to score.

Ben Cohen (ENG 2000–06): 'As I neared the line, I was thinking "I don't have to even get airborne, I have to get the ball over the line. Any second now, there'll be a tackle coming across." So, I flew across the line with a big swallow dive. I know, I know, technically it wasn't the safest way to ground the ball, but all the emotions came flooding through at once and I lost it for a bit. It was incredible to score against the All Blacks like that.'

The emotion was shared by the Twickenham crowd who were in raptures with their side (thanks to the conversion by Wilkinson) now ahead of the All Blacks by 17 points with 20 minutes to play.

Five years earlier, another Woodward-coached England team had held such a lead over the men in black, but the game ended in a draw. An All Black resurgence was sure to come. How would England deal with it?

Jonah Lomu (NZ 1994–2002): '[That] day is one of the gutsiest I've ever been involved in. We struggled in the lineouts and the scrums; we made heaps of mistakes and we turned over way too much ball … We should have been down for the count. But in that final quarter the boys dug deep.'

Mehrtens, then New Zealand's record points-scorer, made a 40-metre penalty look easy and with about 16 minutes to play – plus however much Kaplan was going to add on – the gap was down to 14 points; two converted tries.

The All Blacks started to dominate the forward exchanges, with England appearing to become a bit too cautious with ball in hand and non-committal at the breakdown. When the All Blacks needed tries, who was the man that so often provided them in recent times? Silly question, easy answer. Lomu.

That's who Mehrtens went to after a double-round with his centre Mark Robinson. Lomu hit the pass at pace and Tindall joined the long list of Englishmen steamrolled by Jonah. In the next stride Cohen (no small man himself) was fended away, leaving Johnston and Robinson to merely jump on the giant's back as he crashed to the try-line. Johnson walked back to join his team-mates looking very much like a man who had resigned himself to that fact that Lomu just could not be kept out of the game.

Lewis Moody (1998–2011): 'Lomu was past his prime but he was still a nightmare to deal with.'

Mehrtens' arcing conversion left the All Blacks ten points adrift.

At the 65-minute mark, Wilkinson had the chance to add another three points and stretch the lead but his attempt was one of the least accurate penalty kicks he had struck for some time.

After another charge by Lomu, which began inside his own half and left England players colliding with each other or being swatted away, Mehrtens broke clear and a Randell charge ended very close to the line. England were hugely fortunate to win the scrum put-in after some extremely cynical play by Dallaglio, who firstly came through from an offside position and then quite obviously played the ball on the ground.

John Mitchell (NZ coach 2001–03): 'I thought referee Jonathan Kaplan made some dodgy calls on the day, and he subsequently admitted to me that I may have been right.'

Minutes later, after a surging run by number eight Sam Broomhall, All Black replacement halfback Danny Lee threw a dummy to his right and scooted across for a try. With Mehrtens making the conversion, England were now only three points ahead with roughly ten minutes left to play. Fans at the ground or watching the match on TV were on the edge of their seats as the All Blacks threw everything at England to make the winning score.

With 90 seconds of normal time remaining, from deep inside their half the All Blacks ran the ball. Lomu was the decoy in midfield. This created space for the pace of Howlett, who had come across to the other side of the field. He passed to Blair 40 metres out from the

England line. The fullback had one man to beat to score the match-winning try, the covering Cohen.

Austin Healey (ENG 1997–2003): 'They were going into a move I'd seen them do earlier in the game, so I came out of the defensive line with the intention of hitting Doug Howlett. But … they were around me and it was only a fantastic cover tackle from Ben Cohen that saved us in the corner. Thanks Benny!'

Ben Cohen: 'I said at the time that if I'd missed it I would have gone and packed my bags, got into my car and never played for England again.'

Having shown Blair the sideline, Cohen wrapped up the diminutive fullback and bear-hugged him into touch, a couple of metres short of the corner flag. The England players and crowd breathed a sigh of relief, but there was still time to play.

From the ensuing shaky short England lineout, Kaplan penalised the All Blacks for obstructive play. All Black lock Williams expressed his disagreement with the decision and Kaplan advanced the England penalty a further ten metres in response.

Play continued. The All Blacks stole England's ball from a lineout maul and swept upfield with ease. Inside the England 22, Umaga put a little kick through which the defending Jason Robinson just managed to carry into touch.

So, an All Black lineout on the England line. The last chance for the somewhat green men in black to win the game. The throw from Andrew Hore was snatched out of the air by England lock Ben Kay, his lifters having jettisoned him high above Williams. The ball was cleared safely downfield.

A minute later, Kaplan called time and England had their fifth win over the All Blacks. The match was quite epic in terms of its twists, turns and moments of individual brilliance.

Wilkinson had become the second player (after All Black Don Clarke in 1963) to score four different ways in an England–New Zealand international. His 21-point haul remains the most individual points scored by an Englishman against the All Blacks.

Josh Lewsey (ENG 1998–2008): 'That was the day we actually said, "We are the top team in the world." It was a massive transformation from which England then built for the next few years.'

All Blacks coach Mitchell may have been able to dismiss any damage to his World Cup plans by the resurgence of his young team. But, as Lewsey said, England took enormous confidence from this win. In the following weeks, England beat Australia 32-31, coming back from 19-31 with 20 minutes to play, and then a 14-man South Africa 53-3. They were unstoppable.

Jonah Lomu appeared in the final two Tests of the All Blacks' tour, a draw against France and big win over Wales. After the latter, the last of his 63 Tests, he spent time in hospital as his failing kidneys began to wreak havoc on his body. It makes his two tries on that November day even more remarkable. They took his Twickenham Test tally to five, the most by a non-Englishman, and his overall tally against England to eight.

Referee: J.I. Kaplan (South Africa)

Touch Judges: S.M. Young (Australia), N. Williams (Wales)

Attendance: 73,000

Half-time: ENG 17, NZ 14

Scorers: ENG Moody (t), Cohen (t), Wilkinson (t, 2c, 3p, dg)
NZ Lomu (2t), Howlett (t), Lee (t), Mehrtens (2c), Blair (2c)

ENGLAND: T.J. Woodman (Gloucester), S. Thompson (Northampton), P.J. Vickery (Gloucester), M.O. Johnson (*Capt.* Leicester), D.J. Grewcock (Bath), L.W. Moody (Leicester), R.A. Hill (Saracens), L.B.N. Dallaglio (Wasps), M.J.S. Dawson (Northampton), J.P. Wilkinson (Newcastle), B.C. Cohen (Northampton), M.J. Tindall (Bath), W.J.H. Greenwood (Harlequins), J. Simpson-Daniel+ (Gloucester), J.T. Robinson (Sale)

Reserves: J.B. Johnston (Saracens, 40'), N.A. Back (Leicester, temp 49-62', 70'), B.J. Kay (Leicester, 60'), A.S. Healey (Leicester, 77'), J. Leonard (Harlequins), M.P. Regan (Bath), T.R.G. Stimpson (Leicester)

Coach: C. Woodward

NEW ZEALAND: J.M. McDonnell (Otago), A.K. Hore+ (Taranaki), K.J. Meeuws (Auckland), K.J. Robinson+ (Waikato), A.J. Williams+ (Auckland), T.C. Randell (*Capt*, Otago), M.R. Holah (Waikato), S.R. Broomhall (Canterbury), S.J. Devine+ (Auckland), C.J. Spencer (Auckland), J.T. Lomu (Wellington), K.R. Lowen+ (Waikato), T.J.F. Umaga (Wellington), D.C. Howlett (Auckland), B.A. Blair (Canterbury)

Reserves: D.D. Lee+ (Otago, 24'), M.P. Robinson (Canterbury, temp 33'-40', 46'), A.P. Mehrtens (Canterbury, 40'), B.M. Mika+ (Auckland, 60'), C.J. Hayman (Otago), K.F. Mealamu (Auckland), R. So'oialo (Wellington)

Coach: J. Mitchell

Westpac Stadium, Wellington, 14 June 2003
ENGLAND 15 – ALL BLACKS 13

'That result still irks me.' – Richie McCaw

ON the Monday night before this Test, England beat a strong New Zealand Maori side 23-9. The New Plymouth weather was atrocious, and the Maori had been unbeaten for ten years but that didn't faze England. Their forwards completely dominated the match, quite happy to keep the ball in mauls and drive all night. It was a textbook display of how to make an opposing team forget what the ball looks like, and the likelihood of England playing to a completely different game plan in the Test match was minimal.

Of the 15 All Blacks who had started the Test the previous November, only five remained, just one of which was a member of the forward pack, lock Ali Williams. Once again, All Black coach John Mitchell handed the trump cards to England when he opted for them to be the first home opponents for the All Blacks in the World Cup year, instead of the also visiting Wales or France. Rather than have his side build in confidence before facing the strong northern foe, still in the glow of the previous December's win, a Five Nations crown and with virtually the same starting XV, Mitchell wanted the traditionally slow-starting home side to face some real adversity. That they did!

Australian Peter Marshall was to have refereed the match but due to injury had to hand the whistle over to his pedantic countryman, Stuart Dickinson, a referee who in Super Rugby had dished out more yellow cards than any other officiator.

The day before the match, Jonny Wilkinson went through his practice routine at Westpac stadium. Before he began kicking, he observed something freakish about the ground. When he threw a tuft of grass in the air it immediately blew behind him, then appeared in front of him again. The Wellington stadium, colloquially known as 'The Cake Tin' is a place where even the wind doesn't know where to go once it blows inside the stadium. Come the following evening, the wind wasn't as strong but there was some light rain.

England had a fortuitous penalty in the opening minute of the game following the charge-down of a Carlos Spencer clearance. With Mike Tindall holding the ball so the wind didn't blow it over, Wilkinson kicked the first points of the night.

Spencer's first chance of the evening came after an England indiscretion at a lineout. In his seemingly carefree style, Spencer chipped the kick outside the right-hand upright.

By the tenth minute of the game, referee Dickinson had awarded seven penalties, four of which were to England. But, by half-time the count would be 12-5 to the All Blacks.

At the 20-minute mark the All Blacks had a three-on-two overlap but the final pass from 20-year-old debutant Joe Rokocoko was high and behind his fellow winger Caleb Ralph. Defenders Jason Robinson and Josh Lewsey bundled Ralph into touch a couple of metres short of the corner flag.

Five minutes later, Wilkinson kicked a penalty from the right-hand touchline, just out from the All Blacks' 22. It never looked like missing.

The All Blacks then had a sustained period inside the England 22, but despite players breaking into space, they couldn't breach the defence. At the rucks, however, Dickinson issued his first England team warning for killing the ball.

From an All Black lineout five metres from the England line, after the home side had won the ball, Lawrence Dallaglio came away with the ball which was then cleared downfield by Kyran Bracken. England's defence was proving impregnable.

With five minutes to go in the half, Spencer kicked his second penalty after Neil Back was up too quickly in the defensive line. Three minutes later Spencer had the chance to put the All Blacks in the lead at the break but sent his penalty attempt so wide it came down halfway between the goalposts and the corner flag.

Carlos Spencer (NZ 1997–2004): 'It was only through my poor goal-kicking that we lost the match … The wind was challenging but he [Wilkinson] handled it perfectly while I didn't hit the ball well at all.'

Spencer's reliance on the short, inside pass was also questionable given the express pace out wide of Rokocoko and Howlett. It also meant that for a number of phases the England forwards didn't have to move far from ruck to ruck and just smothered the attacking All Blacks.

Somewhat bemused by Dickinson's rulings, Johnson and he had a long discussion in the tunnel at the conclusion of the half but within the first 60 seconds of the second half, Rowntree came around the side of a ruck to tackle Marshall. In giving the penalty to the All Blacks, Dickinson called out Johnson, who towered over the referee, as imposing and humourless as a Stonehenge pillar.

Dickinson: 'The ball wasn't out, he wasn't at the last feet. The next bloke will go. Okay, the next bloke will go.'

Johnson: 'It's a judgement call, mate.'

Dickinson: 'It's not a judgement call. He's offside. The next bloke will go.'

Two minutes later, the All Blacks were penalised and warned for not rolling away, the irony of which brought a wry smile to the face of captain, Reuben Thorne. Wilkinson had no trouble slotting the kick from near halfway.

In the 45th minute, Back was given a yellow card for playing the ball on the ground and with a one-man advantage the All Blacks suddenly had intent in sending the ball wide. Spencer made a 50-metre break and found Howlett in support but the England defence slowed them down. The ball did find its way to Marshall 15 metres out with a clear run to the line, but he pulled his hamstring, hobbled to a halt and the chance was lost.

However, from the resulting ruck, Dickinson showed Dallaglio a yellow card for 'coming in through the side and killing the ball'.

England were down to 13 men and the All Blacks had a choice; scrum or a kickable penalty to level the scores.

Anton Oliver (NZ 1997–2007): 'We all huddled around Reuben and he told us to scrum them, push them back over the line. I was dying to say, "No, that's silly, let's manipulate the scrum defence as they don't have a full back row." We were eating up valuable time trying to out-scrum them ... But, I didn't want to usurp Reuben's position so I said nothing ... I should have spoken up.'

England, on the other hand, made their call of 'Hit the beach'. Devised by defence coach Phil Larder in the spirit of the Normandy landings, its utterance by Johnson meant that all the England players, and especially the outnumbered forwards, were going to give everything they had in defence of their line. The next eight minutes – with England manipulating the scrum, the referee and the clock – really showed which team was ready for the steely demands of tight RWC knockout rugby.

Richard Hill (ENG 1997–2008): 'Typical of those two guys [Back and Dallaglio] – when things get really tough, they disappear leaving the grunt and grind to me ... We usually practised seven-man scrums; you never know when you are going to lose a man during a game. So, it wasn't down to luck. It was something we prepared for. Mind you, I'm not sure we practised six-man scrums very often.'

The first scrum collapsed and then there were three resets and an injury time-out for Phil Vickery who had some blood on his face.

A penalty eventually came for the All Blacks after those scrums. Rodney So'oialo took a quick tap and looked to have scored but TMO Marshall ruled a triple movement. The England defence had held again.

Not long after, Wilkinson had three more points after the seven-man England scrum forced the All Black front row into a collapse.

After a great charge with ball in hand by Vickery, Wilkinson snapped a right-foot drop goal (his lucky 13th in Tests) from close to the posts (though he did have two men outside him just 15 metres from the line).

With 20 minutes to play, Spencer saw that Lewsey hadn't made his way back after being caught in a ruck, and lobbed a high kick into the England 22. The bounce of the ball went Howlett's way – replays showed he was about a metre ahead of the kicker – and despite desperate defence from Dallaglio, and his usual post-try niggle, a converted try was scored. The advantage to England was down to two points.

The All Blacks should have gone in front, but Spencer continued to show the gulf in goal-kicking class between himself and Wilkinson when his kickable penalty chance went well wide of the posts again.

For the final 15 minutes, apart from another great run by Vickery, all the attacking was from the All Blacks, who grew ever more agitated with their inability to shake free of the England defence.

In a sign of increasing frustration, Williams was penalised by Dickinson for back-chat. Then the All Black lock really lost his cool.

Nearly everybody in the ground saw his knees pumping up and down like a pro-cyclist at the back of a ruck. Television replays showed him rucking the back and head of Lewsey, who was lying on the ball. Tough judge Alan Lewis put out his flag and all money was on Williams being called out for his use of the boot. Instead, as Lewsey received medical attention for cuts to his face (later requiring stitches), Rowntree was first spoken to for rucking a player's leg well away from the ball.

Johnson asked Dickinson, 'You didn't see him [Williams] standing on his head?'

Dickinson replied, 'No, no, that's all we've seen there. If there's anything else, it will be looked after by somebody else with the video.'

Johnson muttered, 'Too late, mate.'

The referee who had been so officious and keen to pull cards from his pocket earlier in the game somehow – along with his touch-judge – missed a dangerous and ugly incident they were both very close to.

Josh Lewsey (ENG 1998–2008): 'There are certain things that are taboo in the game. I got a couple [of stamps] in the face and on the back of the head and then I realised it was coming again, so I turned my head to avoid getting one in the eye.'

For England, the final seconds waiting for the final whistle seemed to take an eternity. When the hooter was heard, Will Greenwood ran into touch with the ball. Then he had the horrible thought that perhaps it hadn't been the right thing to do, that Dickinson would give the All Blacks a lineout and with that a final chance to snatch back the game. Dickinson didn't.

Twenty years after playing in England's 1983 victory at Twickenham, Woodward had coached an England side to their country's second win in New Zealand. He described it as an 'epic game' and credited Johnny Wilkinson for doing 'the business'.

Jonny Wilkinson (ENG 1997–2011): 'The celebrations are a little muted. There's no conscious decision to play it cool. It's just that despite everything we have just been through, most of the team are actually quite disappointed with our performance. The result's not enough now. We've just won in New Zealand, but we feel we could've done better.'

On the All Black bench that night, waiting for his first Test start, was Dan Carter. He had a front-row seat to observe the play of Wilkinson, whom he later said was tactically superb and his kicking from the hand or tee kept the All Blacks at bay.

Dan Carter (NZ 2003–15): 'That's when I realised the All Blacks team just can't lose. Especially not at home. Especially not to England … I looked around the changing room and everyone's head was between their legs. No one spoke and I kept even quieter than usual. I was paralysed by the silence and resolved to sit there until someone else made a move. It took 20 aching minutes.'

Lawrence Dallaglio (ENG 1995–2007): 'I think people have been carried away by the fact we won. We just did what we had to do. We were very good defensively and Jonny kicked a few terrific penalty goals to clinch our victory. No amount of bravery could hide the fact that we hadn't played any rugby … in terms of getting possession and holding on to it, we were poor.'

There had been 18 stoppages for injury breaks, many coming from the England players' call of 'kit-kat' – as in 'take a break' – for one of the tight five to go down and receive attention from the team physio. The All Blacks didn't gain any momentum. Rather, they became more panicky as the match wore on and couldn't get their noses in front.

For the fourth decade in a row, England had beaten the All Blacks in a year ending in the number three, and for the third time their winning total was 15 points.

Ali Williams' stomping on Lewsey was reviewed for 90 minutes by a disciplinary committee. At the conclusion, Australian Michael Goodwin announced that they had found Williams' rucking to be 'inadvertent and incidental', and that he had only made contact with Lewsey's head once. It was even suggested that Lewsey should have known better than to lie on the ball.

To think that the name Cyril Brownlie carries the timeless stigma of being the first man sent off in a rugby international, for something that nobody could agree on, and Williams completely escaped punishment for an incident seen by nearly all who viewed the game.

The morning after the match, one of the New Zealand Sunday newspapers carried an opinion piece by Michael Laws. A former politician turned talk-back host, he liked to court controversy and wind people up. In his piece he described the England forwards as:

> ...giant gargoyles, raw-boned, cauliflower-eared monoliths that intimidated and unsettled. When they ran onto the field it was like watching a tribe of white orcs on steroids. Forget their hardness, has there ever been an uglier forward pack?

Copies of the paper were snapped up by members of the England squad. To some it confirmed their belief that New Zealand journalists were overly negative in their views of the team. For others, it confirmed the maxim, 'Today's news, tomorrow's fish and chip wrapper.'

Referee: S.J. Dickinson (Australia)

Touch Judges: A. Lewis (Ireland), M. Goddard (Australia)

Television Match Official: P.L. Marshall (Australia)

Attendance: 37,500

Half-time: ENG 6, NZ 6

Scorers: ENG Wilkinson (4p, dg)
        NZ Howlett (t), Spencer (2p, c)

NEW ZEALAND: D.N. Hewett (Canterbury), A.D. Oliver (Otago), G.M. Somerville (Canterbury), C.R. Jack (Canterbury), A.J. Williams (Auckland), R.D. Thorne (*Capt.* Canterbury), R.H. McCaw (Canterbury), R. So'oialo (Wellington), J.W. Marshall (Canterbury), C.J. Spencer (Auckland), C.S. Ralph (Canterbury), T.J.F. Umaga (Wellington), M.A. Nonu+ (Wellington), J.T. Rokocoko+ (Auckland). D.C. Howlett (Auckland).

Reserves: S.J. Devine (Auckland, 47'), K.F. Mealamu (Auckland, 56'), J.M. Muliaina+ (Auckland, 72'), J. Collins (Wellington, 73'), D.W. Carter (Canterbury), C.H. Hoeft (Otago), B.C. Thorn (Canterbury)

Coach: J. Mitchell

ENGLAND: G.C. Rowntree (Leicester), S. Thompson (Northampton), J. Leonard (Harlequins), M.O. Johnson (*Capt.* Leicester), B.J. Kay (Leicester), R.A. Hill (Saracens), N.A. Back (Leicester, Y 46'-56'), L.B.N. Dallaglio (Wasps, Y 48'-58'), K.P.P. Bracken (Saracens), J.P. Wilkinson (Newcastle), B.C. Cohen (Northampton), M.J. Tindall (Bath), W.J.H. Greenwood (Harlequins), J.T. Robinson (Sale), O.J. Lewsey (Wasps)

Reserves: P.J. Vickery (Gloucester, 40'), J.P.R. Worsley (Wasps, 72'), D. Luger (Harlequins, 78'), S.W. Borthwick (Bath), A.C.T. Gomarsall (Gloucester), P.J. Grayson (Northampton), D. West (Leicester)

Coach: C. Woodward

Carisbrook, Dunedin, 12 June 2004
ALL BLACKS 36 – ENGLAND 3

'Tough day at the office? Yes, that was tough. It was a thumping.' – Clive Woodward

THERE'S a line of thinking in rugby that the measure of a truly champion side is not just winning the RWC's William Webb Ellis trophy, but continuing to win the year after the tournament. Carrying the tag of world champions, the England side arrived in New Zealand without talismanic leader Martin Johnson, who had retired, and Jonny Wilkinson, who was out injured. But, they had to be regarded as at full strength and were on a winning run of 12 games against the Tri-Nations teams (New Zealand, Australia and South Africa). Clive Woodward told the media that beating the All Blacks remained the ultimate challenge and, having only lost 19 of the 80 matches he had coached England, 'we are trying to build a tradition of success, which is what the All Blacks are built on'.

Lawrence Dallaglio (ENG 1995–2007): 'With the benefit of hindsight, the 2004 summer tour to New Zealand and Australia was a seriously bad idea. That summer we all needed a rest, players and coaches ... Mentally and physically, we didn't have it.'

Mike Catt (ENG 1994–2007): 'We were in pieces while the All Blacks and Wallabies, just starting their new season and out to give the world champions a bloody nose, were as fresh as daisies.'

While on tour, Dallaglio was quietly questioning how motivated Woodward and several assistant coaches were after the success of 2003 and how committed they were to England's cause as they looked ahead to the 2005 Lions tour to New Zealand. There were player mutterings about the excessive length of training sessions and the number of meetings they had to attend.

By contrast, everything about the All Blacks appeared fresh and revitalised. John Mitchell's coaching 'journey', which arrived at the dead end of a RWC semi-final loss to Australia, had been ended by the NZRU. Incidentally, he hadn't beaten the All Blacks when coaching with England or beaten England when coaching the All Blacks.

Mitchell was replaced by a panel when former schoolteacher and coach of Auckland, Wales, and the 2001 Lions, Graham Henry; former All Black player and coach Wayne Smith who had been in charge at Northampton; and former policeman Steve Hansen, who had succeeded Henry as coach of the Red Dragons took over. Joining that trio as a selector was former player and 1987 World Cup-winning coach, Brian Lochore.

Dreadlocked centre Tana Umaga was announced as their captain, the first player of Pacific Island descent accorded that honour.

In the front row for England was 18st farmer Julian White, a scrummager regarded by his peers as one of the toughest to pull on rugby boots. Like Martin Johnson, he had spent time refining his skills in New Zealand, firstly for the Hawke's Bay province – turning out for the rural Dannevirke RFC – and came on as a replacement in one game for the Canterbury Crusaders in Super Rugby. His stay in New Zealand ended when he was in a horrific two-car accident in which both cars caught fire and the driver of the other car died. Initially trapped in the entangled cars, White crawled from the wreckage with a broken ankle and shattered leg.

By the time of the 7.35pm kick-off, it was a cold and clear Dunedin night. Snow had fallen on the hills surrounding the city the previous day.

From the opening whistle the All Blacks played with pace and energy right across the park. They were obviously unburdened by the RWC failings and invigorated by the new coaching panel's directives on how they wanted the game played.

On show for the first 40 minutes was the intensity of the forward pack, the attacking skills of the higher numbers behind them and all-round pressure on the visitors.

Charlie Hodgson had put England on the board with a penalty but was not having his greatest day defensively, weakly missing both All Blacks' wings as they ran in tries. Carlos Spencer scored after the charge-down of a Matt Dawson kick and Dan Carter was chipping over penalty kicks to keep increasing the All Blacks' lead.

In his 22nd Test match, Richie McCaw occasionally looked a little bit off the pace, for reasons that became apparent later.

Richie McCaw (NZ 2001–15): 'I took a hit in the first half. It must've been a decent one. Most of the "lights" went out and when they came back on – it would only have been seconds later – I looked up at the scoreboard and thought, jeez, we've scored a couple of tries. I turned to Xavier Rush and asked him how I was playing. He looked at me like I was stupid. "Yeah, you're going alright."' (Diagnosed with concussion after the game, McCaw was to miss the following Test.)

Come the second half, the All Blacks only added six more points via the boot of Carter but England couldn't muster any additional score.

After the 1998 Dunedin debacle, it was another nightmarish visit to Carisbrook for Woodward and England. In two games there they had now conceded 100 points.

Referee: J.I. Kaplan (South Africa)

Touch Judges: A.J. Cole (Australia), S.J. Dickinson (Australia)

Television Match Official: M. Goddard (Australia)

Attendance: 35,000

Half-time: NZ 30, ENG 3

Scorers: NZ Spencer (t), Rokocoko (t), Howlett (t), Carter (3c, 5p)
ENG Hodgson (p)

NEW ZEALAND: K.J. Meeuws (Auckland), K.F. Mealamu (Auckland), C.J. Hayman (Otago), C.R. Jack (Canterbury), K.J. Robinson (Waikato), J.B. Gibbes+ (Waikato), R.H. McCaw (Canterbury), X.J. Rush (Auckland), J.W. Marshall (Canterbury), C.J. Spencer (Auckland), J.T. Rokocoko (Auckland), D.W. Carter (Auckland), T.J.F. Umaga (*Capt*. Wellington), D.C. Howlett (Auckland), J.M. Muliaina (Auckland)

Reserves: T.D. Woodcock (North Harbour, temp 21'-23', 70'), A.K. Hore (Taranaki, temp 27'-36'), M.R. Holah (Waikato, 60'), N.J. Evans+ (North Harbour, 64'), S. Tuitupou+ (Auckland, 70'), J. Collins (Wellington), B.T. Kelleher (Otago)

Coach: G. Henry

ENGLAND: J. White (Leicester), S. Thompson (Northampton), T.J. Woodman (Gloucester), S.D. Shaw (Wasps), D.J. Grewcock (Bath), C.M. Jones (Sale), R.A. Hill (Saracens), L.B.N. Dallaglio (*Capt.* Wasps), M.J.S. Dawson (Northampton), C. Hodgson (Sale), B.C. Cohen (Northampton), M.J. Catt (Bath), M.J. Tindall (Bath), J. Simpson-Daniel (Gloucester), O.J. Lewsey (Wasps)

Reserves: S. Abbott (Wasps, temp 25'-36', 67'), S.W. Borthwick (Bath, 40'), J.P.R. Worsley (Wasps, 40'), A.C.T Gomarsall (Gloucester, 66'), M.P. Regan (Leeds, 68'), M. Stevens+ (68'), O.J Barkley (Bath)

Coach: C. Woodward

MATCH 27

Eden Park, Auckland, 19 June 2004
ALL BLACKS 36 – ENGLAND 12

'I think I have seen one of the England
players stamping on Keith Robinson's head.'
– Stuart Dickinson, touch judge

I N the week between the two Test matches there had been talk in the media about things 'getting ugly' at some point, such was the noticeable frustration of the England forward pack in being unable to contain their All Black opposites. They were determined to be more confrontational and employ rucking to try and unsettle the home side. The All Blacks wanted to rub salt into raw wounds.

Abrasive All Black lock Keith Robinson was a no-frills bloke who had a touch of old-school provocateur about him. In this two-Test series, he deliberately got up the nose of the England players, particularly captain Lawrence Dallaglio, who himself thrived on a bit of physicality. The one Robinson tactic that really lit the fuse on England tempers was his walking through their side of a lineout being formed for an All Black throw. At one point an enraged Dallaglio grabbed him by the throat to hurry his passage to the correct side of the lineout.

The match began with both forward packs making it apparent they were not going to take a backward step. In the midst of it all was England lock Simon Shaw, at the time the biggest man to have played for his country.

Shaw had only started playing rugby aged 16 and two years later, thanks to the urging of a rugby coach who hailed from New Zealand

and whose brother played for Otago, he had a stint in 1992 with Dunedin's Pirates club. He was only 18, but he was a big boy.

Simon Shaw (ENG 1996–2011): 'It had a big influence on my career. I couldn't have chosen a tougher environment. At that time there were a lot of All Blacks playing club rugby and I learned from the very best.'

One of those Shaw felt the sprigs of was hard man, Jamie Joseph, who would stomp on Kyran Bracken's ankle a year later at Twickenham.

Shaw holds the record for the longest England career in terms of time period. Of his 71 Tests across 15 years, a mere three were against New Zealand. In the tenth minute of the match, at a midfield ruck just on the All Black side of halfway, Shaw put a knee in Robinson's back as the All Black lock lay pinned in a ruck.

All Blacks first-five Carlos Spencer, standing to one side, objected to Shaw's act by pushing Shaw away. He was then barrelled from behind by Dallaglio who drove Spencer on top of the slowly disintegrating ruck. Then it was all on, with players from both sides mouthing off while grabbing necks and jerseys, pushing and shoving.

Ben Cohen came all the way off his wing to grab All Black number eight, Xavier Rush. All the while, referee Nigel Williams tried to restore order by blowing his whistle. As the players reluctantly returned to their respective sides, the last two off the ground were Dallaglio and Spencer.

Shaw's knee to Keith Robinson was brought to the attention of Williams by touch judge Stu Dickinson, he who had been in charge of the Wellington match a year ago. That night he initially couldn't wait to put his hand in his pocket to show yellow cards but then apparently didn't see the rucking of Ali Williams on Josh Lewsey that was happening a few metres in front of him.

While Williams consulted his touch judges and the TMO – with one voice heard to recommend a red card – the incident was shown on the big screen in the ground. Boos and chants of 'Off, off!' grew louder from the crowd. Williams called out Shaw.

'Touch judge report. Deliberate knee. Red card,' said the referee.

As they had been at Dunedin in 1998, England were reduced to 14 men.

Simon Shaw: 'I went to ruck for the ball and realised it was far too high. It was going to look ridiculous if I tried to ruck and when I put my foot back down, I glanced Robinson's head with my knee. There had been no intent to knee him in the head.'

Keith Robinson (NZ 2002–07): 'I got up and there was a scrap going on around me. I didn't know what had happened ... I awoke the next morning and I had a very sore shoulder, so he obviously got me ... I saw the video [later] and regardless of whether he did any damage, if you are going to knee someone in the open like that, you've got to be prepared to be sent off. He got caught and paid the price.'

As abrasive as he could be on the field, Shaw had never before received a red card for club or country.

Simon Shaw: 'You cannot stand there and argue or protest, you just have to take the lonely walk off to the side of the pitch. I was completely alone, and I sat there isolated and in a world of gloom for the rest of the game.'

At the post-match media conference, at which a grumpy Dallaglio stormed out, a disappointed Clive Woodward was very vocal.

Clive Woodward (ENG coach 1997–2004): 'The guy [Robinson] was killing the ball. [Julian] White stood on him but Shaw couldn't get his leg high enough to stand on him, so he put his knee in on him just to make sure he knew he was there. It was a huge call from the touch judge from so far away. I think one of the things that swayed the officials was the reaction of the crowd when it all kicked off. I'm not sure it's very clever to show replays of these incidents on the big screen. It's not something we do at Twickenham. There was nothing in the whole game. It was just a tough Test match. That's what you expect. I asked Shaw what he thought. He said it was absolute bullshit. He's not a dirty player. We thought we could win tonight. I still think we are the better team.'

With England having failed to score a try in the two matches, former England lock Paul Ackford, writing in *The Telegraph*, was having none of Woodward's comments.

> As justifications go, Woodward's lacks credibility. To claim that England are the better side is plain barmy. England have lost two Tests by a combined margin of 72-15. And to attempt

to exonerate Shaw by his failure to do real damage is also indefensible.

At the post-match judicial proceedings Shaw was cleared of the charge against him on a technicality. Referee Williams, who was never appointed to another England–All Blacks Test, should not have confirmed the jersey number of the offending player with the TMO, Matt Goddard.

Danny Grewcock, who had made a similar lonely walk off Carisbrook six years earlier and missed the 2003 Test in Wellington because he had been suspended for punching Dallaglio in the English club competition, came on as a second half substitute. After barely a minute of time on the field he stamped on Dan Carter, who had positioned himself on the wrong side of a ruck. This stomping did not draw the attention of the on-field or sideline officials, but Grewcock was cited – passing the departing Shaw as he went in for his hearing – and suspended for six weeks.

(That was not the last of Grewcock's citings in New Zealand. The following year he was on the plane home early from the Lions tour after a five-hour hearing found him guilty of biting the finger of All Black Keven Mealamu in the first Test.)

Much of the red card controversy took the spotlight off the brilliance of the All Black winger Joe Rokocoko who, with a trio of tries, took his tally in 14 Tests to a remarkable 21 touchdowns.

The match turned out to be Dallaglio's last against the All Blacks. Sadly, he broke his ankle in the first match of the 2005 Lions tour. In his seven Tests against New Zealand he had been a formidable, unrelenting force to be reckoned with. While there may have been relief from New Zealand fans not to see his name on the team sheet, his competitiveness was also genuinely missed.

Jerome Kaino (NZ 2004–17): 'Some of my idols played for England such as Lawrence Dallaglio. I loved the way he played, a big powerful guy who loved carrying the ball.'

It was the second-to-last England game coached by Woodward. The final match, a week later, was a 15-51 loss to Australia.

Mike Catt (ENG 1994–2007): 'In each game we were hammered out of sight and we returned home completely dispirited.'

It is really difficult to judge the success or otherwise of Woodward's teams against the All Blacks. He is the only coach to score two wins over them, plus a draw. But across the seven matches the average scoreline was 35-14 to the All Blacks, his side conceded 31 tries and scored just eight, and the only two red cards shown to Englishmen in the 109 years of competition between the two countries were in his first and last games in New Zealand.

But then, during that time he did win the RWC.

Referee: N. Williams (Wales)

Touch Judges: A.J. Cole (Australia), S.J. Dickinson (Australia)

Television Match Official: M. Goddard (Australia)

Attendance: 49,000

Half-time: NZ 10, ENG 6

Scorers: NZ Rokocoko (3t), Spencer (t), Carter (t, 4c, p)
ENG Hodgson (4p)

NEW ZEALAND: K.J. Meeuws (Auckland), K.F. Mealamu (Auckland), C.J. Hayman (Otago), C.R. Jack (Canterbury), K.J. Robinson (Waikato), J.B. Gibbes (Waikato), M.R. Holah (Waikato, Y 68'-78'), X.J. Rush (Auckland), J.W. Marshall (Canterbury), C.J. Spencer (Auckland), J.T. Rokocoko (Auckland), D.W. Carter (Canterbury), T.J.F. Umaga (*Capt.* Wellington), J.M. Muliaina (Auckland), N.J. Evans (North Harbour)

Reserves: C.A. Newby (North Harbour, temp 29'-37'), T.D. Woodcock (North Harbour, temp 37'-38', 57'), A.P. Mehrtens (Canterbury, 57'), J. Collins (Wellington, 70'), S. Tuitupou (Auckland, 71'), A.K. Hore (Taranaki, 77'), B.T. Kelleher (Otago)

Coach: G. Henry

ENGLAND: T.J. Woodman (Gloucester), M.P. Regan (Leeds), J. White (Leicester), S.D. Shaw (Wasps, R 10'-80'), S.W. Borthwick (Bath), J.P.R. Worsley (Wasps), R.A. Hill (Saracens), L.B.N. Dallaglio (*Capt.* Wasps), A. Gomarsall (Gloucester), C. Hodgson (Sale), B.C. Cohen (Northampton), S. Abbott (Wasps), M.J. Tindall (Bath), T.M.D. Voyce (Wasps), O.J. Lewsey (Wasps)

Reserves: F. Waters (Wasps, 26'), O.J Barkley (Bath, 32'), M. Lipman+ (Bath, 49'), A. Titterrell+ (Sale, 57'), M. Stevens (Bath, 57'), D.J. Grewcock (Bath, 57'), M.J.S. Dawson (Northampton, 57')

Coach: C. Woodward

Twickenham, London, 19 November 2005
ALL BLACKS 23 – ENGLAND 19

'I want 15 against 15, alright, for rugby.'
– Alan Lewis, referee

ONE hundred years after the first meeting between the two sides at Crystal Palace, a new south stand was being built at Twickenham. This meant the ground capacity was 20,000 short of the usual attendance and behind one of the goalposts was an evolving construction site.

There was another significant change, too. For the first time since 1997, the England side to take on the All Blacks was not coached by Clive Woodward. He had resigned in September due to irreconcilable differences of opinion with the RFU, essentially over how best to capitalise on England's 2003 RWC win.

Into his place stepped Andy Robinson, who had been an assistant to Graham Henry on the 2001 Lions tour of Australia and England's forwards' coach in 2003. Like Woodward, he was a former international, having played eight times as a back-row forward for England from 1988–95.

In the days before the Test, with his charges having beaten Australia 26-16 the previous Saturday, Robinson was confidently telling the media that his side would beat the All Blacks because they had the side to do so. They would not take a step back at the contact area, they would take the All Blacks on at the set-piece and use the ball when they had it. New coach, yes, but familiar tactics from the men in jerseys 1-to-8 were sure to prevail.

While the Six Nations teams have the opportunity to achieve a grand slam every winter, southern hemisphere teams are rarely offered such a chance, with their northern visits either only three Tests or including matches in France and Italy.

Graham Henry's 2005 All Blacks had four consecutive Saturdays of Tests, facing Wales, Ireland, England and Scotland. (No fortnight break between games for the southern visitors.)

Henry's solution to keep his squad of 35 players fresh was 'rotation', starting two completely different XVs in the first two Tests. It was audacious and had its critics, but in both matches the All Blacks scored over 40 points and conceded only one try.

Martin Corry's experienced England side was regarded as the biggest obstacle to achieving the 'Slam', with players who had been on the unsuccessful summer Lions tour to New Zealand keen to trip the All Blacks up.

Richie McCaw missed his second consecutive Test against England due to a head knock, while in the reserves for England was the New Zealand-born Mark van Gisbergen, the first of a number of ex-pat Kiwis to be included in England squads over the coming years. The All Blacks performed their new haka, Kapa o Pango, for the first time at Twickenham.

It was an icy afternoon with a milky sun just touching the upper reaches of the East Stand. On a pitch that quickly began to cut up, England made a great start to the match, scoring their first try against the All Blacks in two years after just three minutes. Dan Carter had forced the ball in the in-goal, after Matt Dawson charged down a clearing kick, then rolled it out of play for which he was penalised. As the two teams lined up for the next phase of play, referee Alan Lewis called out Martin Corry.

'I'm looking for controlled aggression, not uncontrolled aggression. I don't want you shouting at the opposition, just deal with your own game. Understand.'

A five-metre lineout and drive by the England forwards saw a try scored, captain Corry rising from the heap with the ball. The maul had got over the All Blacks' line with little resistance, leaving the visitors looking somewhat surprised by the speed at which their line had been crossed.

The Twickenham faithful were hysterical. Charlie Hogdson converted.

England 7, All Blacks 0.

In the following five minutes, referee Lewis had a chat with both captains about 'controlled aggression' and then Danny Grewcock was called out for a slap well away from the ball on his well-known opposite, Ali Williams.

The All Blacks were dropping passes with regularity until, encroaching on the England 22, Carter ran straight, drawing two tacklers, and passed back inside to Tana Umaga. The All Black captain ran around behind the posts for the try. Carter converted, sending the ball into the vast construction site behind the in-goal, where four cranes towered above the uprights.

Within a minute, England had the advantage on the scoreboard again when Hodgson kicked a penalty, the All Blacks having been penalised for diving ahead of the ball.

Carter then levelled the scores, kicking a 45-metre penalty after England were penalised for using hands in a ruck.

The next ten minutes' play was sloppy from both sides. Umaga was brought down inches short of scoring his second try. His popped pass to Chris Masoe, playing in place of McCaw, wasn't controlled. Kicks were charged down, passes didn't go to hand and there were regular stoppages for England players to be tended to by physios. Finally, the All Blacks won another penalty and Carter added another three points.

Play continued in a similar vein with referee Lewis very quick to blow the whistle at the ruck, which was of no benefit to either side.

Hodgson had a chance to even the scores with seven minutes to play in the half but his attempt from almost in front slid to the left of the posts.

After a counter-attack that saw the ball go through eight pairs of All Black hands in advancing from 22 to 22, they then demolished an England scrum but the home side came away with the ball. Paul Sanderson and Ben Cohen combined to take the ball back upfield but the power of the All Blacks' tackling and counter-rucking won the ball back.

Great Test match rugby. Fast and bruising.

Two minutes before half-time, having awarded a penalty to England at a ruck, Lewis called out Corry and Umaga again.

'I want 15 against 15, alright, for rugby. I want it because we've got a good contest here. A very, very good one. But there's bodies going in, there's scooping the ball back. I don't want to go to cards. I don't want to. Let's make a decision. Play the game.'

In the first couple of minutes of the second half, Carter replicated Hodgson's penalty miss but quickly made up for it. With ball in hand he sliced once again through the England midfield from where Rodney So'oialo was held up on the line. The ball was played back, and All Black hooker Keven Mealamu was driven over the line by a couple of his teammates. The conversion by Carter took the All Blacks lead out to ten points with 35 minutes remaining.

All Black prop Tony Woodcock was penalised and warned for a late tackle on Hodgson who had put up a high kick. Getting up off the ground, Hodgson walked to where his kick had been claimed in the All Black 22 and kicked an easy penalty.

Carter added another three for the All Blacks after Dawson was adjudged offside at a scrum. England were starting to feel a bit aggrieved at the way Lewis was adjudicating their play at ruck and tackle situations, but it was to be the All Blacks who would suffer the greatest penalties.

With England looking to maul from a lineout close to the All Blacks line, the move ended in a pile of bodies. A touch judge's call was that Woodcock had pulled the maul down. He was yellow-carded.

Now a man up at scrum time, the England eight was dominant but the All Blacks weren't sitting on their heels defending. Far from it. They suddenly seemed to have greater urgency and intensity.

Hodgson, after being hit on the chin in a tackle by prop Neemia Tialata, again got up off the ground to kick a penalty. This was one from 48 metres, following another All Black ruck infringement.

Just when the All Blacks were due to be back at full numbers again, Tialata was yellow-carded by Lewis for flopping on a player on the ground at a ruck.

'Very cynical and professional. He's got to go. Yellow card.'

Now faced with playing with only 13 men, albeit briefly, Umaga rallied his men while Hodgson kicked another penalty. The margin of the All Blacks' lead was now only four points with 14 minutes remaining. Was kicking for goal the right option for England given the two-man forward advantage and pre-match talk of taking the game to the All Blacks?

Woodcock returned to the field of play, welcomed by the 'chorus of boos'.

Thirteen minutes to play. The score still All Blacks 23, England 19.

Phil Vickery could have considered himself very lucky not to be called out for rucking the head of All Black lock Chris Jack.

A minute after coming back onto the field following the ten minutes of prop Tialata's sin-binning, loose-forward Masoe received a yellow card. Replays suggested it was a harsh call given Masoe had been over the ball but was pulled down into the ruck by Dawson. The England scrum-half had spent much of the afternoon appealing to Lewis like a lower-grade cricket wicketkeeper.

Jerry Collins (NZ 2001–07): 'The way he [Lewis] was waving yellow cards I thought a Boeing 747 was going to land in the middle of the field!'

England once again had a numerical advantage, but time was running out to capitalise on it. Two minutes remained. A try to the home side could seal the match.

It was now or never. From a powerful attacking scrum just inside the All Blacks' 22, the ball went right along the England backline to Ben Cohen. He was bundled into touch. Very tamely, the game was over.

To a man, England's forwards left the ground bloodied and bruised. At the back, Josh Lewsey had been sound under the high ball, but England's problem was the midfield. On defence, Carter had found it easy to find alleys through it and on attack Mike Tindall's play was rather laboured. England needed someone to straighten the line of attack or get over the advantage line and look to offload. Somewhat bizarrely, with the All Blacks having to dig deep while playing without a full complement, Andy Robinson only used one replacement player. Surely fresh legs would have added some spark?

Martin Corry (ENG 1997–2007): 'We got ourselves in a winning position, but we couldn't quite close it out. That final score just eluded us. I do feel we are moving forward but the great thing is everyone is absolutely devastated. We have lost a game and it should hurt like hell.'

Tana Umaga (NZ 1997–2005): 'We saw this as our hardest game, not just on this tour but probably of the whole season. We talked about it like that all week and that is exactly what we got.'

A week later, by beating Scotland 29-10, the All Blacks completed their first Grand Slam since 1978.

Referee Alan Lewis later donated his yellow card to the New Zealand Rugby Museum.

Referee: A. Lewis (Ireland)

Touch Judges: J. Jutge (France), C. Joubert (South Africa)

Television Match Official: M. Changleng (Scotland)

Attendance: 62,000

Half-time: NZ 13, ENG 10

Scorers: NZ Umaga (t), Mealamu (t), Carter (2c, 3p)
ENG Corry (t), Hodgson (4p, c)

ENGLAND: P.J. Vickery (Gloucester), S. Thompson (Northampton), A. Sheridan (Sale), S.W. Borthwick (Bath), D.J. Grewcock (Bath), P.H. Sanderson (Worcester), L.W. Moody (Leicester), M.J. Corry (*Capt.* Leicester), M.J.S. Dawson (Wasps), C. Hodgson (Sale), B.C. Cohen (Northampton), M.J. Tindall (Gloucester), J. Noon (Newcastle), M.J. Cueto (Sale), J.O. Lewsey (Wasps)

Reserves: M. Stevens (Bath, 74'), O.J Barkley (Bath), L. Deacon (Leicester), H.A. Ellis (Leicester), C.M. Jones (Sale), L. Mears (Bath), M. van Gisbergen (Wasps)

Coach: A. Robinson

NEW ZEALAND: T.D. Woodcock (North Harbour, Y 56'-66') K.F. Mealamu (Auckland), C.J. Hayman (Otago), C.R. Jack (Canterbury), A.J. Williams (Auckland), J. Collins (Wellington), M.C. Masoe (Taranaki, Y 77'-80'), R. So'oialo (Wellington), B.T. Kelleher (Waikato), D.W. Carter (Canterbury), S.W. Sivivatu (Waikato), A.J.D. Mauger (Canterbury), J.F. Umaga (*Capt.* Wellington), D.C. Howlett (Auckland), J.M. Muliaina (Auckland)

Reserves: J.J. Eaton (Taranaki, temp 64'-67'), N.S. Tialata (Wellington, Y 66'-77'), P.A.T. Weepu (Wellington, 73'), J.T. Rokocoko (Auckland, 74'), M.M. Tuiali'i (Canterbury, 76'), L.R. MacDonald (Canterbury, 77'), A.K. Hore (Taranaki)

Coach: G. Henry

MATCH 29

Twickenham, London, 5 November 2006
ALL BLACKS 41 – ENGLAND 20

'New Zealand are a killer team on the turnover.'
– Martin Corry, England captain

WHO else but the All Blacks would be invited to appear at Twickenham in a match marking the opening of the new £100m South Stand? Not all in England rugby were happy about the addition of the fixture to the autumn itinerary, though. Arguments for (the RFU) and against (the clubs who had to release the players) ended up in the High Court. A £1m compensation payment from the RFU to Premier Rugby, who represented the clubs, saw an appeal by the clubs dropped.

Though only increasing the ground capacity by 7,000, the total redevelopment (not completed until 2008) included a four-star hotel, offices for the 200-plus RFU staff, a health club with swimming pool and a theatre. The match attendance of 82,076 was a new record for the ground.

A Dan Carter penalty opened the scoring, but England had the first real opportunity for five points when, with four minutes gone, Jamie Noon crossed the line (ignoring the unmarked Grewcock outside him). The TMO ruled that he didn't get the ball down.

Jamie Noon (ENG 2001–2009): 'I was lying on the ball over their line, so I don't understand why the try wasn't given. It was a bizarre decision, but you just have to get on with it.'

After 21 minutes, All Black right-wing Rico Gear stepped on the gas, eluded the England defence and ran from 22 to 22. The only

All Black in support was prop Tony Woodcock who had run the 'fat man's track' upfield. Knowing he didn't have the pace to beat wing Paul Sackey, he ran back towards the posts and arriving team-mates. Quick passing sent the ball to second-five Aaron Mauger who scored in the left corner.

Eight minutes later Noon did score. An England backline move just outside the All Blacks' 22 nearly broke down. Then a pass of questionable trajectory from debutant inside-centre Anthony Allen went behind fullback Ian Balshaw, and to ground. Noon picked up the ball and had a clear run to the line.

A couple of minutes shy of half-time, as England mounted an attack inside the All Blacks' half, a floating pass from Allen was plucked out of the air by All Black wing Joe Rokocoko. The speedster was never going to be caught and he dived in under the England posts.

With the half-time whistle due to be blown, another England error was costly. Moody lost possession and the All Blacks sent the ball to Rokocoko on the left. He sped upfield and spun one would-be tackler away before being taken to ground just over halfway. From the ruck, the ball went right to a line of ten All Blacks. The ball was passed all the way to the touchline where Ma'a Nonu flicked it inside to lock Chris Jack. He then fed the ball to big prop Carl Hayman who was rumbling up in support, and he crossed for a try.

Martin Corry (ENG 1997–2007): 'On the whole, we weren't good enough. When we had the ball, we looked quite dangerous at times, but when New Zealand got in behind us we really struggled ... New Zealand are a killer team on the turnover.'

On top of that bad five minutes, Carter had been adding penalties and the half-time lead for the All Blacks had blown out to 28-5.

Andy Robinson (ENG coach 2004–06): 'We lost our shape a bit, the game was gone and it was about how we responded.'

England had to start the second half with intensity, look to eliminate simple errors and provide a better scrum platform for the backs to work from. Initially they did. Ben Cohen scored in the left corner after quick hands from Corry, George Chuter and Moody.

The All Blacks' first try of the second stanza was ridiculously easy. Following an England 22-drop out, Richie McCaw took a pass inside his own half, ran ten metres and passed to Dan Carter who fended off Allen and then glided half the length of the field unopposed to score his 15th Test try. Several England players returning to the goal line could only shake their heads.

England fans did have cause for celebration in the 57th minute when an attempted kick through the defensive line by Mauger went straight to the chest of England scrum-half Shaun Perry, who bobbled the ball then scooted 70 metres to score.

All Black flanker Chris Masoe had a second yellow card in as many visits to Twickenham, but even with a numerical advantage England couldn't add any further points.

This was England's sixth straight loss. The All Blacks' 41 points was a record home defeat for England and the first time they had conceded more than 30 points at the 'home of rugby'.

Lewis Moody (1998–2011): 'We tried to attack New Zealand, gave it a go and were beaten ... by the best attacking team in the world.'

The following week, Argentina had their first ever victory at Twickenham and Andy Robinson's time as England coach was all but over.

Richie McCaw (NZ 2001–15): 'Andy Robinson stopped me for a chat and was particularly complimentary. I thought that was a nice touch.'

Referee: J. Jutge (France)

Touch Judges: S.J. Dickinson (Australia), M. Goddard (Australia)

Television Match Official: C. Berdos (France)

Attendance: 82,076

Half-time: NZ 28, ENG 5

Scorers: NZ Mauger (t), Rokocoko (t), Hayman (t), Carter (t, 5p, 3c)
ENG Noon (t), Cohen (t), Perry (t), Hodgson (c, p)

ENGLAND: A. Sheridan (Sale), G. Chuter (Leicester), J. White (Leicester), D.J. Grewcock (Bath), B.J. Kay (Leicester), M.J. Corry (*Capt.* Leicester), L.W. Moody (Leicester), P.H. Sanderson (Worcester), S. Perry+ (Bristol), C. Hodgson (Sale), B.C. Cohen (Northampton), A. Allen+ (Gloucester), J. Noon (Newcastle), P. Sackey+ (Wasps), I. Balshaw (Gloucester)

Reserves: M. Lund (Sale, 60'), P. Richards (Gloucester, 66'), L. Mears (Bath, 75'), A. Goode (Saracens), C.M. Jones (Sale), S. Turner (Sale), M. van Gisbergen (Wasps)

Coach: A. Robinson

NEW ZEALAND: T.D. Woodcock (North Harbour), K.F. Mealamu (Auckland), C.J. Hayman (Otago), C.R. Jack (Canterbury), K.J. Robinson (Waikato), R.D. Thorne (Canterbury), R.H. McCaw (*Capt.* Canterbury), M.C. Masoe (Wellington, Y 64'-74'), B.T. Kelleher, D.W. Carter (Canterbury), J.T. Rokocoko (Auckland), A.J.D. Mauger (Canterbury), M.A Nonu (Wellington), R.L. Gear (Tasman), J.M. Muliaina (Waikato)

Reserves: A.M. Ellis (Canterbury, 67'), S.W. Sivivatu (Waikato, 70'), C. Dermody (Southland, 71'), R. So'oialo (Wellington, 71'), A.K. Hore (Taranaki, 75'), I.F. Afoa (Auckland, 75'), L.R. MacDonald (Canterbury)

Coach: G. Henry

MATCH 30

Eden Park, Auckland, 14 June 2008
ALL BLACKS 37 – ENGLAND 20

*'Test match rugby is a brutal place and if you make
simple mistakes then you will be punished.'*
– Rob Andrew, caretaker England coach

AFTER their sensational semi-final exit from the 2007 RWC at the hands of cup nemesis France – the All Blacks' worst tournament result – Graham Henry was controversially reappointed coach after a very heated national debate. The losing candidate, Robbie Deans, promptly headed across the Tasman to become coach of Australia. Ten players involved in the All Blacks' cup campaign left New Zealand to take up offers with overseas clubs.

England, despite losing a pool game to South Africa where they failed to score a point, had made the cup final. Again, the South Africans prevailed.

The 2008 England team arrived in New Zealand without a number of injured and unavailable players, including Jonny Wilkinson, Simon Shaw, Josh Lewsey, Lewis Moody, Dan Hipkiss, Phil Vickery, Harry Ellis and Paul Sackey.

They were also without new coach, Martin Johnson, who had taken over from Brian Ashton who had been shown the door by the RFU after a mixed Six Nations campaign. Johnson did not travel with the team as his wife was due to give birth to their second baby. Rob Andrew, who had been appointed RFU Director of Rugby in 2007, deputised for him with some reluctance.

England lock Tom Palmer, whose first cap was in 2001 and the second five years later, had been born in Kenya and spent time in New Zealand at Otago Boys' High School. There, in 1997, he played alongside Richie McCaw in the college first XV and then the national Secondary Schools' side.

Returning to the All Blacks was Brad Thorn, an absolute ironman of oval ball codes. The New Zealand-born forward had represented Australia in rugby league and was regarded as one of the toughest and fittest players in the National Rugby League competition. He turned to union in 2001 and declined his first opportunity to appear for the All Blacks, finally making his debut for them in 2003. Two years later he went back to the 13-man game in Australia. He is the only man to have represented New Zealand at rugby union and Australia at rugby league.

The All Blacks had been unbeaten in their previous 17 internationals at Eden Park and their last loss at home was that against England in 2003. In the rounds of Super Rugby that preceded the June internationals, the New Zealand players had become versed in the new Experimental Law Variations (ELVs) – more free kicks awarded than penalties – but went back to the 'old' rules for this series.

On a cool night when light rain occasionally fell, England came out full of intent from the kick-off.

Richie McCaw (NZ 2001–15): 'The first five or ten minutes they throw big numbers into all the breakdowns and, after the Super 14 where there's seldom more than a couple of guys to clean out, we're shocked out of our stride. They knock us off our own ball a couple of times, and it's like, holy hell, back to Test rugby!'

Penalty kicks by Olly Barkley and Dan Carter opened the scoring before, with about 16 minutes gone, England had the first chance for five points after a period of aerial ping-pong. Mike Brown returned a kick with a bomb which came down just on the All Blacks' 22. Lock Ali Williams made a mess of the catch and it rebounded into the hands of Brown. The ball was then spun left to David Strettle. He only had the covering Jerome Kaino to beat but his attempted fend allowed the imposing All Black loose-forward to drag him into touch where he also lost the ball forward. A golden opportunity was squandered.

England remained on the attack, however, and had three more points from another Barkley penalty.

Graham Henry (NZ coach 2004–11): 'After 20 minutes we were under the cosh. The England forwards had control of the game and were beating us at the tackle.'

John Wells (ENG forwards' coach 2006–11): 'For a young combination, I thought they gave the All Blacks a bloody rough time by getting stuck in, showing no fear and challenging them on their own ball.'

The All Blacks responded several minutes later through Carter. On the England 22 and right in front of the posts, with the All Blacks playing under advantage, he put a deft grubber kick towards the England line. Rolling end over end, the ball drew two England players to claim it, but it bounced into the arms of All Black centre Conrad Smith, who stumbled over the line to score.

As the clock ticked towards the 30-minute mark, the All Blacks had a scrum on the left of the England 22. Calling an 8-9-11-10 move, Kaino passed to Andy Ellis who turned the ball inside to Sitiveni Sivivatu at his shoulder. The wing beat two tackles before popping a pass to Carter who slid in by the left-hand upright.

England prop Andrew Sheridan, who had been the subject of newspaper reports (dismissed by England management) that he had been out drinking a couple of nights before the Test, was yellow-carded for not rolling away at a ruck.

Just before half-time, after Thorn strode into the England half, the ball went left to Carter who dummied his way through England's midfield defenders. With two men outside him and only one to beat he flicked a short pass, which was grabbed by England wing Topsy Ojo. He set off from his own 22 with nothing but vacant field ahead of him.

All Black fullback Mils Muliaina raced across from the other side of the field and closed in on Ojo but the big man was just too quick and dived in by the right-hand corner flag, sliding all the way to the dead-ball line for a try on debut.

The All Blacks struck back when Ma'a Nonu took a flat pass on halfway and broke free of two England defenders with one quick fend. He ran on into the England 22 and sent a long (forward?) pass out to Muliaina who crossed untouched, mid-way between the posts and left-hand corner flag.

The All Blacks scored again after a series of dropped passes by players from both sides and an England knock-on. Nonu was the provider again, this time for Sivivatu who had a short run to the line. Referee Nigel Owens ruled that the first spill, from the hands of Carter, had been knocked away by an England tackler.

Nigel Owens (referee): 'New Zealand won quite comfortably but it was a very difficult match to referee.'

The English midfield and Ojo were continually being caught horribly out of position when defending but on attack Ojo was again in the right place when, with eight minutes to go, from halfway Danny Care kicked deep into open territory. Muliaina and Sivivatu were both beaten by the bounce of the ball and the speed of Ojo who ran between them, claiming the ball and calmly strolling around behind the posts for his second try. The 22-year-old joined Prince Obolensky and Bob Lloyd as the only Englishmen to have scored two tries against New Zealand on their international debut.

Referee: N. Owens (Wales)

Touch Judges: S.J. Dickinson (Australia), M. Jonker (South Africa)

Television Match Official: A.J. Ayoub (Australia)

Attendance: 45,000

Half-time: NZ 23, ENG 13

Scorers: NZ Smith (t), Muliaina (t), Sivivatu (t), Carter (t, 4c, 3p)
ENG Ojo (2t), Barkley (2c, 2p)

NEW ZEALAND: N.S. Tialata (Wellington), A.K. Hore (Taranaki), G.M. Somerville (Canterbury), B.C. Thorn (Tasman), A.J. Williams (Tasman), R. So'oialo (Wellington), R.H. McCaw (*Capt.* Canterbury), J. Kaino (Auckland), A.M. Ellis (Canterbury), D.W. Carter (Canterbury), S.W. Sivivatu (Waikato), M.A Nonu (Wellington), C.G. Smith (Wellington), A.S.M. Tuitavake (North Harbour), J.M. Muliaina (Waikato)

Reserves: K.F. Mealamu (Auckland, temp 7'-8', 48'), S.T.H. Lauaki (Waikato, 48'), A.F. Boric (North Harbour, 52'), L.R. MacDonald (Canterbury, 52'), Q.J. Cowan (Southland, 60'), S.R. Donald (Waikato, 69'), J.E. Schwalger (Wellington)

Coach: G. Henry

ENGLAND: A. Sheridan (Sale, Y 32'-42'), L. Mears (Bath), M. Stevens (Bath), T. Palmer (Wasps), S.W. Borthwick (*Capt.* Bath), J. Haskell (Wasps), T. Rees (Wasps), L. Narraway (Gloucester), R. Wigglesworth (Sale), C. Hodgson (Sale), D. Strettle (Harlequins), O.J Barkley (Bath), M.J. Tindall (Gloucester, Y 76'-80'), T. Ojo+ (London Irish), M. Brown (Harlequins)

Reserves: J. Noon (Newcastle, 49'), B.J. Kay (Leicester, 53'), T. Payne (Wasps, 62'), J.P.R Worsley (Wasps, 62'), D. Paice+ (London Irish, 76'), D. Care+ (Harlequins), M. Tait (Newcastle)

Coach: R. Andrew

AMI Stadium, Christchurch, 21 June 2008
ALL BLACKS 44 – ENGLAND 12

'Embarrassing that we should lose like that.'
– James Haskell, England loose-forward

TOURING rugby and cricket teams have often found some countries harder to visit than others. In the amateur days, the big obstacle to rugby success in the Republic of South Africa was the open bias of rugby referees. In France it was the brutality of forward play in games against a variety of 'selections'. In recent years, the England rugby team has found New Zealand difficult to tour because of its nightclubs!

The number of non-playing staff travelling with international rugby sides has continued to swell in size over the decades. When for so long it was simply players and a coach, numerous support staff attendant to the coaching or general needs of players now have boarding passes for international trips. Since the Woodward years, a seat on the plane with England squads has been reserved for a Queen's Counsel (QC). This legal professional is an important figure when players have to face disciplinary hearings. Sadly, they have also earned their salt dealing with players' off-field indiscretions.

In the week after the first Test loss, allegations of sexual misconduct were levelled at four England players. A woman, one of two to accompany the players back to the Hilton Hotel after drinking at an Auckland club (where Dan Carter and Ali Williams had joined some of the Englishmen), sought hospital treatment and then made a statement to police. The allegations were denied by the players, but the British tabloid newspapers soon had journalists winging their way to New Zealand. The second woman sold her story, which ran in *The Sun*.

No charges were laid by the police but Mike Brown and Topsy Ojo were later fined by an RFU disciplinary officer for breaches of team protocol, i.e., 'staying out all night'.

Rob Andrew (ENG interim coach 2008): 'You can lay down as many laws as you like about tour standards, and employ every security guard on the planet in an effort to save players from themselves, but unless those players have a sense of their own vulnerability, unless they understand the importance of self-control in the face of a thousand temptations, there is no guarantee of safe passage through a rugby weekend.'

On a clear Canterbury night, against the backdrop of construction machinery rebuilding the park's eastern stand, England, with six changes to their starting XV, looked to turn around the week of bad news with a positive performance. Unfortunately, from the third minute of the game, the downward spiral continued. Debutant All Black centre Richard Kahui touched down behind the posts after a trademark glide into space by Dan Carter which left Mike Tindall almost turning circles.

The tussle was a good one for the next 20 minutes and England, who had the better of the lineouts all night, nearly profited from a high, deep kick as they had at Eden Park. This time Matthew Tait punted the ball and no All Black committed themselves to claiming it. England number eight Luke Narraway grabbed the bouncing ball and passed left to wing Tom Varndell, just in from touch on the All Blacks' 22. He ran straight but with the line only metres away was pushed into touch by All Black fullback Leon McDonald.

Sixteen further points to Carter via the boot and a try blew the score out to 23-0.

The England fightback was led by Danny Care, who took a quick tap from a scrum penalty five metres from the All Blacks' line. He ran wide and untouchable through the retreating defenders to score.

Having been the man to give the last pass to All Black try-scorers the previous Saturday, Ma'a Nonu got on the scoresheet himself after a simple inside-outside passing move opened up space in the England midfield once again.

With 20 minutes to play, the All Blacks extended their lead to 30 points when replacement number eight Sione Lauaki picked up from a five-metre scrum and threw a huge dummy that left Ojo sprawling. Lauaki then dived over by the left-hand post.

Ojo nearly had his third Test try when he jinked and barged his way through players from both sides in the shadow of the All Blacks' posts. The ball then went wide to Yarndell, who dived over in the corner for his third Test try.

With time up on the clock, replacement All Black halfback Jimmy Cowan kicked a cross-field bomb to the England in-goal. The ball looked to have come off Yarndell before All Black flanker Adam Thomson caught it and rolled over for a try, but the TMO ruled Yarndell had been played in the air.

The reprieve was brief for England, who were penalised for holding on to the ball when trying to wind down the clock. Cowan took a quick tap and scored an almost identical try to Care's. It was awarded after Kaplan asked the TMO to confirm the try had been scored.

As the England players milled about after the match, they knew they should have scored more points. Poor final execution of basic skills, such as placing the ball for a try and staying in the field of play, saw tries to Tait and Yarndell bombed.

Veteran local rugby scribe Wynne Gray wrote in the *New Zealand Herald* that:

> England brought the beef and most of the bluster and in the washup, they just maintained their reputation as one of the game's great pretenders. Take them away from their own dung-heap at Twickenham, from the safety of their own grounds, officials and crowds, and they morph into one of rugby's great pretenders.

Except for the description of Twickenham as a 'dung-heap'(!), English rugby journos were pretty much in agreement with him.

This was the third and last visit by an England team to AMI Stadium, formerly known as Lancaster Park. The home of Canterbury rugby, with a stand named after the Deans family – Bob had played against England in 1905 and grand-nephew Robbie in 1983 – was destroyed by the 7.4 magnitude earthquake in 2011. The playing field, scene of many famous rugby, cricket and athletics moments, oozed with liquefaction while the stands suffered irreparable cracks and, in some areas, even moved off their foundations.

Referee: J.I. Kaplan (South Africa)

Touch Judges: M. Jonker (South Africa), M. Goddard (Australia)

Television Match Official: J. Meuwesen (South Africa)

Attendance: 26,000

Half-time: NZ 20, ENG 0

Scorers: NZ Kahui (t), Nonu (t), Lauaki (t), Cowan (t), Carter (t, 4c, 3p), Donald (c)
ENG Care (t), Varndell (t), Barkley (c)

NEW ZEALAND: N.S. Tialata (Wellington), A.K. Hore (Taranaki), G.M. Somerville (Canterbury), B.C. Thorn (Tasman), A.J. Williams (Tasman), A.J. Thomson (Otago), R.H. McCaw (*Capt.* Canterbury), R. So'oialo (Wellington), A.M. Ellis (Canterbury), D.W. Carter (Canterbury), R.N. Wulf (North Harbour), M.A. Nonu (Wellington), R.D. Kahui+ (Waikato), S.W. Sivivatu (Waikato), L.R. MacDonald (Canterbury)

Reserves: A.F. Boric (North Harbour, 15'), S.T.H. Lauaki (Waikato, 27'), K.F. Mealamu (Auckland, temp 34'-37', 50'), T.D. Woodcock (North Harbour, 40'), Q.J. Cowan (Southland, 67'), S.R. Donald (Waikato, 74'), J.M. Muliaina (Waikato, temp 72'-74')

Coach: G. Henry

ENGLAND: T. Payne (Wasps), L. Mears (Bath), M. Stevens (Bath), T. Palmer (Wasps), S.W. Borthwick (*Capt.* Bath), J. Haskell (Wasps), T. Rees (Wasps), L. Narraway (Gloucester), D. Care (Harlequins), T. Flood (Newcastle), T. Varndell (Leicester), J. Noon (Newcastle), M.J. Tindall (Gloucester), T. Ojo (London Irish), M. Tait (Newcastle)

Reserves: P. Richards (London Irish, 29'), J.P.R. Worsley (Wasps, 52'), T. Croft (Leicester, 57'), B.J. Kay (Leicester, 68'), O.J Barkley (Bath, 72'), J. Hobson+ (Bristol, 72'), D. Paice (London Irish, 75')

Coach: R. Andrew

Twickenham, London, 29 November 2008
ALL BLACKS 32 – ENGLAND 6

'Are you trying to kill yourselves here or what?'
– Alain Rolland, referee

FOR the third meeting between the two sides in the calendar year, unveiled for the first time was the Hilary Shield. It was named in honour of Sir Edmund Hilary who in 1953, with Sherpa Tensing Norgay, were the first men to summit Mt Everest. They did so as part of a British expedition. 'Ed', as he was known to many, had passed away aged 88 in January 2008. According to his widow, Lady June, Ed 'really loved his rugby and the shield is going to be a great honour'.

Richie McCaw (NZ 2001–15): 'It was a prize that was very important to us – much more so than the Grand Slam. We talked a lot about Sir Ed and what he had done for New Zealand.'

Following a record loss to South Africa (6-42) England's coach Martin Johnson, his assistant coaches and captain Steve Borthwick had been copping all sorts of negative comments from the press and public. Among those firing barbs was Sir Clive Woodward, who continued to be as critical of the overall England set-up as he had been when he stepped down as coach in 2004.

In the England backline was New Zealand-born Riki Flutey, who had played in a world championship-winning Under-19 New Zealand team and for the New Zealand Maori. He had four seasons with the Wellington Hurricanes Super Rugby franchise before taking up a contract with London Irish. He had qualified for England thanks to a three-year residency. In 2009 he was selected for the Lions to South Africa and, having played against the 2005 tourists to New Zealand, became the first player to have played for and against the Lions.

The All Blacks spoke openly of fearing a backlash from England after their humiliation at the hands of South Africa, but the home side gave the impression of a side merely trying to stop the All Blacks playing rather than take the initiative themselves. By half-time, England had conceded ten penalties and referee Alain Rolland looked to be growing increasingly frustrated with them. He was particularly annoyed by Borthwick, who he felt offered no courtesy in listening to him or communicating instructions to his players.

Alain Rolland (referee): 'Two of the best sides in the world in front of a full house but one of those sides had no interest in playing ... I don't think I ever encountered that level of wilful negativity before, where one team was trying to play and the other did not want to play. Neither had I been confronted by such a blatant unwillingness to cooperate.'

Not only were England doing their best to disrupt the All Blacks' ball at the ruck, they also showed no urgency or inclination to use the ball when they had it. There was much mustering of his forwards by halfback Danny Care, but all the while the ball wasn't used. This meant the All Blacks had time to settle their defensive line, mutterings from the crowd grew more urgent and Rolland, in his own words, got 'pissed off' and dished out four yellow cards.

The first was after only 23 minutes. Hooker Lee Mears was sent to the sidelines for ten minutes after stepping across to the All Black side of the ruck and picking up the ball.

James Haskell, who spent time in Dunedin playing for the Otago Highlanders in Super Rugby, was sent to join Mears a few minutes later. His unsubtle swinging arm and shoulder collected the jaw of All Black number eight, Rodney So'oialo.

England began the second half with Haskell still in the bin, but an attacking move from inside their own half saw Nick Easter with a clear run to the line. Fifteen metres out, his ankle was tapped by a desperate All Black and the move broke down.

Two minutes later, with Haskell having just returned to the field, the All Blacks ran the ball from inside their 22. Halfback Jimmy

Cowan was allowed to run and run until fly-half Toby Flood came across and hooped him around the head. Flood immediately admitted his guilt and may have got away with only being penalised if Rolland's temper hadn't been on the boil. Another yellow card. Coach Martin Johnson's own blood pressure was reaching dangerous levels, as was that of critics of the disciplinary record during his time as coach.

Players involved during that period put the poor discipline down to frustration and desperation brewing from the desire to turn around poor results, rather than any intentional foul play.

Simon Shaw (ENG 1996–2011): 'England were at their best when they had the best "cheaters" in the world and very few of those guys collected yellow cards. Lawrence [Dallaglio], Neil Back and Johnno [Martin Johnson] himself were brilliant at pushing things to the absolute limit and getting away with it. The ironic thing was that here we were in team meetings listening to Johnno telling everyone not to give away penalties when he had given quite a few away in his own career.'

Approaching the 60-minute mark, England had played for half the game with only 14 men on the park and the physical effort to hold the All Blacks to just 12-6 finally told. In the last quarter the All Black tries came. Fullback Mils Muliaina slid across in the right-hand corner twice, once after claiming a deft kick-pass from Dan Carter. Ma'a Nonu ran from his own 10-metre line for a try under the posts after receiving a short pass from Sitiveni Sivivatu (whose progress had been stopped by another tackle around the head).

With five minutes to go, despite the game drawing to a close, Rolland still deemed England's tactics worthy of punishment and replacement Tom Rees became the fourth player to see yellow.

Martin Johnson (ENG coach 2008–11): 'I put down indiscipline sometimes to mistakes. Maybe our guys have really got to learn that Test match rugby is about pressure. When you make mistakes, they'll kill you. They made mistakes, but we didn't take advantage, and that's the difference in the game. But you're not helping yourself, obviously, when you have 14 men for half the game.'

Fortunately for England, Carter only kicked six penalties from 11 attempts, as the 2008 All Blacks became the third New Zealand side to secure a Grand Slam.

Referee: A. Rolland (Ireland)

Touch Judges: N. Owens (Wales), G. Clancy (Ireland)

Television Match Official: T. Hayes (Wales)

Attendance: 81,180

Half-time: NZ 12, ENG 3

Scorers: NZ Muliaina (2t), Nonu (t), Carter (5p, c)
   ENG Armitage (p), Flood (p)

ENGLAND: T. Payne (Wasps), L. Mears (Bath, Y 24'-34'), P.J. Vickery (Wasps), S.W. Borthwick (*Capt.* Saracens), N. Kennedy (London Irish), J. Haskell (Wasps, Y 32'-42'), M. Lipman (Bath), N. Easter (Harlequins), D. Care (Harlequins), T. Flood (Leicester, Y 43'-53'), U.C.C. Monye (Harlequins), R. Flutey (Wasps), J. Noon (Newcastle), P. Sackey (Wasps), D. Armitage (London Irish)

Reserves: M. Stevens (Bath, 53'), T. Rees (Wasps, 58', Y 76' -80'), H.A. Ellis (Leicester, 61'), T. Croft (Leicester, 67'), D.M. Hartley (Northampton, 67'), D.J. Hipkiss (Leicester, 73'), D.J. Cipriani (Wasps, 75')

Coach: M. Johnson

NEW ZEALAND: T.D. Woodcock (North Harbour), K.F. Mealamu (Auckland), N.S. Tialata (Wellington), B.C. Thorn (Tasman), A.J. Williams (Tasman), J. Kaino (Auckland), R.H. McCaw (*Capt.* Canterbury), R. So'oialo (Wellington), Q.J. Cowan (Southland), D.W. Carter (Canterbury), S.W. Sivivatu (Waikato), M.A. Nonu (Wellington), C.G. Smith (Wellington), J.T. Rokocoko (Auckland), J.M. Muliaina (Waikato)

Reserves: I.F. Afoa (Auckland, 55'), K.J. Read (Canterbury, 55'), A.F. Boric (North Harbour, 69'), P.A.T. Weepu (Wellington, 70'), I. Toeava (Auckland, 76'), S.R. Donald (Waikato), H.T.P. Elliot (Hawke's Bay)

Coach: G. Henry

Twickenham, London, 21 November 2009
ALL BLACKS 19 – ENGLAND 6

'I'm never happy losing but we threw everything at them.'
– Lewis Moody, England loose-forward

THIS All Blacks end-of-year tour was not the try-fest of previous trips. Though Italy and Wales had been defeated, the visitors only crossed the try-line once in each match. It was a trend that continued at Twickenham. But, a lack of tries does not necessarily mean a dull match. Far from it.

One of the great games-within-a-game, on a typically cool late-November afternoon where handling was sometimes affected by the light rain that fell, was the battle between the opposing loose-forwards, Richie McCaw and Lewis Moody. The speed with which both got to the breakdown to lay claim to the ball was amazing, along with the fearless physicality and split-second decision-making. Moody was at the peak of his powers (voted by the media as the English player of the autumn series) and McCaw ... well, when did he ever play a bad game?

Lewis Moody (ENG 1998–2011): 'There were a couple of moments in that game when I beat McCaw, the arch scavenger, to the ball, and once, when we confronted each other, I turned him over.'

From the kick-off, England wing Matt Banahan scragged his opposite Sitiveni Sivivatu as he claimed Wilkinson's kick and Dan Carter nearly had his clearing kick charged down by a flying Moody. England had signalled their intent to harrass and harry the All Blacks.

Nearly 20 minutes later with England leading 3-0 thanks to a Wilkinson penalty, and Carter's inability to dissect the posts twice, the All Black first-five went on a long run. Twice he fended off Hipkiss before passing to Conrad Smith who sent a short pass to Mils Muliaina looking for another Twickenham try. The covering Ugo Monye rolled him into touch just short of the corner.

Two minutes later, England prop Tim Payne was called out from a ruck by referee Kaplan for, not one, but two punches to the face of All Black hooker Andrew Hore.

'If I see that again,' said Kaplan, pointing to the stands.

Both the England and New Zealand television commentary teams were unanimous in wondering why Kaplan hadn't issued a yellow card. The penalty, however, was languidly kicked from near halfway by Carter.

In the 49th minute, hooker Steve Thompson resumed his duel with the men in black when he came on as a replacement. An opinionated, steely presence in the front row who took a lot of stopping with ball in hand, he had retired from all rugby nearly three years earlier due to a neck injury.

Despite the best exertions of forwards Steve Borthwick, James Haskell, Simon Shaw and Moody, there was a lack of creativity from the England backline. The next 40 minutes only saw nine more points scored, via two penalties to Carter and one to Wilkinson.

Then came the game breaker. All Black halfback Jimmy Cowan had the ball from a ruck 15 metres from the England line. Standing close to his left was Sivivatu.

To his right, the rest of the backline waited. Cowan called McCaw, who had just got up off the ground, to go left with him, before passing to Sivivatu. In a two-man tackle, he in-passed to McCaw who, as he was felled by Croft, passed out again to Cowan who crossed untouched. It was a tremendous example of how the All Blacks of that era could manipulate opposition defenders and work moves in narrow areas of the field.

Richie McCaw (NZ 2001–15): 'I remember looking at the scoreboard and thinking, yeah, this might just about do it.'

Carter's conversion was unerring, and he finished the day with a final penalty.

Graham Henry (NZ coach 2004–11): 'We thought England would be right up for it and it proved that way. I was very impressed with the way they played. They were very physical.'

Referee: J.I. Kaplan (South Africa)

Assistant referees: A. Lewis (Ireland), S. McDowell (Ireland)

Television Match Official: N.C. Whitehouse (Wales)

Attendance: 80,676

Half-time: NZ 6, ENG 6

Scorers: NZ Cowan (t), Carter (c, 4p)
ENG Wilkinson (2p)

ENGLAND: T. Payne (Wasps), D.M. Hartley (Northampton), D.S.C. Bell (Bath), S.D. Shaw, S.W. Borthwick (*Capt.* Bath), J.P.R. Worsley (Wasps), L.W. Moody (Leicester), J. Haskell (Wasps), P.K. Hodgson (London Irish), J.P. Wilkinson (Toulon), U.C.C. Monye (Harlequins), A.O. Erinle (Biarritz), D.J. Hipkiss (Leicester), M.A. Banahan (Bath), M.J. Cueto (Sale)

Reserves: S. Thompson (49'), D.G. Wilson (Bath, 50'), S.J.J. Geraghty (Northampton, 63'), L. Deacon (Leicester, 64'), T. Croft (Leicester, 2'), D. Care (Harlequins, 69'), M. Tait (Newcastle, 72')

Coach: M. Johnson

NEW ZEALAND: T.D. Woodcock (North Harbour), A.K. Hore (Taranaki), O.T. Franks (Canterbury), B.C. Thorn (Canterbury), T.J.S. Donnelly (Otago), A.J. Thomson (Otago), R.H. McCaw (*Capt.* Canterbury), K.J. Read (Canterbury), Q.J. Cowan (Southland), D.W. Carter (Canterbury), S.W. Sivivatu (Waikato), M.A Nonu (Wellington), C.G. Smith (Wellington), Z.R. Guildford (Hawke's Bay), J.M. Muliaina (Waikato)

Reserves: I.F. Afoa (Auckland, 59'), A.F. Boric (North Harbour, 59'), J. Kaino (Auckland, 59'), A.M. Ellis (Canterbury, 70'), A.P. de Malmanche (Waikato), S.R. Donald (Waikato), T.E. Ellison (Otago)

Coach: G. Henry

MATCH 34

Twickenham, London, 6 November 2010
ALL BLACKS 26 – ENGLAND 16

'We've got to learn not to be crap in the first half.'
– Dan Cole, England prop

WITH New Zealand hosting the 2011 RWC, England, Ireland and Canada accepted invitations to play the New Zealand Maori side in their centenary series. All sides were defeated by the hosts but the loss by a second-string England side (28-35), was a particularly exciting game.

Enroute to London to begin their end-of-year tour, the All Blacks had played a dead-rubber Bledisloe Cup match against Australia in Hong Kong (of all places), suffering a frustrating last-minute defeat, 24-26.

Among the talking points of England selections were the return of prop Andrew Sheridan after a period away with injury and the presence of Kiwi league convert, Shontayne Hape, on the wing. Another former New Zealand rugby league international, Sonny Bill Williams, made his union debut for the All Blacks. Williams' pairing with Ma'a Nonu meant the midfield combination was the heaviest in All Black history at over 33st.

As a piece of pure trivia, this game was the first time England players were able to wear GPS packs in the back of their jerseys.

England started well, with All Blacks fans wondering just when their team was going to have any time with the ball. As the clock ticked on and on towards the 15-minute mark, England were making all the play. The first real try-scoring chance of the match came when Williams charged in midfield following an All Black lineout win near halfway.

In the tackle of two England players he offloaded to Jerome Kaino who ran into the 22 before throwing a looping pass to Hosea Gear on the left-hand touchline. A desperate covering tackle from Chris Ashton looked to have taken one of Gear's legs into touch but the TMO advised referee Roman Poite he could award the try. Luckily for Poite the ground's big screen had gone blank so the crowd could not see the contentious score.

Five minutes later, from an All Black attacking scrum, Gear came in off his wing and was wrestled to the ground a couple of metres short of the line. Number eight Kieran Read picked the ball up and drove low across the line, with additional impetus from Kaino. With both conversions by Carter, the All Blacks led by 14-0.

Toby Flood gave England their first points a couple of minutes later, thanks to an offside penalty on the All Blacks' 22.

A ruck penalty on the half-hour was landed by Carter from over 40 metres out.

Chris Ashton (ENG 2010–14): 'The first 30 minutes were a bit of a shock to me … It's hard to work out why but we just didn't do any of what we said we were going to do. We started completely the wrong way.'

Throughout the game, scrums had been twisting and turning with little direction from Poite and a penalty against the All Blacks gave Flood his second penalty and the first points of the second half. This was followed closely by a penalty from Carter as England were again sloppy at the ruck.

Trailing by 14 points again, England needed some luck and they got two doses of it as they scored their first try. Ashton quick-tapped a mark and sprinted upfield, before passing to Flood who put a grubber kick into the All Black half. It was toed on awkwardly by Ashton, who had been a couple of metres ahead of Flood. From a ruck, replacement hooker Dylan Hartley drove over the line with, as several pressmen wrote, 'the suggestion' of a double-movement.

Dylan Hartley (ENG 2008–18*): 'It was good to score a try, but I didn't really feel like celebrating. The game was there to be won but the All Blacks are good at closing matches out. They were a lot more clinical than us.'

The arrival of Hartley at the 50-minute mark had not only stoked new fire in England's play, but it also brought some unnecessary niggle. At a ruck, Hartley rammed his forearm into the face of Richie McCaw which drew a response from big Brad Thorn.

Richie McCaw (NZ 2001–15): 'Things deteriorated in the second spell – and not just on the scoreboard. There were a few penalties dished out for off-the-ball incidents ... Dylan Hartley had a go at me on the deck. He never really connected, just clipped the side of my head.'

Replacement England wing Dylan Armitage introduced himself to All Black replacement Isaia Toeava with a stiff-arm tackle to the chin which was penalised by Poite, gifting three more points to Carter. The margin of the All Blacks' lead was back to ten points.

With 20 minutes to go neither side was giving an inch but both were guilty of giving away silly penalties. None more so than when, with nine minutes to play, Jerome Kaino walked around a ruck to lift the ball from the England side and was sin-binned.

With a one-man advantage, England upped the ante and spun the ball wide from a ruck close to the All Black line on the right-hand side of the field. As the ball went along the backline, England had a big overlap. Isaia Toeava (and a trailing Read) were defending against Ben Foden, Ashton and Hape. It looked as though Ashton could well have made the line, but he passed to Hape who lost the ball in the tackle of Toeava as he was taken out in the corner. Curiously, despite Poite and the TMO having two reasons not to award the try, the decision was met with loud boos.

Lewis Moody (ENG 1998–2011): 'By the end, with the All Blacks a man down in the sin bin, and with us pressing hard on their line, you might have thought we were the world's number-one side, rather than them, but the lesson from the day was that the best teams finish their chances, and also seize them when offered. We would have won in 2003 but seven years later we did not possess the nous to close the deal.'

Post-match, All Blacks' hooker Keven Mealamu was cited for a dangerous tackle, though a head-butt on Moody went without attention from the match officials. He initially received a four-week ban, which was halved.

If there was any consolation for England it was that they had won the second half 13-9. But it was still their ninth successive loss to the All Blacks.

Chris Ashton: 'Straight after the game I had to do a television interview and Dan Carter was right there walking past ... I'll never forget seeing him come around the corner and I went out of my way to offer my hand. He shook it and said well done. I didn't want him to think the defeat was bothering me that much. "Next time we play you," I thought, "I'll remember today and how it felt to be on the losing side."'

Lewis Moody: 'At the post-match function, Richie McCaw ... mentioned in his speech how much he enjoyed playing at Twickenham. When it was my turn, I began by stating how the last thing I wanted the New Zealand captain to say was how much fun it was playing at the home of English rugby. I wanted him and every other visiting captain to hate having to play at headquarters. It was all friendly banter, of course, even though I wanted to make the point.'

Referee: R. Poite (France)

Assistant referees: S.J. Dickinson (Australia), D. Changleng (Scotland)

Television Match Official: G. De Santis (Italy)

Attendance: 80,350

Half-time: NZ 17, ENG 3

Scorers: NZ Gear (t), Read (t), Carter (2c, 4p)
ENG Hartley (t), Flood (c, 3p)

ENGLAND: A. Sheridan (Sale), S. Thompson (Leeds), D.R. Cole (Leicester), C.L. Lawes (Northampton), T. Palmer (Stade Francais), T. Croft (Leicester), L.W. Moody (*Capt.* Bath), N. Easter (Harlequins), B.R. Youngs (Leicester), T. Flood (Leicester), M.J. Cueto (Sale), S. Hape (Bath), M.J. Tindall (Gloucester), C.J. Ashton (Northampton), B. Foden (Northampton)

Reserves: D.M. Hartley (Northampton, 50'), D.G. Wilson (Bath, 57'), D.M.J. Attwood+ (Gloucester, 63'), H. Fourie+ (Leeds, 67'), D. Armitage (London Irish, 67'), D. Care (Harlequins, 72'), C. Hodgson (Sale)

Coach: M. Johnson

NEW ZEALAND: T.D. Woodcock (North Harbour), K.F. Mealamu (Auckland), O.T. Franks (Canterbury), B.C. Thorn (Canterbury), S.L. Whitelock

(Canterbury), J. Kaino (Auckland, Y 71'-80'), R.H. McCaw (*Capt.* Canterbury), K.J. Read (Canterbury), A.S. Mathewson (Wellington), D.W. Carter (Canterbury), H.E. Gear (Wellington), M.A Nonu (Wellington), S.W. Williams+ (Canterbury), J.T. Rokocoko (Auckland), J.M. Muliaina (Waikato)

Reserves: A.M. Ellis (Canterbury, 51'), I. Toeava (Auckland, 57'), A.F. Boric (North Harbour, 68'), I.F. Afoa (Auckland, 75'), H.T.P. Elliot (Hawke's Bay), S.R. Donald (Waikato), L.J. Messam (Waikato)

Coach: G. Henry

MATCH 35

Twickenham, London, 1 December 2012
ENGLAND 38 – ALL BLACKS 21

'The greatest ever England victory, ever, at Twickenham.'
– Matt Dawson, former England scrum-half

THERE are wins, and then there are WINS! England's 2011 Rugby World Cup campaign had been calamitous. They were issued early tickets home after being bundled out in the quarter-finals but garnered greater media coverage for off-field incidents in Queenstown (Mike Tindall, a 'mystery blonde' and a bouncer trying to sell photos to the highest bidder) and Auckland (Manu Tuilagi deciding to swim to the quay as a ferry docked).

Following the obligatory RFU review there was some surprise, not that Martin Johnson was replaced as coach but that the reins were handed over to Stuart Lancaster. As a player he had turned out for Scotland's Under-21 side and for the previous three years had been coaching the England Saxons (formerly known as England 'A').

Seasoned stars such as Lewis Moody, Jonny Wilkinson and Steve Thompson called time on their stellar careers. An array of other older players were told their time was up. The new broom was sweeping clean, with the fresh-faced squad being runners-up in the Six Nations. On the back of those results, Lancaster was formally appointed coach.

Much has always been made of the fact that Will Carling was appointed England captain after only six Test appearances. Lancaster's choice of leader, Chris Robshaw, was even less experienced. He had only played 53 international minutes in a match against Argentina, and that had been back in 2009. But, he quickly proved a 'follow-me' player and captain.

Brothers Tom (hooker) and Ben Youngs (scrum-half) were the sons of Nick who had worn the England nine jersey in the 1983 win over the All Blacks.

In the autumn series matches, England had suffered narrow losses to Australia (14-20) and South Africa (15-16), managing only four line-breaks and 13 offloads in total. England players' caps only totalled 206 to the All Blacks' 788. Just three England players had participated in the previous meeting against the All Blacks.

The bookies gave England no chance of toppling the world champions who had not lost in 20 games and, in their 14th Test of the year, were looking to complete an unbeaten season.

During the week, several All Blacks had visited Stamford Bridge as guests of the Chelsea Football Club, while flanker Adam Thomson and hooker Andrew Hore made appearances before the citing commissioners after foul-play incidents in the wins over Scotland and Wales.

In the days before the match, there were whispers that most of the All Blacks had been spending a lot of time in bathrooms thanks to the outbreak of a stomach bug. Coach Steve Hansen tried to downplay its effects, hoping that the team doctors had managed the recoveries well and the players would have enough fuel in the tanks for the match.

Dan Carter (NZ 2003–15): 'Even at the Thursday training there were a few guys who couldn't train – they simply couldn't get out of bed ... The energy of the team was really sapped, which would have been hard at any time, but was particularly difficult at the end of a gruelling season. We didn't want that to be an excuse, and still prepared as well as we could have.'

So often England teams had spoken before games of taking their opportunities and then afterwards of their failure to do so. If the All Blacks were all 5–10% off their physical peak, the best game plan for England to employ was one that sapped the legs of their opponents. Be physical at the breakdown, pick and go, and make them return kicks from deep in their territory.

Dan Cole (ENG 2010–17): 'Take the game to the All Blacks. That was the mentality all week. We looked at the [2011] World Cup Final, when they weren't as dominant as they had been. France dominated by taking it to the All Blacks and that's what we did in the first half. Defensively we tried to shut them down. The mentality was not to sit back and let them dictate. We wanted to try and take that away from them and put them on the back foot.'

Tom Youngs (ENG 2012–17): 'It was a week where we were thinking, "What have we got to lose? Let's just go out there and throw everything at it." The atmosphere at Twickenham was one of the best I've ever experienced. It was unbelievable, and things just clicked out there. It happens sometimes in a game of rugby where everything goes your way – the bounce of the ball, decisions – and we could just feel it that day.'

It was 12 minutes before the All Blacks managed to make their way into the England 22 during which time there had been unremarkable passages of play with aerial ping-pong and passes going astray. A long counter-attacking run from Mike Brown briefly lit up the match. There was pressure on the All Black scrum and lineout due to England controlling the pace at which play was restarted.

Whistles from the crowd as Carter lined up the first penalty attempt of the day turned to cheers as the ball floated high past the right-hand upright.

England spent five minutes in the All Blacks' 22, during which time the visitors made a number of uncharacteristic mistakes and they were unable to clear the ball any great distance. Under advantage from referee George Clancy, England had several phases before the ball went right. The final pass to Chris Ashton, right on the sideline, was at head-height and he spilled the ball with the line open. Returning to the other side of the field for a penalty, Owen Farrell kicked the first points of the match.

England should have immediately lost their advantage when Ben Morgan was penalised at a ruck but Carter's second penalty kick of the afternoon scraped past the left-hand upright.

The All Blacks were trying to use the ball in hand but the English defence, both at the ruck and in the midfield, was putting players on the ground and disrupting quick ball. It was apparent after just 30 minutes that the All Blacks' forwards were starting to look a bit disjointed. It was often only Richie McCaw and lock Brodie Retallick who were on the spot to try and compete against England forwards such as Cole and Joe Launchbury (who was having the sort of game that had been a trademark of Martin Johnson for many years).

After 33 minutes, Farrell kicked his second penalty to give his side a six-point lead.

Two minutes later Tom Youngs made ground through the middle of the All Black forwards and when the ball went wide, centre Manu Tuilagi was just grabbed by Dan Carter.

In the best tradition of Jonny Wilkinson, Farrell dropped a goal (his first in Tests) from close range to extend the lead and then right on half-time he kicked a long-range penalty from directly in front. England had a dozen points and the All Blacks had to find answers to the question, how do they break through the England defence?

After 40 minutes, the tight match was looking very much like it was going to be decided by the boots of the respective kickers. Instead, it would be perhaps the most exhilarating and extraordinary half witnessed at the ground.

A minute into the second half, Farrell dissected the uprights thanks to a scrum penalty against the All Blacks. McCaw was starting to look a bit concerned at the way England were creeping further away on the scoreboard.

All Black wing Cory Jane danced 30 metres down the right-hand touchline before England were penalised for diving off their feet to prevent the ball being played. The All Blacks opted for a short line-out. With McCaw leading the charge, the All Blacks began to bend the English defensive line and Julian 'The Bus' Savea crashed over in the tackle of three defenders in the left-hand corner. Carter converted.

Within the blink of an eye, the All Blacks had another try in the same spot. This time it was Kieran Read, after great skill from the elusive Jane and England not clearing the ball to touch. Carter converted and suddenly it was only a one-point advantage to England.

England's riposte came almost immediately. Launchbury crashed forward in centre field, then the ball went left to where South African-born Brad Barritt ran into a large gap left by Conrad Smith rushing up on Tuilagi. Skipping away from Read's attempted ankle-tap and with only Israel Dagg in front of him, he perhaps could have gone all the way to the line. Instead, he passed to Tuilagi 15 metres out. Just as he was dragged into touch, the big centre passed the ball back to Barritt who rolled over in a tackle for his first Test try. Farrell's sideline conversion came down on the crossbar and bounced back into the field of play. It had taken 52 minutes, but England had their first try and it had been superb.

Just as the All Blacks had scored their twin tries in a matter of minutes, so did England. Their second came after Tuilagi took the ball right in the centre of the field and crashed through the midfield, fending off Carter and leaving McCaw and Aaron Smith in his wake. On the 22 he fired a pass left to Chris Ashton who had no one in front of him. He delighted the crowd with his 'Ash Splash' dive to celebrate the try. Farrell's conversion drifted wide of the right-hand upright.

The All Blacks looked to seize back the initiative and created space on the right wing but a soft pass from Read – intended for Carter – was intercepted by Tuilagi. With a smile on his face he coasted away and over the line.

Three England tries in ten minutes. The crowd couldn't believe what they were seeing. With Farrell finally putting a conversion between the posts, England led by 18 points, 32-14.

Now the question was, with 16 minutes to play, could the fading All Blacks rally or would the margin become even greater?

England threatened the try-line once more after a Ben Youngs break again saw Conrad Smith caught out. Compliments have to be paid to the All Black defence (even though England were playing under advantage), especially a pile-driving tackle on Alex Corbisiero by Read that stopped the big prop on the spot, leaving him struggling to get off the ground.

Nevertheless, referee Clancy came back for a penalty right in front of the posts and Freddie Burns, who had only just come on to the field of play, added more nails to the All Blacks' coffin. The lead was an astonishing 21 points.

England, with absolutely nothing to lose, were running the ball at every opportunity until they were awarded a penalty 30 metres out in front of the posts. It was time for a breather. Burns kicked the goal. 38-14. England had scored 23 unanswered points against the team who had been unbeaten all year.

Cynical play by Mako Vunipola with six minutes remaining saw the replacement prop yellow-carded before he could even get his jersey dirty and the All Blacks, through offloads and quick passing, had a consolation try to Julian Savea which replacement first-five Aaron Cruden converted.

In the final two minutes of play, the All Blacks should have twice scored in the left-hand corner but long passes from Conrad Smith were spilled by Sam Whitelock and Victor Vito. This was cause for ironic cheers from the England crowd, the likes of which were usually heard across town at Lord's Cricket Ground when bumbling fielders dropped catches.

The All Blacks continued their quest for more points, without reward. Right on full-time prop Charlie Faumuina was held up over the line. With a whistle and the sweep of an arm, Clancy ended the game. Now the England players and their fans could celebrate a stunning victory.

Matt Dawson (ENG 1995–2006): 'Not only has this got to be the greatest game I've seen England play at Twickenham, we've got to put this among one of the world's greatest upsets, maybe even in any sport. It was an absolutely astonishing performance to win by 17 points. England harried, hounded and were just relentless. They said to New Zealand, "We will tackle you wherever you go and then we'll pinch the ball and see if we can live off scraps." New Zealand cracked.'

Stuart Lancaster (ENG coach 2012–15): 'We had played the world champions, coming in unbeaten in twenty, and had put in a performance that had beaten a hugely talented and experienced team fair and square.'

Paul Ackford, so often a critic of England's play, waxed effusively in *The Telegraph* about the result.

> It wasn't the fact of the victory which was so astonishing, but the manner of it. New Zealand were butchered, hung, drawn and quartered by an England side who played with passion, bite, style and, at long, long last, accuracy. There was nothing remotely fortuitous about this triumph. It was close to a humiliation for New Zealand.

Writing for the *New Zealand Herald*, Gregor Paul opined that:

> The season has ended in stunningly bad fashion with England bursting into astonishing life at Twickenham to not only beat the All Blacks – but to beat them well and to beat them playing inspired rugby. England looked a lot more like the All Blacks than New Zealand did ... England are peppered with criticism for not playing a southern hemisphere style of rugby. But why should they? When they play their own style, they can be deadly.

It was coach Hansen's first loss since taking over from Graham Henry as coach, following the 2011 RWC. But, as he always did, without hesitation he congratulated England.

Steve Hansen (NZ coach 2012–18*): 'They should be proud of what they achieved. We don't have an excuse. We just got beaten by the better side. England's win was thoroughly deserved. They played some magnificent football. We had 80 minutes to do our best, and we got beaten by a side that was better than us.'

Richie McCaw (NZ 2001–15): 'We just couldn't match them in the last 25 minutes. I know *my* legs were gone. Sure, the illness hadn't helped things, but I'd never use it as an excuse. I think even a fully fit team would have struggled. That night I sat through my only Test dinner as a member of a losing All Blacks side in Twickenham. I never wanted to go through that experience again.'

Chris Robshaw (ENG 2009–18*): 'You can talk about a good performance but today we had to go out there and deliver. It was the best possible response, to beat the current world champions and score the tries we did was something in itself. Everyone delivered. Everyone rose to the occasion and proved a few people wrong. All week we were quietly confident.'

This was England's 350th Test win. It was their highest score and biggest winning margin against New Zealand, the latter beating that of 1936. They joined the 1928 South Africans (17-0, Durban) for inflicting the second heaviest defeat on the All Blacks. It was the first time in ten years, since the 2002 loss to England at Twickenham, that the All Blacks had lost an end-of-year Test to a northern hemisphere opponent. The All Blacks had played 183 Tests since they last failed to register a point in the first half (1998, and a 3-13 loss to South Africa in Wellington).

No one who was at the ground, watched or listened to broadcasts of the game will ever forget it. Nor will those who played in it!

Referee: G. Clancy (Ireland)

Assistant referees: N. Owens (Wales), L. van der Merwe (South Africa)

Television Match Official: G. De Santis (Italy)

Attendance: 82,000

Half-time: ENG 12, NZ 0

Scorers: ENG Barritt (t), Ashton (t), Tuilagi (t), Farrell (1c, 4p, dg), Burns (2p)
NZ Savea (2t), Read (t), Carter (2c), Cruden (c)

ENGLAND: A.R. Corbisiero (Northampton), T.N. Youngs (Leicester), D.R. Cole (Leicester), J.O. Launchbury (Wasps), G.M.W. Parling (Leicester), T.A. Wood (Northampton), C.D.C. Robshaw (*Capt.* Harlequins), B.J. Morgan (Gloucester), B.R. Youngs (Leicester), O.A. Farrell (Saracens), M. Brown (Harlequins), B.M. Barritt (Saracens), E.M. Tuilagi (Leicester), C.J. Ashton (Saracens), A.D. Goode (Saracens)

Reserves: J. Haskell (Wasps, 57'), F.S. Burns+ (Gloucester, 64'), J.J.B. Joseph (66'), C.L. Lawes (Northampton, 66'), M.W. Vunipola (Saracens, 66', Y 74'-80'), D. Care (Harlequins, 68'), D. Paice (London Irish, 72'), D.G. Wilson (Bath, 72'),

Coach: Stuart Lancaster

NEW ZEALAND: T.D. Woodcock (North Harbour), K.F. Mealamu (Auckland), O.T. Franks (Canterbury), B.A. Retallick (Hawke's Bay), S.L. Whitelock (Canterbury), L.J. Messam (Waikato), R.H. McCaw (*Capt.* Canterbury), K.J. Read (Canterbury), A.L. Smith (Manawatu), D.W. Carter (Canterbury), S.J. Savea (Wellington), M.A. Nonu (Wellington), C.G. Smith (Wellington), C.S. Jane (Wellington), I.J.A. Dagg (Hawke's Bay)

Reserves: L. Romano (Canterbury, 48'), C. Faumuina (Auckland, 52'), D.S. Coles (Wellington, 62'), V.V.J. Vito (Wellington, 63'), A.W. Cruden (Manawatu, 64'), P.A.T. Weepu (Wellington, 64'), W.W.V. Crockett (Canterbury, 66'), B.R. Smith (Otago, 71')

Coach: S. Hansen

MATCH 36

Twickenham, London, 16 November 2013
ALL BLACKS 30 – ENGLAND 22

'This was one for the connoisseurs.'
– Sir Ian McGeechan, former Scotland international
and four times Lions coach

DESPITE having knocked the All Blacks off their perch the year before, Stuart Lancaster wanted to learn what made the All Blacks the most successful team in the history of the game. To do that he made a flying visit to Sir Brian Lochore when England were in Australia and heard from the legendary New Zealand player and coach about the national obsession. He also tried to lure former All Black player and coach, Wayne 'The Professor' Smith, to join his management team. It is believed negotiations had reached the point of financial terms being agreed before Smith had a change of heart.

A couple of days before the match, much to the displeasure of the All Blacks' management, a journalist gained access to the team's hotel meeting room where written on a whiteboard was the phrase, 'We are the most dominant team in the history of the world.' For a team whose recent image was built on modesty and who would grind their molars when watching the celebrations of teams who have beaten them, to have such a statement made public was very irritating.

Star All Black first-five Dan Carter (by then having usurped Jonny Wilkinson as the highest points scorer in the history of international rugby) was playing his 100th Test while England hooker Dylan Hartley and All Black lock Sam Whitelock were both making their 50th Test appearances. Hartley had made his Test debut two years before Whitelock, but a series of well-publicised suspensions – few players have been banned for eye-gouging two players in one match or calling a referee a cheat – were interruptions to his mounting tally of caps.

The All Blacks came off a 26-19 win over France in Paris, while England had disposed of Argentina 31-12.

Richie McCaw (NZ 2001–15): 'The English were obviously keen to make it two in a row while we were equally determined to win and put that memory behind us.'

In the first minute of the game, the All Blacks had the throw to a lineout five metres from the England line. They called a ten-man lineout, with the front three being backs Julian Savea, Carter and Ma'a Nonu! Brodie Retallick was shadowed and challenged by Courtney Lawes and the ball was tapped back to Liam Messam who faced a swarm of England forwards. The ruck ball was won by the All Blacks and Aaron Smith sent his pass left from the 15-metre line towards the touchline where four All Blacks faced four England defenders. Kieran Read, on his way to being named International Rugby Player of the Year, drew three tacklers as he ran diagonally towards the touchline and then slipped a pass behind him to Savea who crossed the line untouched.

Once again, the All Blacks had created a try in the narrow confines of the field.

Carter converted and knocked over a penalty, as did Owen Farrell to give England their first points. Then Read had a try of his own. Owen Franks took a pass from Retallick in midfield and charged ahead, into the England 22. Quick ball came right to where Israel Dagg ran across the field creating a three-on-one overlap. Dagg passed to Read who, having beaten the flying attempted tackle of Ben Foden, slid over near the corner. Carter duly converted.

17-3; the All Blacks scoring a point a minute.

From an England attacking scrum, the ball was kicked through towards the All Blacks' line. Read failed to secure the ball. Tom Wood did his best to control the rolling ball with both feet. Joe Launchbury picked the ball up and fell over the line for his second Test try. Referee Craig Joubert consulted with the TMO to check that Chris Robshaw hadn't touched the ball from an offside position before Launchbury picked it up. In the eyes of the officials he hadn't. Try awarded and Farrell converted.

17-10 to New Zealand.

There were problems for the All Blacks when Carter, wearing special red and gold boots to commemorate a century of caps, left the field after only 25 minutes.

Dan Carter (NZ 2003–15): 'As I went down, I felt my Achilles. It wasn't just tight – it was a sharp pain. I got up and hobbled through the next five minutes. But I knew it was over. I realised I wasn't helping my team, hanging around on one leg, and very reluctantly went off.'

His replacement Aaron Cruden added a penalty as did Farrell, right on half-time. Trailing by only four points, England had ground their way back into the game after the All Blacks' dynamic first 15 minutes.

After half-time, England went in front thanks to two more Farrell penalties. Leading 22-20 it looked as though England might have only their second back-to-back victory against the All Blacks. But, the men in black had been stung by the 2012 result and didn't want another painful summer pondering a loss to England.

In the 63rd minute, after using the full width of the pitch and midfield runners straightening the attack, Nonu ran the line between two defenders to draw them both in to tackle him. He then threw a miracle pass over the back of Courtney Lawes to Savea who rolled over the line in a ball-and-all tackle from Mike Brown.

Cruden converted and then added a long-range penalty to push the All Blacks out beyond the seven-point margin. That is how the score remained.

Chris Robshaw (ENG 2009–18*): 'Everyone is pretty battered and beaten up. That's what Test rugby is all about.'

Centre Joel Tomkins, a convert from rugby league, had a match to forget but Billy Vunipola had carted the ball forward with all the subtlety of a lorry whose brakes have failed and at the back, Mike Brown's all-round play was outstanding.

Tom Wood (ENG 2011–15): 'We gave them a 14-point head start and I don't remember that being in the game plan.'

If you look at the match stats that favoured England, you wonder just how they didn't win the game. Territory: 62%. Possession: 40%.

Rucks won: 109-52. Tackles made: 81-153. But then comes the one that perhaps counts for the most when trying to beat the All Blacks. Line breaks: 0-5.

Referee: C. Joubert (South Africa)

Assistant referees: N. Owens (Wales), F. Pastrana (Argentina)

Television Match Official: G. Simmonds (Wales)

Attendance: 81,739

Half-time: NZ 20, ENG 16

Scorers: NZ Savea (2t), Read (t), Carter (2c, p), Cruden (2p, c)
    ENG Launchbury (t), Farrell (c, 5p)

ENGLAND: J.W.G. Marler (Harlequins), D.M. Hartley (Northampton), D.R. Cole (Leicester), J.O. Launchbury (Wasps), C.L. Lawes (Northampton), T.A. Wood (Northampton), C.D.C. Robshaw (*Capt.* Harlequins), V.M.L. Vunipola (Saracens), L.A.W. Dickson (Northampton), O.A. Farrell (Saracens), B. Foden (Northampton), W.W.F. Twelvetrees (Gloucester), J.A. Tomkins (Saracens), C.J. Ashton (Saracens), M. Brown (Harlequins)

Reserves: G.M.W. Parling (Leicester, 46'), T.N. Youngs (Leicester, 50'), B.J. Morgan (Gloucester, 57'), B.R. Youngs (Leicester, 65'), T. Flood (Leicester, 67'), A.D. Goode (Saracens, 76'), M.J. Mullan (Worcester, 76'), D.G. Wilson (Bath, 76')

Coach: S. Lancaster

NEW ZEALAND: T.D. Woodcock (North Harbour), K.F. Mealamu (Auckland), O.T. Franks (Canterbury), B.A. Retallick (Hawke's Bay), S.L. Whitelock (Canterbury), L.J. Messam (Waikato), R.H. McCaw (*Capt.* Canterbury), K.J. Read (Canterbury, Y 32-42'), A.L. Smith (Manawatu), D.W. Carter (Canterbury), S.J. Savea (Wellington), M.A. Nonu (Wellington), B.R. Smith (Otago), C.T. Piutau (Auckland), I.J.A. Dagg (Hawke's Bay)

Reserves: A.W. Cruden (Manawatu, 26'), W.W.V. Crockett (Canterbury, 40'), C. Faumuina (Auckland, 42'), D.S. Coles (Wellington, 60'), L. Romano (Canterbury, 65'), D.S. Luatua (Auckland, 65'), T.N.J. Kerr-Barlow (Waikato, 71'), R.S. Crotty (Canterbury, 71')

Coach: S. Hansen

Eden Park, Auckland, 7 June 2014
ALL BLACKS 20 – ENGLAND 15

'It was one of those games which someone had to take by the scruff of the neck.' – Steve Hansen, All Blacks coach

IF there's one way to ruin a coach or captain's winning average, it's to arrange a clutch of Tests against the All Blacks, in New Zealand. This was the first time England played a three-Test series in New Zealand. Traditionally they were the privilege of South Africa, Australia or the British and Irish Lions. Also included in the itinerary was a game against Super Rugby side the Canterbury Crusaders.

To the chagrin of the New Zealand public, and coach Lancaster, England were without 14 players for the first of three Test matches in New Zealand thanks to Northampton and Saracens contesting the Premiership final. The competitiveness of England in this first Test was questioned in the days before the game but All Blacks coach Steve Hansen spoke of England being 'the most improved side in world rugby in the past two years' and that 'those who think England will be fielding a weak side in the first Test are completely underestimating the depth of quality in the England squad'.

Come match time, on a clear night with the pitch in perfect order, the players given starts in the white jerseys played with cohesion and growing confidence.

Jerome Kaino (NZ 2004–17): 'I catch the ball from the kick-off and get smashed by three England blokes. I have my eye on Manu Tuilagi flying in, so my main aim is to catch the ball and set up the ruck. He smashes into me and then another two do: bang, bang!

They made their intentions clear early in that game that they were out for blood.'

Leading the way for England in a real arm wrestle of a match were forwards Ben Morgan, Geoff Parling and the ever-physical James Haskell. Kyle Eastmond at inside-centre – a convert from league in 2011 – was a threat with ball in hand. Their combined efforts were putting pressure on the All Blacks as well as bringing reward on the scoreboard. Freddie Burns, ably running the cutter at fly-half, was knocking over penalty kicks.

At one stage England's lead was 9-3.

With just over ten minutes to play – and the scores locked at 12-12 – neither side had been able to score a try, though had Mike Brown held a pass from his captain Chris Robshaw early in the match things might have been very different.

Then came an England error that proved oh-so costly.

Halfback Ben Youngs went to pick the ball up from a ruck on the All Black ten-metre line but spilled it. All Black lock Brodie Retallick lowered his huge frame to scoop it up and took off, head down like an Olympic sprinter leaving the starting blocks. He made it as far as the England 22 before Marland Yarde brought him down.

Despite calls from referee Nigel Owens for Yarde to release his hold on Retallick and move away from the wrong side of the ruck, he was well and truly pinned there by arriving All Blacks. Owens went to his pocket, produced a yellow card and England were down to 14 men for the rest of the game. Plus, Aaron Cruden had an easy penalty from right in front of the posts.

Three points down with eight minutes to play, England had to throw everything they had at the All Blacks if they were to emulate the 1973 team and win on Eden Park.

Attacking just inside the All Blacks' half, they were awarded a ruck penalty and the decision was made to kick for goal. Danny Cipriani coolly struck a beautiful long-range kick to level the scores once more.

The All Blacks swung back on attack. Their 20-year unbeaten record at the ground was still at stake.

A kickable penalty to the All Blacks saw Cruden given the ball. Fully conscious of the fact England were a man short in the backline and with several England players with their backs to him, instead of preparing to take the shot at goal he tapped and ran towards the right-hand corner.

After a five-metre scrum and several charges at the line by All Blacks' forwards were repulsed by England, halfback 'TJ' Perenara sent the ball right to the short blind-side. Johnny May had his opposite Ben Smith covered. Unfortunately for England, Smith's quick hands sent the ball on to Conrad Smith and he dived over in the corner for the 78th-minute try. Cruden's audacious gamble had (eventually) paid off. Though he couldn't convert the try, the All Blacks' lead was five.

A seven-pointer would win it for England. They were on attack right on full time, making their way into the All Blacks' half. But, after making a half-break, Kyle Eastmond held onto the ball as All Black replacement loose-forward Victor Vito stood over him trying to claim it. Owens penalised Eastmond. McCaw settled his men. The ball was kicked into the crowd. Game over.

Stuart Lancaster (ENG coach 2011–15): 'We created lots of opportunities, made line breaks and our set piece was good, but it's fine margins. At 15-15 it's all about territory and how you manage and close out the game. We're desperately disappointed, having fought so hard to be in the game for so long. It was a tremendous effort and it's tough not to come away with anything.'

It had been a gripping game and one in which a group of England players, some of whom were labelled as lucky to be in the side, proved their pride in the jersey and the depth that Lancaster had built in his squad.

Chris Robshaw (ENG 2009–18*): 'As a squad, we're in a good place. But it's one thing being in a good place and it's another thing winning. We will get better.'

Looking ahead to the next match, All Blacks coach Steve Hansen stated that his side would improve, too. By about 30–40%. That sounded ominous.

Referee: N. Owens (Wales)
Assistant referees: J. Peyper (South Africa), J. Garces (France)
Television Match Official: A.J. Ayoule (Australia)
Attendance: 48,000
Half-time: NZ 9, ENG 9

Scorers: NZ C. Smith (t), Cruden (5p)
ENG Burns (4p), Cipriani (p)

NEW ZEALAND: T.D. Woodcock (North Harbour), D.S. Coles (Wellington), O.T. Franks (Canterbury), B.A. Retallick (Hawke's Bay), S. Whitelock (Canterbury), L.J. Messam (Waikato), R.H. McCaw (*Capt.* Canterbury), J. Kaino (Auckland), A.L. Smith (Manawatu), A.W. Cruden (Manawatu), C.S. Jane (Wellington), M.A Nonu (Wellington), C.G. Smith (Wellington), B.R. Smith (Otago), I.J.A. Dagg (Hawke's Bay)

Reserves: B.J. Barrett (Taranaki, 54'), C. Faumuina (Auckland, 54'), M.F. Fekitoa (Auckland, 59'), W.W.V. Crockett (Canterbury, 59'), K.F. Mealamu (Auckland, 59'), T.T.R. Perenara (Wellington, 70'), V.V.J. Vito (Wellington, 71'), P. T. Tuipulotu (Auckland)

Coach: S. Hansen

ENGLAND: J.W.G. Marler (Harlequins), R.W. Webber (Bath), D.G. Wilson (Bath), J.O. Launchbury (Wasps), G.M.W. Parling (Leicester), J. Haskell (Wasps), C.D.C. Robshaw (*Capt.* Harlequins), B.J. Morgan (Gloucester), B.R.Youngs (Leicester), F.S. Burns (Gloucester), J.J. May (Gloucester), K.O. Eastmond (Bath), E.M. Tuilagi (Leicester), M.X.G. Yarde (London Irish, Y 69'-79' min), M. Brown (Harlequins)

Reserves: D.M.J. Attwood (Bath, 70'), J.G. Gray+ (Harlequins, 70'), T.A. Johnson (Exeter, 70'), H.M. Thomas (Sale, 70'), D.J. Cipriani (Sale, 71'), L.A.W. Dickson (Northampton, 79'), C.J. Pennell+ (Worcester, 79'), M.J. Mullan (Wasps)

Coach: S. Lancaster

Forsyth Barr Stadium, Dunedin, 14 June 2014
ALL BLACKS 28 – ENGLAND 27

*'The All Blacks remain masters of all that they
survey, still the untouchables of world rugby.'*
– Mick Cleary, The Telegraph

ENGLAND'S two previous trips to Dunedin had ended in the All Blacks romping to victory at Carisbrook stadium, known as 'The House of Pain'. That long-standing venue, steeped in the traditions of southern football was no more, demolished as it was no longer deemed fit for purpose. The two teams now faced each other at an indoor venue for the first time.

It wasn't the first outing to the Forsyth Barr Stadium for England, however. During the 2011 RWC they had played three matches there, coming from behind late in the game to beat Argentina and then romping past Georgia and Romania. Oddly enough, Jonny Wilkinson found the venue difficult for place-kicking, notching only three from eight against the Argentinians. Blame was variously put on the new balls or a draught that blew in one end of the venue and out the other. Members of the England sideline medical team had found themselves in trouble for cheekily switching balls when it came time for kicks to be taken.

England took much heart from the closeness of the contest at Eden Park the week before and knew that by eliminating errors, and having had another week of solid preparation together, a third win by an England side on New Zealand soil was achievable.

They needed a good start. They got it.

From a Chris Robshaw-claimed lineout five metres from the All Blacks' line, their maul stalled. Danny Care ran to his right and drew the defending Richie McCaw towards him for a millisecond then popped up a pass. Flying onto it was Marland Yarde who came in off his wing, escaped the clutches of McCaw and stretched out for a try in the tackle of Aaron Cruden.

Another England try in the first minutes of a game.

Richie McCaw (NZ 2001–15): 'I hesitated, just for a split second. Too late. I fell off Marland Yarde and he was through for the try. I copped a fair bit of grief for that. Rightly so, I guess.'

Farrell added the conversion and a penalty, while Cruden knocked over a penalty for the All Blacks. England ahead 10-3.

As the first half ticked to a close, the All Blacks spent a sustained period of time hammering away inside the England 22. The defence continued to hold and when the All Blacks ran left with space and numbers it looked like trouble for England. A pass from Cruden to wing Cory Jane was dropped cold and Manu Tuilagi, playing in the unfamiliar position of wing, picked up the ball 15 metres from his own line. Off he went, powering out of the despairing grasp of the chasing Cruden.

Crossing halfway, in his peripheral vision he would've seen a black jersey, that of home-town fullback Ben Smith who, in his first game at 15 for the All Blacks, was sprinting across from the other side of the field. It was, as they say, a footrace.

Inside the All Blacks' 22, Smith produced a play of absolute brilliance. A game-changer. He dragged down Tuilagi and got back to his feet to win the tackled ball from the fast-arriving Mike Brown. From there the All Blacks counter-attacked and won a penalty back in England territory, which Cruden kicked.

What could have been an England half-time lead of at least 12 points was instead just four.

In some ways, the Ben Smith turnover showed the different philosophies of the two teams. The previous week, Yarde had been in a similar situation, chasing down Brodie Retallick. He hauled him in but instinctively held onto the player to slow the release of the ball. Smith did the opposite. He tackled a man not much lighter than

Retallick and was up on his feet and fighting for the ball to turn defence into attack.

England began the second half with the same intent as they had at the beginning of the game. A promising backline attack took them towards the All Blacks' 22. With a four-on-one overlap, instead of sending the ball to the players outside him, Billy Twelvetrees looked for a gap in the covering defence and threw an inside pass that went to ground.

Claimed by the All Blacks, Ben Smith had no hesitation in sending the ball wide. Cruden slipped through a gap between two England forwards and fired a pass to Julian Savea. With only Robshaw to beat he passed inside where Ben Smith – that man again – took the pass and scored under the posts. In five minutes of play Smith had saved a try and scored a try. The All Blacks were in front, but not for long as Owen Farrell kicked a penalty to level the scores.

Tom Wood (ENG 2011–15): 'At half-time, it was there for us. When they came at us after the interval – we needed to get our hands on the ball and build some pressure. We didn't do it. They're the ones with the biggest targets on their heads, so they're used to teams getting out of the blocks and really going after them. They know what they're doing – they back their fitness and their skills – and when they establish ascendancy, you can sense their belief growing. They're the most dangerous team of all.'

Further All Blacks scores were made by Savea and Ma'a Nonu as the All Blacks' backline showed no signs of the hiccups of the week before and the lead blew out to 28-13.

Farrell, whose territorial and tactical kicking had not been a thing of precision, conceded another England yellow card for not releasing a player in the tackle.

Mike Brown did get over the try-line an hour after England had scored their first try. That narrowed the scores to 28-20 with ten minutes remaining. Chris Ashton's consolation try in injury time, and Farrell's subsequent conversion, were the final acts in a match that had somehow ended up an All Blacks win by a solitary point.

Referee: J. Peyper (South Africa)

Assistant referees: N. Owens (Wales), J. Garces (France)

Television Match Official: A J. Ayoub (Australia)

Attendance: 24,870

Half-time: ENG 10, NZ 6

Scorers: NZ B. Smith (t), Nonu (t), Savea (t), Barrett (p, c), Cruden (c, 2p)
ENG Yarde (t), Brown (t), Ashton (t), Farrell (3p, 2c)

NEW ZEALAND: T.D. Woodcock (North Harbour), D.S. Coles (Wellington), O.T. Franks (Canterbury), B.A. Retallick (Hawke's Bay), S.L. Whitelock (Canterbury), L.J. Messam (Waikato), R.H. McCaw (*Capt.* Canterbury), J. Kaino (Auckland), A.L. Smith (Manawatu), A.W. Cruden (Manawatu), S.J. Savea (Wellington), M.A. Nonu (Wellington), C.G. Smith (Wellington), C.S. Jane (Wellington), B.R. Smith (Otago)

Reserves: B.J. Barrett (Taranaki, 50') K.F. Mealamu (Auckland, 59'), W.W.V. Crockett (Canterbury, 65'), C. Faumuina (Auckland, 65'), V.V.J. Vito (Wellington, 65'), T.T.R. Perenara (Wellington, 76'), P.T. Tuipulotu (Auckland, 76'), M.F. Fekitoa (Auckland)

Coach: S. Hansen

ENGLAND: J.W.G. Marler (Harlequins), R.W. Webber (Bath), D.G. Wilson (Bath), J.O. Launchbury (Wasps), G.M.W. Parling (Leicester), T.A. Wood (Northampton), C.D.C. Robshaw (*Capt.* Harlequins), B.J. Morgan (Gloucester), D. Care (Harlequins), O.A. Farrell (Saracens, Y 58'-68'), M.X.G. Yarde (London Irish), W.W.F. Twelvetrees (Gloucester), L.D. Burrell (Northampton), E.M. Tuilagi (Leicester), M. Brown (Harlequins)

Reserves: D.M. Hartley (Northampton, 47'), C.L. Lawes (Northampton, 56'), V.M.L. Vunipola (Saracens, 56'), C.J. Ashton (Saracens, 71'), M.J. Mullan, (Wasps, 71'), B.R. Youngs (Leicester, 71'), K. Brookes+ (Newcastle, 76'), F.S. Burns (Gloucester)

Coach: S. Lancaster

MATCH 39

Waikato Stadium, Hamilton, 21 June 2014
ALL BLACKS 36 – ENGLAND 13

'I have to hand it to our strategy group, they nailed it.'
– Jerome Kaino, All Black loose-forward

B Y THE time of the third Test, thanks to the arrival of the initially absent players, the England tour party had grown to 46 members. With many players needing to fill their days, they undertook a variety of goodwill community activities, not all of which were covered by the media. The second-string team played an All Blacks-less Canterbury Crusaders and ran in six tries to one with a commanding 38-7 win.

When the players took to the field on a chilly Hamilton night punctuated by light showers of rain, the All Blacks were looking to join their 1965–69 predecessors and the Springboks of 1997/98 as the only tier one teams to have won 17 Test matches in a row. On top of that, they had not been beaten in New Zealand since a 2009 loss to South Africa at the same ground.

England were looking to rid their game of the errors and missed opportunities that had been costly in the previous two matches. They dearly wanted to leave New Zealand on a high.

After less than ten minutes, England's chances of a win were slim. By the end of the first half they were virtually nil.

Julian Savea scored two tries in the left corner in the first nine minutes as the All Blacks utilised the full width of the field to create space beyond the narrow England defence. Even when passes went to ground they could still carry on with the intended move and leave England scrambling, particularly in midfield. Savea could have had a third try five minutes later but the final pass from Ben Smith went forward.

Jerome Kaino (NZ 2004–17): 'It was all about how we manipulated their transition defence. With our lineout, the key was to speed it up and put pressure on their defence, especially in the midfield where their combination of Kyle Eastmond and Manu Tuilagi wasn't too solid. I have to hand it to our strategy group, they nailed it.' (Eastmond was dragged by coach Lancaster at half-time.)

The English cause wasn't helped by a malfunctioning lineout, nor Billy Vunipola being shown a yellow card for a clumsy high tackle on Aaron Cruden.

The All Blacks' third try, to halfback Aaron Smith, came after 25 minutes when they used short, quick passes to beat poor England tackling in the tramlines of the right-hand side of the field.

Minutes later Smith had another try after fullback Ben Smith made an easy break through the England defence by throwing a dummy and then slipping a couple of tackles.

Down by 6-29 at the break, England started the second half as they no doubt wished they had started the first. Joe Launchbury made a great offload to Ben Youngs who weaved his way into the All Blacks' 22. Tuilagi ran onto the ball and nearly slid up to the line in the tackles of two All Blacks. The ball was laid back and Yarde dived over to score, midway along the left-hand try-line. All Blacks prop Wyatt Crockett was yellow-carded with eight minutes to play.

There were no further points scored by either team until a minute after the full-time hooter had sounded. From halfway, Ben Smith, Cory Jane and Savea used quick passing in the right-hand tramlines again – leaving defenders bewildered by rugby's version of the cups and balls magic trick – and Savea jogged across the line for his hat-trick of tries. In doing so he equalled Lomu's All Blacks record of eight tries against England.

Though he had made numerous blunders on defence in the first half, Yarde was very threatening on attack in the second 40 minutes, in what was only the second double-figure loss by a Lancaster-coached side.

Stuart Barnes (ENG 1984–93): 'England have to look at [the All Blacks] first half and say, those are the levels we want to aspire to.'

England had been hamstrung by the RFU scheduling overseas internationals that clashed with the English domestic showcase. Perhaps as a concession to that and considering the one-point loss in Dunedin as a triumph for the coach, Lancaster's contract was extended until after the 2019 Rugby World Cup.

Stuart Lancaster (ENG coach 2011–15): 'It was tough losing in New Zealand … it was difficult, if I'm being honest.'

Referee: J. Garces (France)

Assistant referees: N. Owens (Wales), J. Leckie (Australia)

Television Match Official: A.J. Ayoub (Australia)

Attendance: 25,800

Half-time: NZ 29, ENG 6

Scorers: NZ Savea (3t), Smith (2t), Cruden (3c, p), Barrett (c)
ENG Yarde (t), Burns (2p, c)

NEW ZEALAND: T.D. Woodcock (North Harbour), D.S. Coles (Wellington), O.T. Franks (Canterbury), B.A. Retallick (Hawke's Bay), S.L. Whitelock (Canterbury), J. Kaino (Auckland), R.H. McCaw (*Capt.* Canterbury), K.J. Read (Canterbury), A.L. Smith (Manawatu), A.W. Cruden (Manawatu), S.J. Savea (Wellington), M.A. Nonu (Wellington), M.F. Fekitoa (Auckland), C.S. Jane (Wellington), B.R. Smith (Otago)

Reserves: L.J. Messam (Waikato, 40'), B.J. Barrett (Taranaki, 44'), K.F. Mealamu, (Auckland, 44'), C. Faumuina (Auckland, 58'), W.W.V. Crockett (Canterbury 63', Y 72'-80'), R.S. Crotty (Canterbury, 63'), P.T. Tuipulotu (Auckland, 76'), T.T.R. Perenara (Wellington, 74')

Coach: S. Hansen

ENGLAND: J.W.G. Marler (Harlequins), D.M. Hartley (Northampton), D.G. Wilson (Bath), J.O. Launchbury (Wasps), C.L. Lawes (Northampton), T.A. Wood (Northampton), C.D.C. Robshaw (*Capt.* Harlequins), V.M.L. Vunipola (Saracens, Y 20'-30'), B.R. Youngs (Leicester), F.S. Burns (Leicester), M.X.G. Yarde (London Irish), K.O. Eastmond (Bath), E.M. Tuilagi (Leicester), C.J. Ashton (Saracens), M. Brown (Harlequins)

Reserves: D.M.J. Attwood (Bath, temp 21'-28', 65'), L.D. Burrell (Northampton, 40'), K. Brookes (Newcastle, 56'), B.J. Morgan (Gloucester, 56'), R.W. Webber (Bath, 58'), D.J. Cipriani (Sale, 59'), M.J. Mullan (Wasps, 65'), L.A.W. Dickson (Northampton, 71')

Coach: S. Lancaster

MATCH 40

Twickenham, London, 8 November 2014
ALL BLACKS 24 – ENGLAND 21

'TV producers are starting to have an influence on the game.' – Steve Hansen, All Blacks coach

IN the year since England last hosted the All Blacks, Twickenham had undergone further refurbishment and upgrades, this time to the tune of £76m. Among the improvements were shadow-free floodlights and two 169m² high-definition television screens. As the game wore on, the person who took the most interest in the almost mesmerising new screens was referee Nigel Owens.

For the first time, the two sides played each other for a fourth time in a calendar year. Media eyes were already being cast ahead to the 2015 RWC which would be hosted by England. Was this a dress rehearsal for the final? Who would have the psychological advantage after the match?

The crowd of 82,223, including Prince Harry, was a new record for Twickenham and many had barely settled in their seats – the most expensive of which cost £89 – when England wing Jonny May sensationally channelled the spirit of Obolensky to score his first Test try.

Prior to the match, much attention had focused on the selection of blockbusting Fijian officer in the British Army Semesa Rokoduguni on the England right wing. But it was his team-mate Jonny May on the other side of the field who had the Twickenham faithful jumping for joy. May received a pass just on his side of halfway and ghosted past All Black centre Conrad Smith, then sped towards the left-hand corner with only the covering Israel Dagg to beat. Dagg showed him the sideline but in return May – who at one point looked as though he could barely believe no one had yet caught him – showed Dagg the underside of his boots as he raced past him to dot down for a sensational try. Yet again England had crossed the try-line in the first four minutes of a game against the All Blacks.

The fairy-tale start could have been greater as May nearly bagged another try following a kick by Owen Farrell. Big Billy Vunipola then went close to scoring from short range and poor Mike Brown dropped the ball with nothing but the try-line in front of him.

Ten minutes later the All Blacks responded when, after a fairly pedestrian series of passes along the backline, Kieran Read fed Jerome Kaino in the tramlines. Kaino put his head down and went through two tackles before being brought down just short of the line. With quick ruck ball, All Black halfback Aaron Smith passed left to his namesake first-five Aaron Cruden who ... barged? ... at the line. While at first viewing it looked as though he had been brought down just short, in the eyes of referee Owens he had 'touched the line', having rolled the ball forward to the white paint. Suggestions by English players that Owens consult the TMO were ignored.

Cruden converted his try and kicked a penalty while Farrell kicked a trio of penalties to give England a three-point lead (14-11) at half-time. Did anyone dare suggest England would have their first win over the All Blacks of the year?

Five minutes into the second half All Black prop Owen Franks burst into open space in the England 22. The ball was spun left to an All Black overlap. Dagg sent a pass to Richie McCaw, which went slightly behind him. McCaw juggled it before turning back to cross the line in a stiff-arm tackle from the arriving Dylan Hartley.

Several minutes later, All Black lock Sam Whitelock nearly became the first grandson of an All Black Twickenham try-scorer when he cheekily reached through a ruck on the England try-line to force the ball. In the eyes of Owens there was no merit in Whitelock's appeal nor any need to consult the TMO. The scowl on the bearded face of Whitelock, who was having a stellar game, said it all.

The TMO, Simon McDowell, was then called on by Owens in what became a farcically long period of discussion and consultation of the big screens. Dylan Hartley, a man never far from the matches when on-field fireworks are lit, needled his opposite, the feisty Dane Coles. While lying on the ground Coles aimed a kick at Hartley. (Said Steve Hansen after the game, 'He fell to a sucker punch, didn't he?')

The assistant referee waved his flag, the crowd jeered. Owens blew his whistle and replay after replay, each slower than the one before, spread across the big screens. Finger to his ear, Owens consulted McDowell as they reviewed the incident. McDowell recommended the offence be punishable by a penalty only. Owens asked McDowell to repeat his decision and promptly dismissed it, sending Coles to the sideline to cool his heels for ten minutes.

Jerome Kaino (NZ 2004–17): 'Dane's yellow card strengthened our resolve. We refused to let them back in and in fact they failed to score a point while he was off.'

Then the heavens opened, and buckets of rain fell on the stadium.

Replacement All Black first-five Beauden Barrett missed a simple penalty attempt before making amends with another to give the All Blacks a five-point lead.

The match was still there for England, but they just could not get the ball.

After attacking the England line for 24 phases, a gap in the stoic defence was finally found and All Black prop Charlie Faumuina barrelled over for a try.

But, as the All Blacks returned to their half and Beauden Barrett prepared to take the conversion, repeated replays on the big screen suggested Faumuina hadn't made the goal line. The 'chorus of boos' boomed around inside the stadium like rolling thunder.

Owens seemed to be uncharacteristically off his game and was drawn into doubt. He halted Barrett's conversion and asked for replays of the try. They showed conclusively that Faumuina had scored and the uncertainty had been caused by a painted border of an advertising logo on the turf.

Steve Hansen (NZ coach 2011–18*): 'TV producers are having too big a say and I don't think it's a positive thing for the game. The game is not all about TV. The game has always been played with a referee, who is sole judge of time and what happens out there. If we start letting TV dictate to us, where is our game going to go? My biggest concern is not the ref or TMO, it is that TV producers are starting to have an influence on the game. It's not on the away side, I might add. If something goes wrong, we see a replay ten times. We don't need a TV producer replaying it 100 times. That's not the spirit of our game.'

(See Clive Woodward's similar complaint when Simon Shaw was sent off at Eden Park in 2004. It is also worth noting that in English football, such replays are not shown to the spectators inside the ground.)

When Barrett did finally get to take his conversion attempt, it missed, but the All Blacks were in front by ten points.

With a minute remaining, an attacking England scrum may well have driven to the line for a push-over try. Instead it was rewarded by Owens with a penalty try, the only one awarded in the first 40 games between the two sides. George Ford's quick drop-goal conversion left England three points behind with a minute to play but the All Blacks made certain there wasn't going to be a last-gasp draw (at the least).

The four losses in the year to the All Blacks gave Chris Robshaw an unwanted record, that of the England captain to suffer the most defeats against New Zealand.

Richie McCaw was named Man of the Match. His 98th Test appearance as captain and 135th Test overall was his last against England. Like 1905 All Black captain Dave Gallaher, he was often a target for barbs by journalists questioning the legality of his play and scurrilous actions by teams trying to put him off his game. The match jerseys he swapped with his opposites are prized possessions for those that received them, and few England fans wouldn't agree with the widely held view that he is one of the greatest players the game has seen.

Referee: N. Owens (Wales)

Assistant referees: J. Garces (France), D. Phillips (Ireland)

Television Match Official: S. McDowell (Ireland)

Attendance: 82,223

Half-time: ENG 14, NZ 11

Scorers: NZ Cruden (t), McCaw (t), Faumuina (t), Cruden (2p), Barrett (c)
ENG May (t), penalty try, Ford (c), Farrell (3p)

ENGLAND: J.W.G. Marler (Harlequins), D.M. Hartley (Northampton), D.G. Wilson (Bath), D.M J. Attwood (Bath), C.L. Lawes (Northampton), T.A. Wood (Northampton), C.D.C. Robshaw (*Capt.* Harlequins), V.M.L. Vunipola (Saracens), D. Care (Harlequins), O.A. Farrell (Saracens), J.J. May (Gloucester), K.O. Eastmond (Bath), B.M. Barritt (Saracens), S. Rokoduguni+ (Bath), M. Brown (Harlequins)

Reserves: G.E.J. Kruis+ (Saracens, 22'), B.J. Morgan (Gloucester, 52'), M.J. Mullan (Wasps, 54'), A.K.C. Watson+ (Bath, 61'), B.R. Youngs (Leicester, 61'), G.T. Ford (Bath, 64'), K. Brookes (Newcastle, 73'), R.W. Webber (Bath, 73')

Coach: S. Lancaster

NEW ZEALAND: W.W.V. Crockett (Canterbury), D.S. Coles (Wellington, Y 56'-66') O.T. Franks (Canterbury), B.A. Retallick (Hawke's Bay), S.L. Whitelock (Canterbury), J. Kaino (Auckland), R.H. McCaw (*Capt.* Canterbury), K.J. Read (Canterbury), A.L. Smith (Manawatu), A.W. Cruden (Manawatu), S.J. Savea (Wellington), S.W. Williams (Auckland), C.G. Smith (Wellington), B.R. Smith (Otago), I.J.A. Dagg (Hawke's Bay)

Reserves: P.T. Tuipulotu (Auckland, 40'), R.S. Crotty (Canterbury, 47'), C. Faumuina (Auckland, 47'), B.J. Barrett (Taranaki, 59'), B.J. Franks (Wellington, 59'), K.F. Mealamu (Auckland, temp 60'-66', 66'), L.J. Messam (Waikato, 66'), T.T.R. Perenara (Wellington, 66')

Coach: S. Hansen

The Game That Never Was (Going To Be)

Twickenham, London, 4 November 2017

THE final game of 2014 didn't turn out to be a shadow RWC 2015 final. England's campaign faltered with poor decision-making in a loss to Wales and ended meekly in quarter-final defeat to Australia who, having controversially edged Scotland, lost the final to the All Blacks.

Stuart Lancaster, unsurprisingly, went the way of those before him and was sacked. In his place, the first non-Englishman was appointed, Australian Eddie Jones.

The All Blacks marched on to a world record of 18 successive victories. Their run was ended by Ireland – who had never beaten them before – in, of all places, Chicago.

Eddie Jones' England chalked up win after win until they had equalled the All Blacks' record (without actually playing the number one side in the world). In the week that England prepared to face Ireland in Dublin to claim not only a second successive Grand Slam but also to set a new tier one record for most consecutive Test wins, things at the RFU got a bit giddy.

It was reported by the *Daily Mail* that RFU chief executive Ian Richie had, for several weeks, been pursuing the arrangement of an out-of-schedule Test between England and the All Blacks, replacing the soon-to-be finalised fixture between the All Blacks and Barbarians to celebrate the latter's 125th anniversary.

The ever-confident Eddie Jones was reportedly very keen for the game to go ahead.

In both hemispheres, media – both mainstream and social – went crazy with talk of the match. NZR chief executive Steve Tew down-played the prospect of the game being played at all. He and Richie had previously butted heads over revenue sharing from the All Blacks' visits to 'HQ'. Richie had been quoted as saying that if NZR wanted more money from international matches they should build bigger stadiums.

It was then alleged that the All Blacks were demanding half the stadium revenue, an estimated £3m.

A week later, with England having lost 9-13 to Ireland, media reported that the match was not going to happen.

All Black coach Steve Hansen said, 'People are desperate for England and the All Blacks to play. It will happen and hopefully it will live up to the hype when it does.'

In February 2018, the *Daily Mail* reported that top-priced tickets for the November match at Twickenham would be an eye-watering £195!

Red Roses and
Black Ferns

FOR the past couple of decades, running parallel to the rivalry of the England and New Zealand men's teams is that of their female counterparts.

England's Red Roses (a name bestowed on the side in 2016) and New Zealand's Black Ferns have contested the final of the Women's Rugby World Cup (WRWC) four times: in 2002, 2006, 2010, and 2017. Unfortunately for England, they have lost all four of the encounters (9-19, 17-25, 10-13, 32-41).

The Red Roses did claim the title of world champions in 1994 when the IRB was yet to sanction the event and in 2014 when they beat the consistent Canada in the final. The Black Ferns had crashed out after the pool stages thanks to a shock loss to Ireland.

A 42-Test stalwart of the Red Roses was Bristol Ladies flanker Izzy Noel-Smith who debuted in 2011 and retired in 2018. She also played Sevens for England from 2011–13.

Though they lost the final of the WRWC to New Zealand in August 2017, earlier in the year the Red Roses had savoured a rare win over the Black Ferns *in* New Zealand, 29-21. It saw them clinch a quadrangular tournament that also featured Australia and Canada. What's more, the Rotorua match was the curtain-raiser to the British and Irish Lions' 32-10 victory over the New Zealand Maori.

'It meant absolutely everything. It had been such a long time since we had gone out there and won. For some in our team, they had never beaten New Zealand before. The feeling was that we had achieved something for all the Red Roses who had gone before us.

The atmosphere in the stadium was electric. By the end of the game it was so loud and there was such a buzz it was truly amazing. I'll never forget walking around the pitch at the end of our game and shouting "Lions, Lions" at the crowd and them shouting it back at us!'

Not only did the Red Roses dominate at the set piece in the traditional English style, they also scored five tries to three. Noel-Smith sees similarities between the way the England men and women play the game.

'I think we are both quite structured in how we play our rugby. We use our kicking game to gain field position and then either attack or defend based on that. We are passionate and driven.'

Noel-Smith's hero when she was growing up was Lewis Moody. 'He was my main role model as a back-row forward. I wanted to be just like him. I also loved Jonah Lomu and Jonny Wilkinson. For me they were game changers.'

Her earliest memories of watching England's encounters against New Zealand, be it the All Blacks or Black Ferns, are inter-related. 'They always seemed to be teams that were in another league from anyone else. The pinnacle of the game would be to beat them. They were respected but also feared.'

When her time came to represent her country against New Zealand, one of the highlights was facing the haka. 'I love it! For me it's an incredible privilege as it is something so laced in heritage and tradition. It gets me fired up. There's so much adrenaline coursing through you as you watch it.'

Another highlight was scoring a try in the 2017 WRWC final, though it was only to be savoured some time later.

'To be honest, as soon as I grounded it I was just thinking we need to get the ball back to centre field. We still needed another try with five minutes to go. As forwards, when we got to the lineout that close to the line, it was our job to make sure we left with five points. I was just doing my role.'

Unsurprisingly, given that they are consistently the two top women's teams in world rugby, there is great rivalry between the Red Roses and Black Ferns.

'I think there is a huge rivalry between us on and off the field. Where there is respect there is also an intense desire to beat each other. We don't spend too much time together and during tournament time we often seem to almost blank each other at functions and out and about. I think both teams recognise they have a job to do and don't want anything to break that focus. It was difficult during the World Cup 2017 as we shared the same hotel. [Not something the men would ever experience!] So, on the morning of the World Cup Final you would be taking the lift down to breakfast and they would be in the same lift with you. We're all human but that is pretty awkward!'

Noel-Smith's advice to those who follow in her sprig marks on how to consistently beat New Zealand could apply equally to the men as to the women.

'Play more heads-up rugby. New Zealand are very good at showing you one picture, then completely changing their game plan. They are very spontaneous and have a serious amount of flair.'

Series Statistics

	ENGLAND	NEW ZEALAND
Matches won total	7	32
By era: amateur/ professional	4/3 + 1 draw	14/18 + 1 draw
Total points scored	560	969
Longest winning streak	2 (2002–03)	9 (2004–10)
Most points – home	38 (Twickenham 2012)	64 (Carisbrook 1998)
Most points – away	27 (Forsyth Barr Stadium 2014)	45 (Newlands 1995)
Biggest winning margin – h	17 (Twickenham 2012)	42 (Carisbrook 1998)
Biggest winning margin – a	6 (Eden Park 1973)	26 (Twickenham 2008)
Most game points (player)	21 (1t, 2c, 3p, dg) J. Wilkinson (2002)	26 (1t, 3c, 5p) D.W.Carter (2006)
Most series points (player)	55 O.Farrell	178 D. Carter
Most match tries (player)	2 A.Obolensky (1936), B.Lloyd (1963), W.Carling, R.Underwood (1985), T.Ojo (2014)	4 D.McGregor (1905), J.T.Lomu (1995)

Most match conversions (player)	3 R.Andrew (1995, 4 tries scored)	5 A.Mehrtens (1998, 9 tries scored)
Most match penalty goals (player)	5 O.Farrell (2013)	6 K.Crowley (1985)
Yellow cards	13 N.A. Back; L.N. B.Dallaglio (Westpac Stadium, 2003); A.Sheridan, M.Tindall (Eden Park, 2008); M.Tindall (AMI Stadium, 2008); L.Mears, J.Haskell, T.Flood, T.Rees (Twickenham, 2008) M.W.Vunipola (Twickenham, 2012); M.X.G.Yarde (Eden Park, 2014); O.A.Farrell (Forsyth Barr Stadium, 2014); V.M.L.Vunipola (Waikato Stadium, 2014)	9 M.R.Holah (Eden Park, 2004); T.Woodcock, N.Tialata, M.C.Masoe (Twickenham, 2005); M.C.Masoe, (Twickenham, 2006) J.Kaino (Twickenham, 2010); K.J.Read (Twickenham, 2013); W.W.V.Crockett (Waikato Stadium, 2014); D. Coles (Twickenham, 2014)
Red cards/sent off	2 D.J.Grewcock (Carisbrook, 1998); S.D.Shaw (Eden Park, 2004)	1 C. Brownlie (Twickenham, 1926)

Bibliography

Andrew, Rob. *Rugby, the game of my life: battling for England in the professional era.* (London: Hodder & Stoughton, 2017).

Ashton, Chris. *Splashdown: the story of my world cup year.* (London: Simon & Schuster, 2011).

Assorted match programmes.

Becht, Richard. *Carlos.* (Auckland: Celebrity Books, 2004).

Beaumont, Bill. *Thanks to rugby.* (London: Stanley Paul & Co. Ltd, 1982).

Bennetts, Julian. *The official England rugby heroes: the greatest England rugby internationals of all time.* (London: Carlton Books, 2015).

Bowker, Barry. *England rugby: a history of the national side, 1871–1978.* (London: Cassell Ltd, 1978).

Cameron, Don. *Retreat from glory.* (Auckland: Hodder and Stoughton Ltd, 1980).

Carling, Will and Paul Ackford. *Will Carling: my autobiography.* (London: Hodder and Stoughton, 1998).

Carter, Dan and Duncan Grieve. *Dan Carter: my story.* (Auckland: Upstart Press, 2015).

Catt, Mike. *Landing on my feet: my story.* (London: Hodder & Stoughton, 2007).

Chester, R.H. and N.A.C. McMillan. *Centenary: 100 years of All Black rugby.* (Auckland: Moa Publications, 1984).

Chester, R.H. and N.A.C. McMillan. *The encyclopaedia of New Zealand rugby.* (Auckland: Moa Publications, 1981).

Chester, R.H. and N.A.C. McMillan. *The visitors: the history of international rugby teams in New Zealand.* (Auckland: Moa Publications, 1990).

Clarke, Don and Pat Booth. *The Boot: Don Clarke's story.* (Wellington: A.H. & A.W. Reed, 1966).

Cohen, Ben with Sarah Lawrence. *Carry me home: my autobiography.* (London: Ebury Press, 2015).

Cotton, Fran. *Fran: the autobiography.* (London: Queen Anne Press, 1981).

Dallaglio, Lawrence. *It's in the blood: my life.* (London: Headline, 2007).

Dallaglio, Lawrence with David Trick. *World Cup Rugby tales.* (London: Simon and Schuster, 2011).

Dawson, Matt. *Nine lives.* (London: HarperCollins, 2012).

Elliott, Matt. *Dave Gallaher: the original All Black captain.* (Auckland: HarperCollins, 2011).

Elliott, Matt. *Kieran Read: tribute to a great eight.* (Auckland: David Bateman, 2015).

Elliott, Matt. *War Blacks: the extraordinary story of New Zealand's World War I All Blacks.* (Auckland: HarperCollins, 2016).

Fox, Grant with Alex Veysey. *The Game, the Goal: the Grant Fox story.* (Auckland, Rugby Press Ltd, 1992).

Frost, David. *The All Blacks 1967 tour of the British Isles and France.* (London: Wolfe Publishing Ltd, 1968).

Gillies, Angus. *Justin Marshall.* (Auckland: Hodder Moa, 2005).

Guscott, Jeremy. *Jeremy Guscott: the autobiography.* (London: Headline, 2001).

Greenwood, Will. *Will: the autobiography of Will Greenwood.* (London: Random House Group, 2004).

Haden, Andy. *Boots and all.* (Auckland: Rugby Press Ltd, 1983).

Hawkes, Chris. *The new official England rugby miscellany.* (London: Carlton Books, 2015).

Hawkes, Chris. *World rugby records 2012.* (London: Carlton Books, 2011).

Healey, Austin. *Me and my mouth.* (London: Monday Books, 2006).

Hill, Richard. *Richard Hill: the autobiography.* (London: Hachette, 2010).

Howitt, Bob. *A perfect gentleman: the Sir Wilson Whineray story.* (Auckland: HarperCollins, 2010).

Howitt, Bob. *Beegee: the Bryan Williams story.* (Auckland: Rugby Press Ltd, 1981).

Howitt, Bob. *Grant Batty: a biography*. (Auckland: Rugby Press Ltd, 1977).

Howitt, Bob (ed.) *Rugby annual*. (Auckland: Rugby Press/Moa, various).

Howitt, Bob. *Midfield liaison: the Frank Bunce, Walter Little story*. (Auckland: Rugby Publishing Ltd, 1996).

Howitt, Bob. *New Zealand rugby greats. Volumes 1, 2, & 3*. (Auckland: Hodder Moa Beckett, 1997).

Jarden, Ron. *Rugby on attack*. (Wellington: Whitcombe and Tombs Ltd, 1961).

Johnson, Martin. *Martin Johnson: the autobiography*. (London: Headline Book Publishing, 2003).

Kaino, Jerome with Patrick McKendry. *My story*. (Auckland: Penguin Random House, 2015).

Kaplan, Jonathan and Mike Behr. *Call it like it is: the Jonathan Kaplan story*. (Zebra Press, 2014).

Kirwan, John with Paul Thomas. *Running on instinct*. (Auckland: Moa Beckett Publishers Ltd, 1992).

Knight, Lindsay. *Kirky*. (Auckland: Rugby Press Ltd, 1979).

Kronfeld, Josh with Brian Turner. *On the loose*. (Dunedin: Longacre Press, 1999).

Laws, Michael. *Gladiator: the Norm Hewitt story*. (Wellington: Darius Press, 2001).

Laidlaw, Chris. *Mud in your eye*. (Wellington: A.H. & A.W. Reed, 1973).

Leonard, Jason. *Full time: the autobiography of a rugby legend*. (London: HarperCollins, 2001).

Lewsey, Josh. *One chance: my life and rugby*. (London: Virgin Books, 2009).

Llewellyn, David. *A century of Twickenham legends*. (Leicestershire: Matador, 2011).

Lomu, Jonah. *Jonah: my story*. (Auckland: Hodder Moa, 2004).

McCarthy, Winston. *Haka! the All Blacks' story*. (Bristol: Pelham Books, 1968).

McCaw, Richie. *148*. (Auckland: Mower, 2016).

McCaw, Richie with Greg McGee. *Richie McCaw: the open side*. (Auckland: Hodder Moa, 2012).

McConnell, Robin. *Iceman: the Michael Jones story.* (Auckland: Rugby Press Ltd, 1994).

McGeechan, (Sir) Ian. *The Lions: when the going gets tough.* (London: Hodder & Stoughton, 2017).

McGowan, Phil. *Twickenham: the home of England rugby.* (Gloucestershire: Amberley Publishing, 2014).

McIlraith, Matt. *Robbie Deans: red, black & gold.* (Auckland: Mower, 2014).

McKay, Alex. *The team that changed rugby forever: the 1967 All Blacks.* (Auckland: New Holland, 2017).

McKechnie, Brian with Lynn O'Connell. *McKechnie: double All Black.* (Invercargill: Craig's Publishers, 1983).

McLean, Terry. *All Black magic: the triumphant tour of the 1967 All Blacks.* (Wellington: A H and A W Reed, 1968).

McLean, Terry. *Willie away: Wilson Whineray's All Blacks of 1963/64.* (Wellington: A H & A W Reed, 1964).

Masters, R.R. *With the All Blacks in Great Britain, France, Canada and Australia 1924-5.* (Christchurch: Christchurch Press, 1928).

Mitchell, John and Gavin Rich. *Mitch: the real story.* (Cape Town: Zebra Press, 2014).

Moody, Lewis. *Mad dog, an Englishman: my life in rugby.* (London: Hodder & Stoughton, 2011).

Moore, Brian. *Beware of the dog: rugby's hard man reveals all.* (London: Simon & Schuster, 2010).

Mourie, Graham with Ron Palenski. *Graham Mourie: captain.* (Auckland: Moa, 1982).

Muliaina, Malili with Lynn McConnell. *Mils Muliaina: living the dream.* (Auckland: Hodder Moa, 2009).

Nepia, George and Terry McLean. *I, George Nepia.* (Wellington: A.H. & A.W. Reed, 1963).

Oliver, Anton with Brian Turner. *Anton Oliver inside.* (Auckland: Hodder Moa, 2005).

Quinn, Keith and Joseph Romanos. *Legends of the All Blacks.* (Auckland: Hodder Moa Beckett Publishers Ltd, 1999).

Oliver, C.J. and E.W. Tindall. *The tour of the third All Blacks, 1935.* (Wellington: Sporting Publications, 1936).

O'Meagher, Steven. *Fronting up: the Sean Fitzpatrick story.* (Auckland: Moa Beckett Publishers Ltd, 1994).

Owens, Nigel with Lynn Davies. *Half time: the autobiography*. (Wales: Y Lolfa, 2009).

Palenski, Ron, Rod Chester and Neville McMillan. *Men in Black*. (Auckland: Hodder Moa, 2006).

Peatey, Lance. *In pursuit of Bill: a complete history of the Rugby World Cup*. (Sydney: New Holland, 2011).

Rolland, Alain with Daragh Ó Conchúir. *The whistle blower: a journey deep into the heart of rugby*. (Dublin: Hero Books, 2015).

Scott, R W H with Terry McLean. *The Bob Scott story*. (Wellington: A H and A W Reed, 1956).

Shaw, Simon. *The hard yards: my story*. (Edinburgh: Mainstream Publishing Co. Ltd, 2009).

Slatter, Gordon. *On the ball: the centennial book of New Zealand rugby*. (Christchurch: Whitcombe & Tombs, 1970).

Squires, Neil. *The house of Lancaster: how England rugby was reinvented*. (London: Yellow Jersey Press, 2015).

Stead, W.J. *Billy's trip home: the remarkable diary of an All Black on tour*. (Dunedin: New Zealand Sports Hall of Fame, 2005).

Tibballs, Geoff. *Great rugby heroes: a history of rugby legends of yesteryear*. (London: Michael O'Mara Books, 2003).

Tuigamala, Va'aiga with Bob Howitt. *Inga the winger*. (Auckland: Rugby Press Ltd, 1993).

Uttley, Roger with David Norrie. *Pride in England: a rugby biography*. (London: Stanley Paul, 1981).

Verdon, Paul. *The power behind the All Blacks: the untold story of the men who coached the All Blacks*. (Auckland: Penguin, 1999).

Veysey, Alex. *Ebony and ivory: the Stu Wilson and Bernie Fraser story*. (Auckland: Moa Publications Ltd, 1984).

Veysey, Alex. *Fergie*. (Christchurch: Whitcoulls Ltd, 1976).

Veysey, Alex with Gary Caffell and Ron Palenski. *Lochore: an authorised biography*. (Auckland: Hodder Moa Beckett Publishers Ltd, 1996).

Wheeler, Peter. *Rugby from the front*. (London: Stanley Paul, 1983).

Whineray's men: a pictorial record of the 1963-64 All Blacks in the British Isles. (Auckland: New Zealand Newspapers Ltd, 1964).

Wilkinson, Jonny. *Jonny: my autobiography*. (London: Headline Publishing Ltd, 2011).